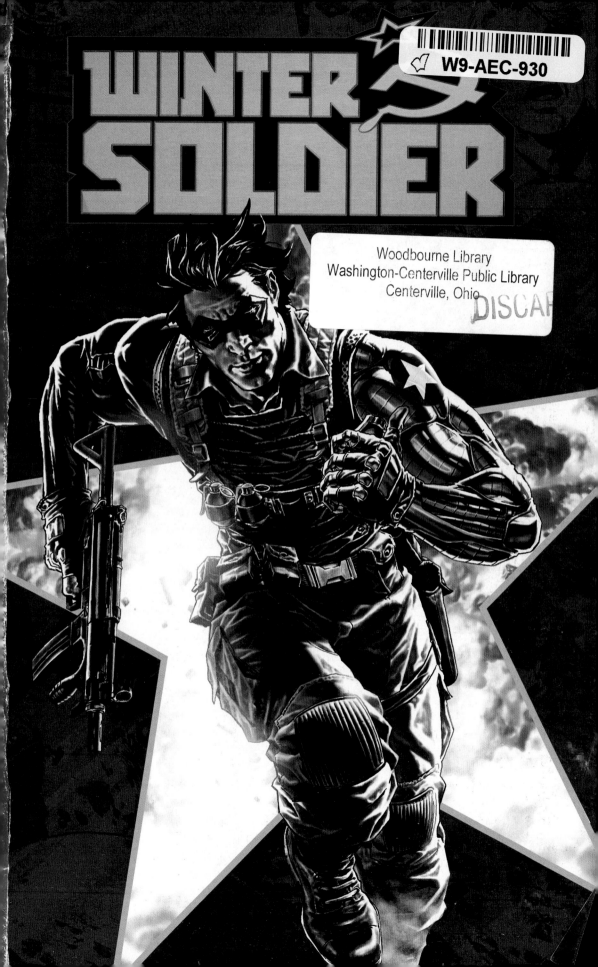

WINTER SOLDIER

WINTER SOLDIER

THE LONGEST WINTER

WRITER
ED BRUBAKER

ARTIST
BUTCH GUICE

INKERS, #3-5
STEFANO GAUDIANO, BRIAN THIES, TOM PALMER & BUTCH GUICE

COLOR ARTIST **BETTIE BREITWEISER**
WITH **JORDIE BELLAIRE** (#3) & **MATTHEW WILSON** (#4)

LETTERER **VC'S JOE CARAMAGNA**

COVER ART **BUTCH GUICE & BETTIE BREITWEISER** (FEAR ITSELF #7.1)
AND **LEE BERMEJO** (WINTER SOLDIER #1-5)

ASSISTANT EDITOR **JOHN DENNING** EDITOR **LAUREN SANKOVITCH**

EXECUTIVE EDITOR **TOM BREVOORT**

COLLECTION EDITOR **JENNIFER GRÜNWALD**
ASSISTANT EDITORS **ALEX STARBUCK & NELSON RIBEIRO**
EDITOR, SPECIAL PROJECTS **MARK D. BEAZLEY**
SENIOR EDITOR, SPECIAL PROJECTS **JEFF YOUNGQUIST**
SENIOR VICE PRESIDENT OF SALES **DAVID GABRIEL**
SVP OF BRAND PLANNING & COMMUNICATIONS **MICHAEL PASCIULLO**
BOOK DESIGN **JEFF POWELL**

EDITOR IN CHIEF **AXEL ALONSO**
CHIEF CREATIVE OFFICER **JOE QUESADA**
PUBLISHER **DAN BUCKLEY**
EXECUTIVE PRODUCER **ALAN FINE**

WINTER SOLDIER VOL. 1: THE LONGEST WINTER. Contains material originally published in magazine form as FEAR ITSELF #7.1: CAPTAIN AMERICA and WINTER SOLDIER #1-5. First printing 2012. ISBN# 978-0-7851-4440-3. Published by MARVEL WORLDWIDE, INC., a subsidiary of MARVEL ENTERTAINMENT, LLC. OFFICE OF PUBLICATION: 135 West 50th Street, New York, NY 10020. Copyright © 2011 and 2012 Marvel Characters, Inc. All rights reserved. $15.99 per copy in the U.S. and $17.99 in Canada (GST #R127032852); Canadian Agreement #40668537. All characters featured in this issue and the distinctive names and likenesses thereof, and all related indicia are trademarks of Marvel Characters, Inc. No similarity between any of the names, characters, persons, and/or institutions in this magazine with those of any living or dead person or institution is intended, and any such similarity which may exist is purely coincidental. **Printed in the U.S.A.** ALAN FINE, EVP - Office of the President, Marvel Worldwide, Inc. and EVP & CMO Marvel Characters B.V.; DAN BUCKLEY, Publisher & President - Print, Animation & Digital Divisions; JOE QUESADA, Chief Creative Officer; TOM BREVOORT, SVP of Publishing; DAVID BOGART, SVP of Operations & Procurement, Publishing; RUWAN JAYATILLEKE, SVP & Associate Publisher, Publishing; C.B. CEBULSKI, SVP of Creator & Content Development; DAVID GABRIEL, SVP of Publishing Sales & Circulation; MICHAEL PASCIULLO, SVP of Brand Planning & Communications; JIM O'KEEFE, VP of Operations & Logistics; DAN CARR, Executive Director of Publishing Technology; SUSAN CRESPI, Editorial Operations Manager; ALEX MORALES, Publishing Operations Manager; STAN LEE, Chairman Emeritus. For information regarding advertising in Marvel Comics or on Marvel.com, please contact Niza Disla, Director of Marvel Partnerships, at ndisla@marvel.com. For Marvel subscription inquiries, please call 800-217-9158. Manufactured between 7/26/2012 and 8/28/2012 by QUAD/GRAPHICS, DUBUQUE, IA, USA.

10 9 8 7 6 5 4 3 2 1

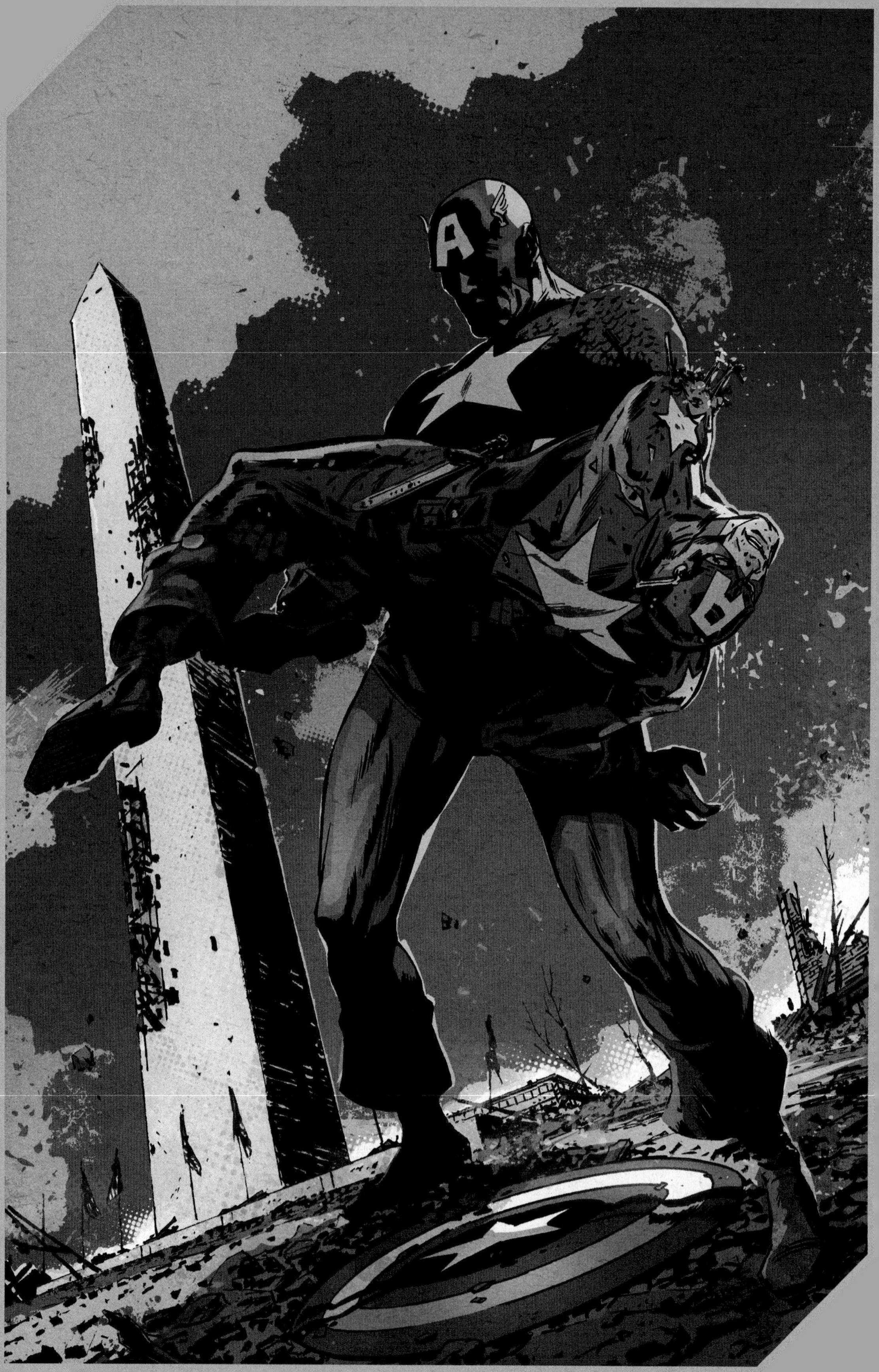

FEAR ITSELF

CHAPTER 7.1: CAPTAIN AMERICA

A time of uncertainty and fear grips the world.

Sin, daughter of the Red Skull, has released the mysterious Serpent from entombment at the bottom of the Marianas Trench. The Serpent's mystic hammer empowers Sin, transforming her into his herald, Skadi.

The Serpent summons his Worthy, causing seven additional hammers to fall from the heavens and strike all over the world. Each hammer transforms its destined wielder into an unstoppable engine of destruction to rampage in the Serpent's name.

Withdrawing from Earth, Odin and the Asgardians begin preparations to burn the planet in order to destroy the Serpent. When Thor attempts to intercede, the Serpent reveals to him that he is Odin's brother, the true, exiled King of Asgard, and that Thor is fated to fall in battle with him.

In a last-ditch attempt to fend off the Serpent's army from the World Tree in Broxton, Tony Stark forges a set of weapons made of enchanted uru metal to even the odds for the Avengers. The heroes manage to hold the enemy at bay long enough for Thor to defeat the Serpent, take nine steps and die in his father's arms.

In the aftermath, the Avengers tend to the wounded and mourn their losses, including one of the early casualties of the Serpent's deadly campaign, the current Captain America, Bucky Barnes.

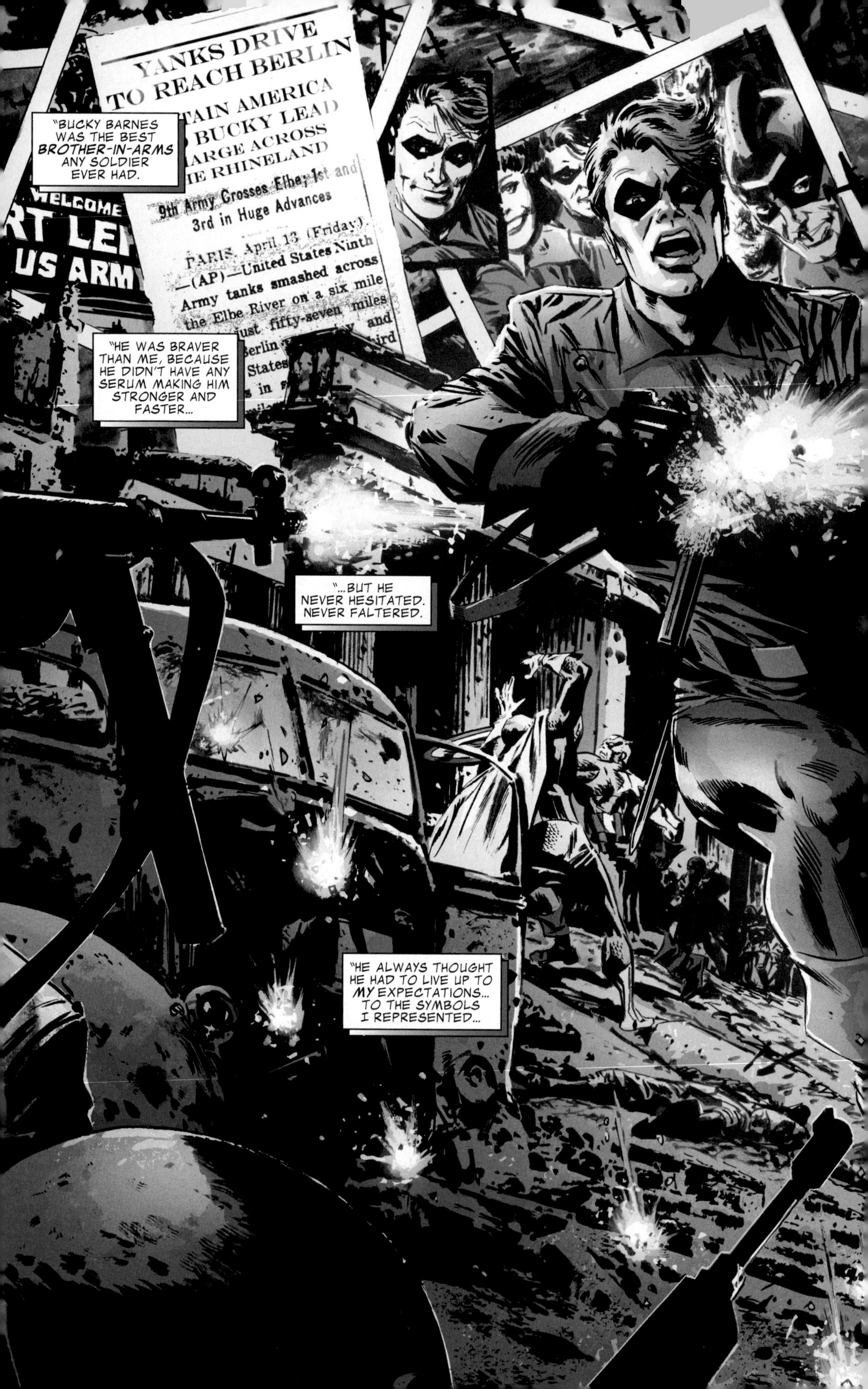
YANKS DRIVE TO REACH BERLIN
9th Army Crosses Elbe; 1st and 3rd in Huge Advances
WELCOME
US ARMY
"BUCKY BARNES WAS THE BEST BROTHER-IN-ARMS ANY SOLDIER EVER HAD.
"HE WAS BRAVER THAN ME, BECAUSE HE DIDN'T HAVE ANY SERUM MAKING HIM STRONGER AND FASTER...
"...BUT HE NEVER HESITATED. NEVER FALTERED.
"HE ALWAYS THOUGHT HE HAD TO LIVE UP TO MY EXPECTATIONS... TO THE SYMBOLS I REPRESENTED...

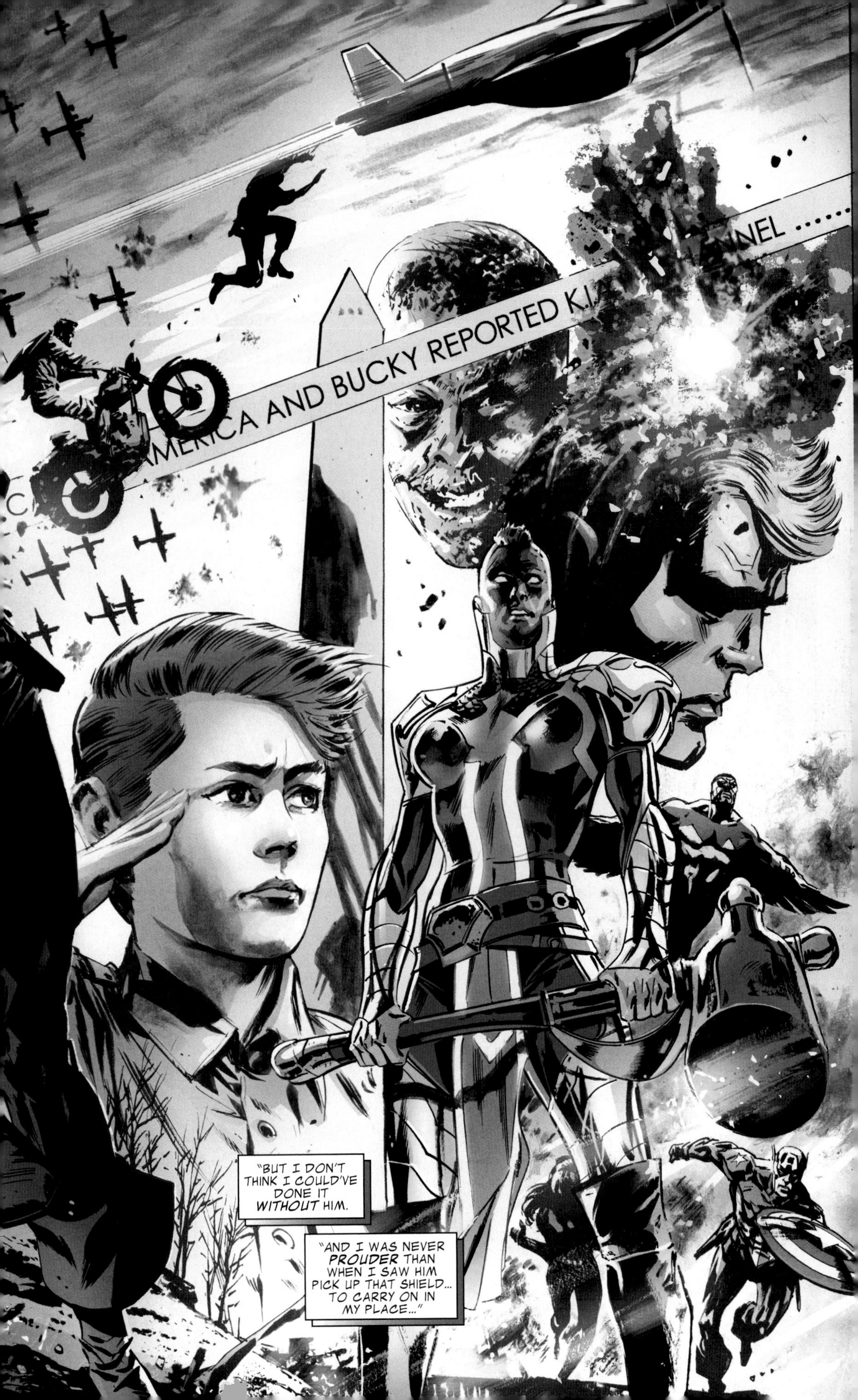
AMERICA AND BUCKY REPORTED K.I.
"BUT I DON'T THINK I COULD'VE DONE IT *WITHOUT* HIM.
"AND I WAS NEVER *PROUDER* THAN WHEN I SAW HIM PICK UP THAT SHIELD... TO CARRY ON IN MY PLACE..."

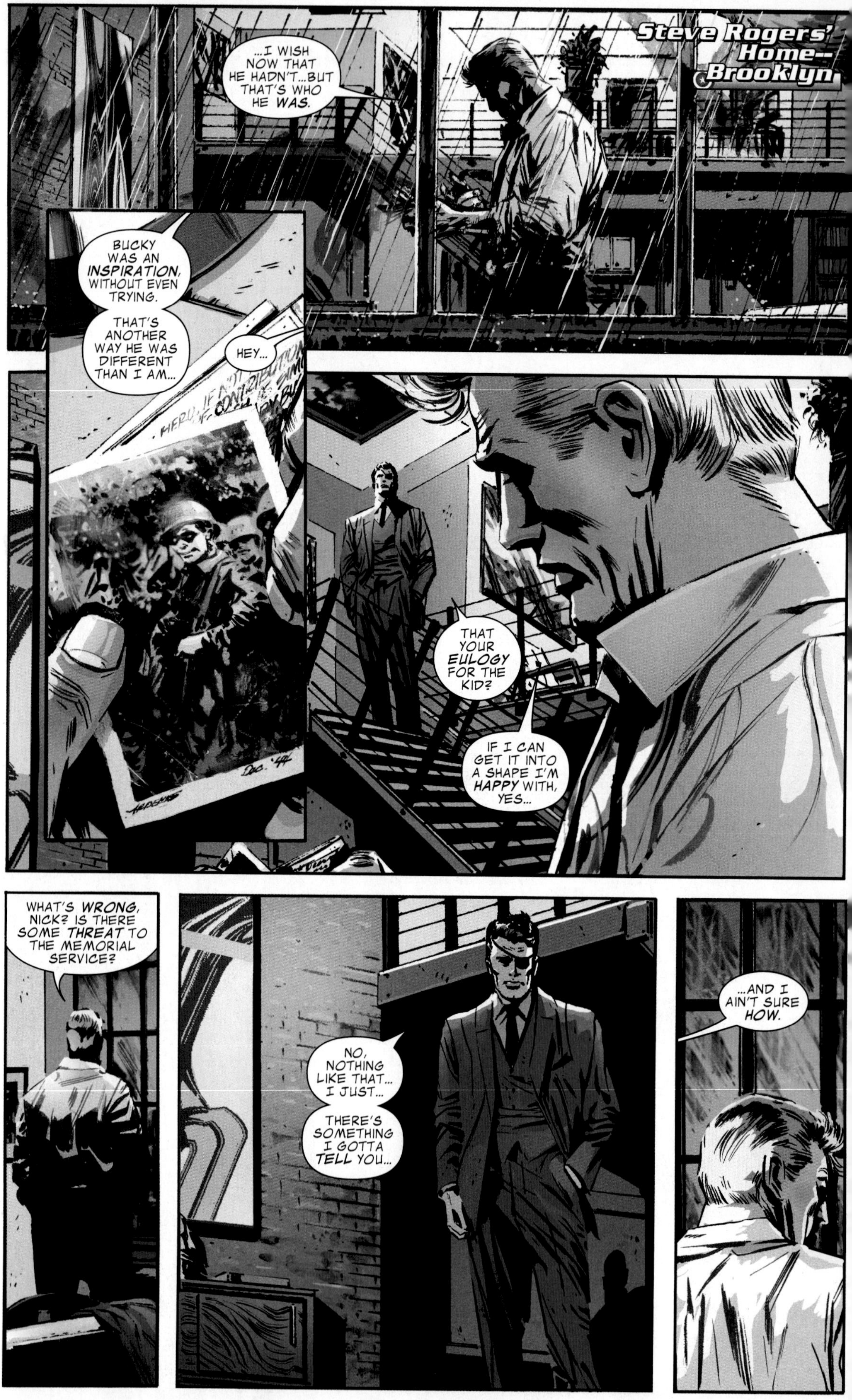

Steve Rogers' Home-- Brooklyn
...I WISH NOW THAT HE HADN'T...BUT THAT'S WHO HE WAS.
BUCKY WAS AN INSPIRATION, WITHOUT EVEN TRYING.
THAT'S ANOTHER WAY HE WAS DIFFERENT THAN I AM...
HEY...
THAT YOUR EULOGY FOR THE KID?
IF I CAN GET IT INTO A SHAPE I'M HAPPY WITH, YES...
WHAT'S WRONG, NICK? IS THERE SOME THREAT TO THE MEMORIAL SERVICE?
NO, NOTHING LIKE THAT... I JUST...
THERE'S SOMETHING I GOTTA TELL YOU...
...AND I AIN'T SURE HOW.

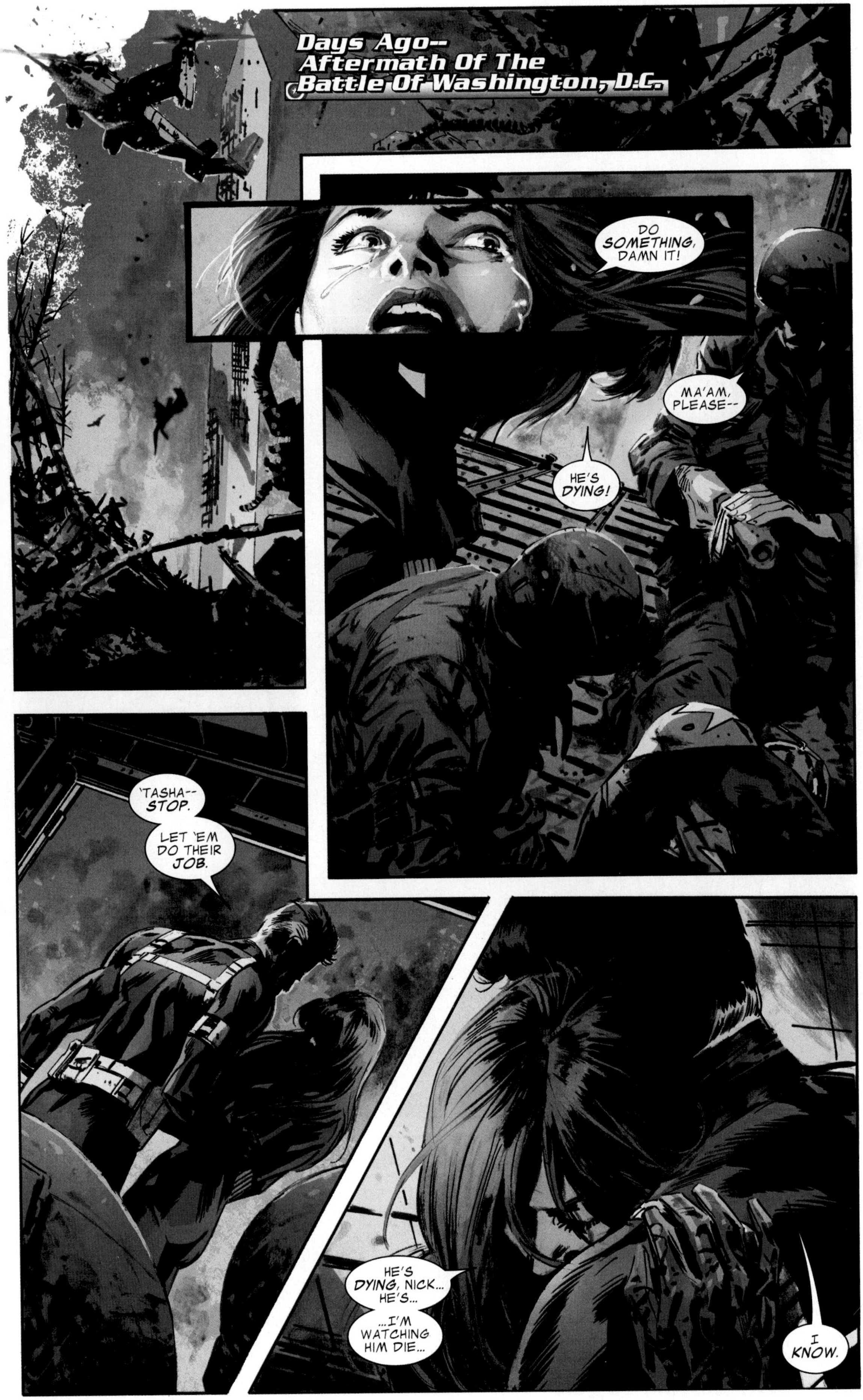
Days Ago--
Aftermath Of The
Battle Of Washington, D.C.
DO SOMETHING, DAMN IT!
MA'AM, PLEASE--
HE'S DYING!
'TASHA-- STOP.
LET 'EM DO THEIR JOB.
HE'S DYING, NICK... HE'S...
...I'M WATCHING HIM DIE...
I KNOW.

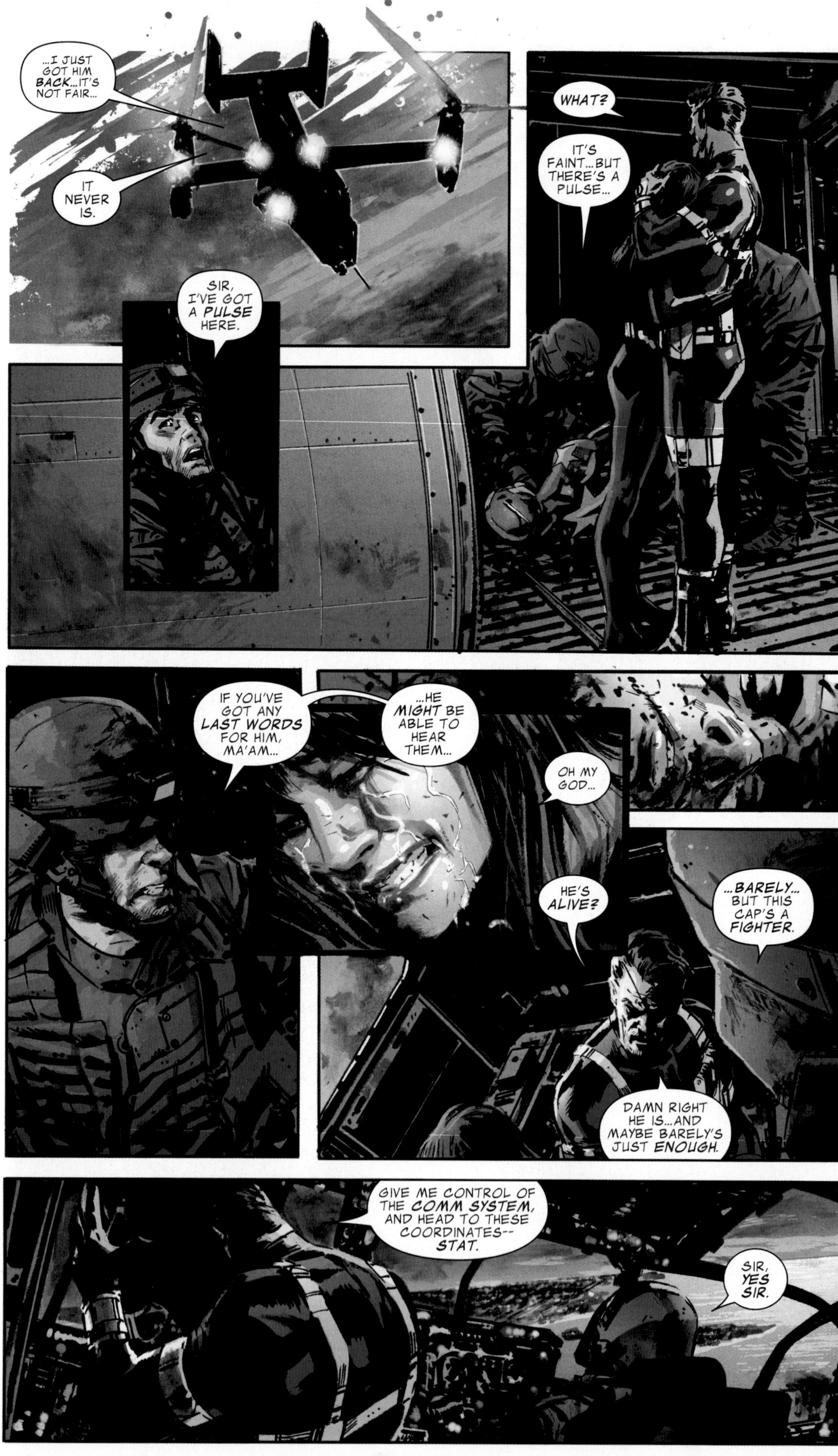
...I JUST GOT HIM BACK...IT'S NOT FAIR...
IT NEVER IS.
WHAT?
IT'S FAINT...BUT THERE'S A PULSE...
SIR, I'VE GOT A PULSE HERE.
IF YOU'VE GOT ANY LAST WORDS FOR HIM, MA'AM...
...HE MIGHT BE ABLE TO HEAR THEM...
OH MY GOD...
HE'S ALIVE?
...BARELY... BUT THIS CAP'S A FIGHTER.
DAMN RIGHT HE IS...AND MAYBE BARELY'S JUST ENOUGH.
GIVE ME CONTROL OF THE COMM SYSTEM, AND HEAD TO THESE COORDINATES-- STAT.
SIR, YES SIR.

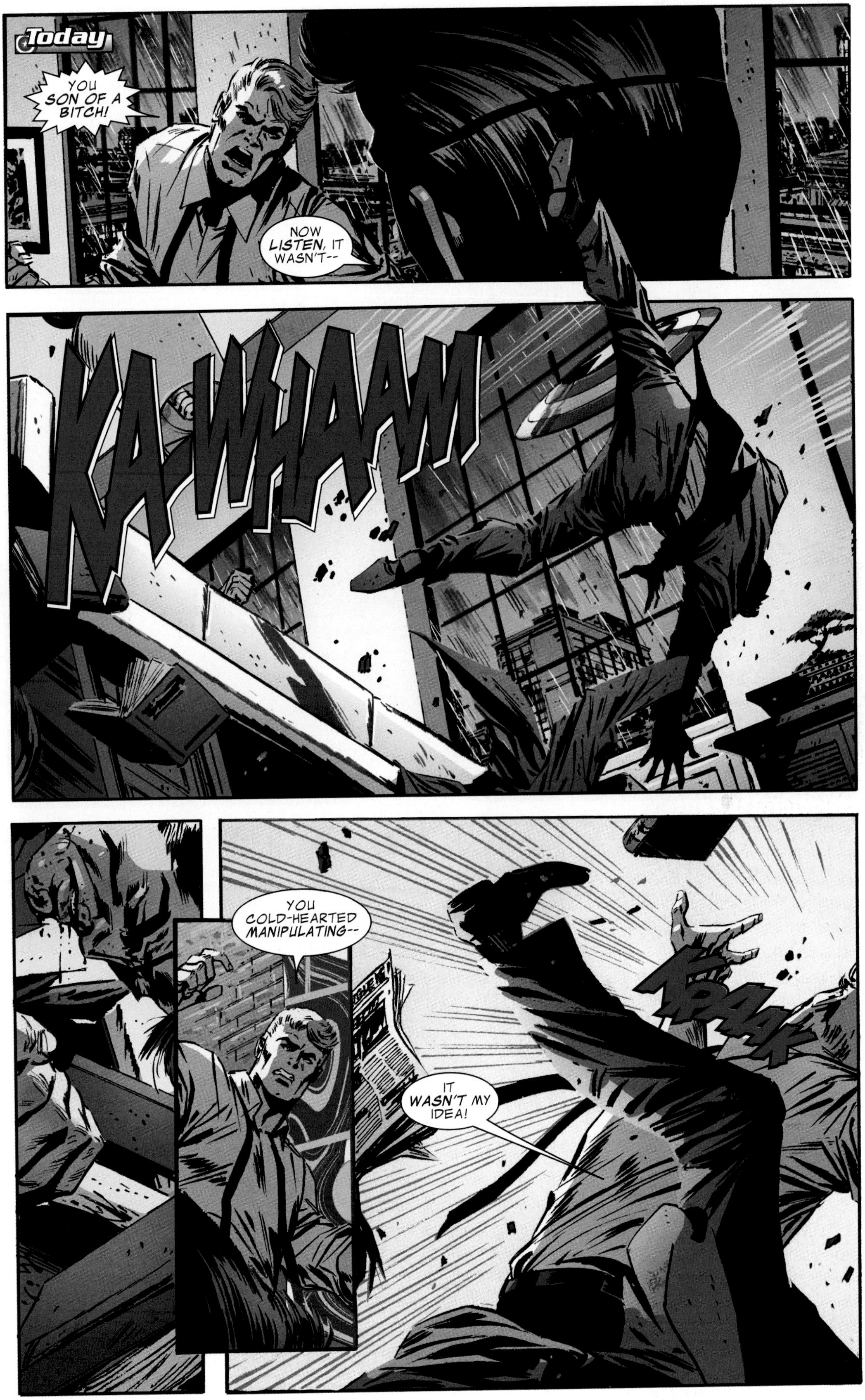
Today
YOU SON OF A BITCH!
NOW LISTEN, IT WASN'T--
KA-WHAAM
YOU COLD-HEARTED MANIPULATING--
KRAAK
IT WASN'T MY IDEA!

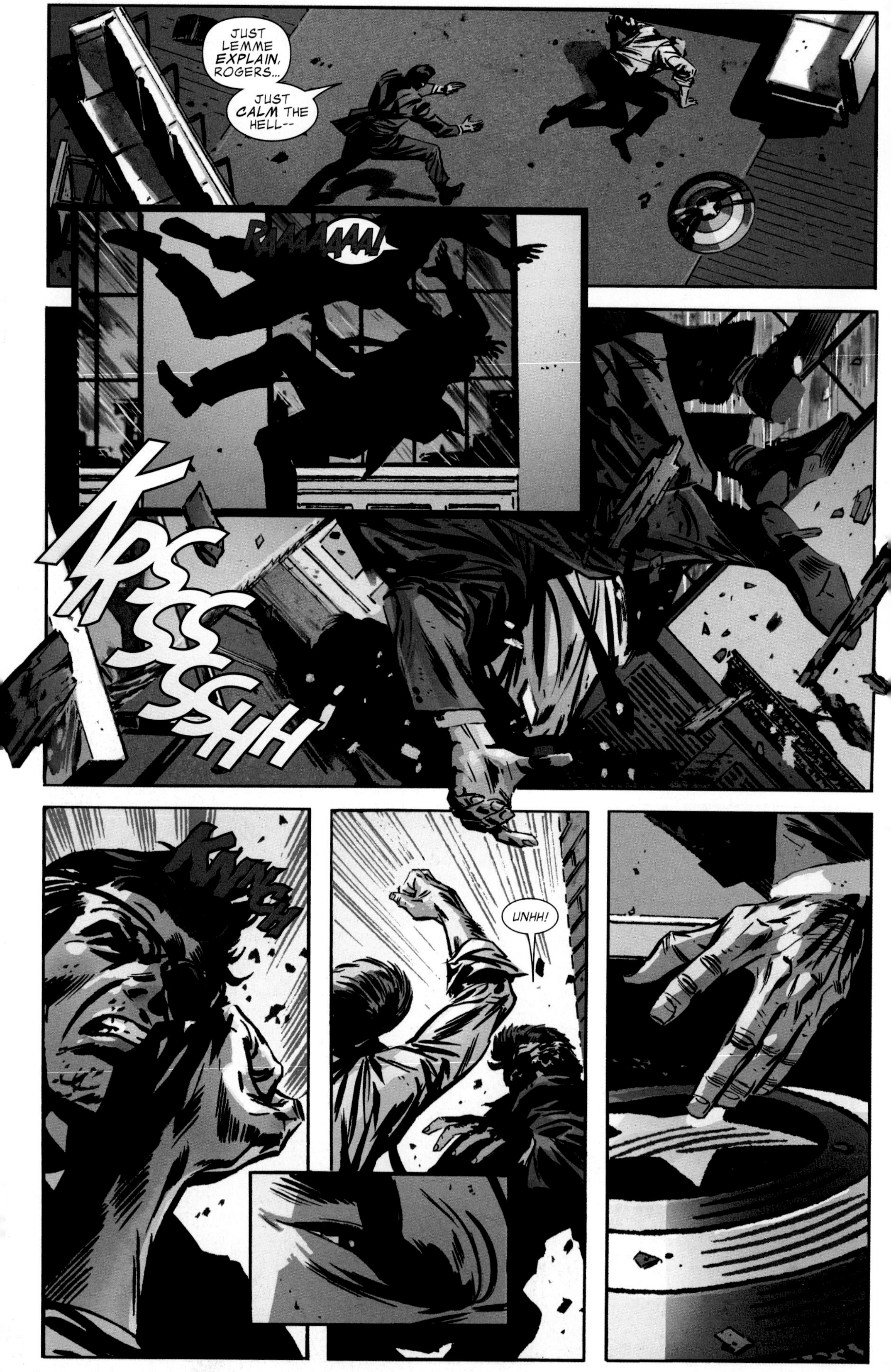
JUST LEMME EXPLAIN, ROGERS...
JUST CALM THE HELL--
RAAAAAAA!
KRSSSSHH
KNNCH
UNHH!

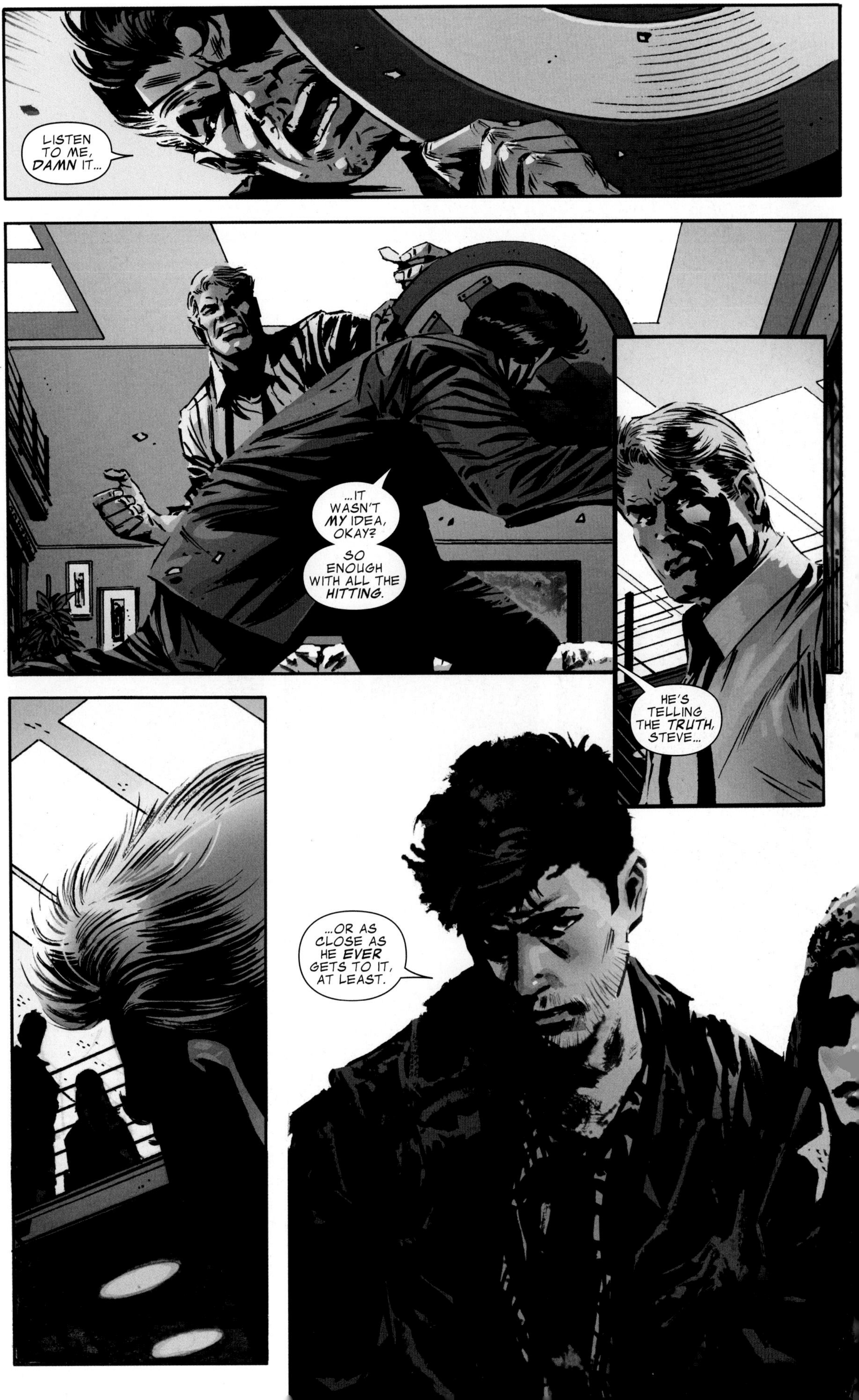
LISTEN TO ME, DAMN IT...
...IT WASN'T MY IDEA, OKAY?
SO ENOUGH WITH ALL THE HITTING.
HE'S TELLING THE TRUTH, STEVE...
...OR AS CLOSE AS HE EVER GETS TO IT, AT LEAST.

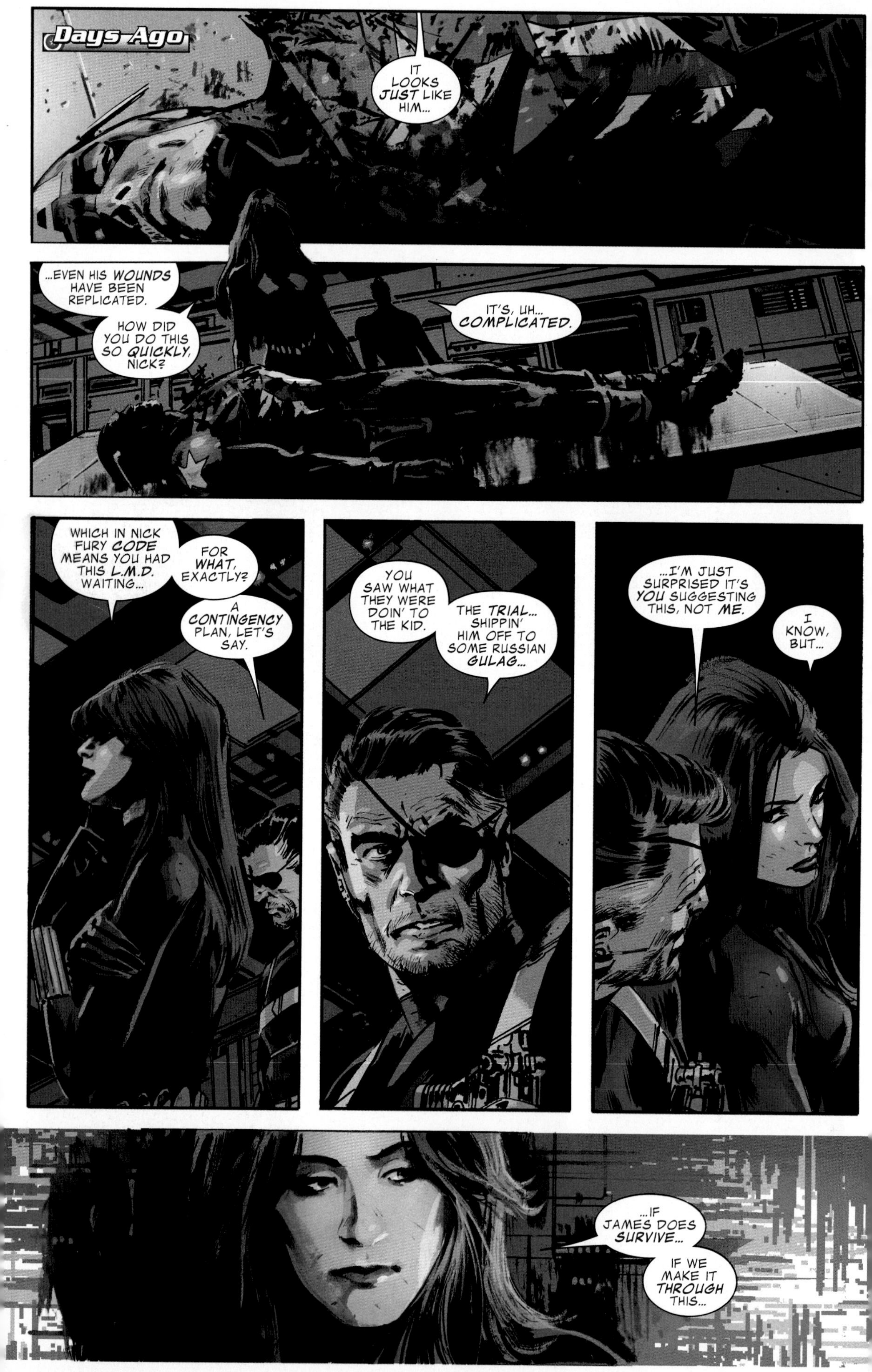
Days Ago
IT LOOKS JUST LIKE HIM...
...EVEN HIS WOUNDS HAVE BEEN REPLICATED.
HOW DID YOU DO THIS SO QUICKLY, NICK?
IT'S, UH... COMPLICATED.
WHICH IN NICK FURY CODE MEANS YOU HAD THIS L.M.D. WAITING...
FOR WHAT, EXACTLY?
A CONTINGENCY PLAN, LET'S SAY.
YOU SAW WHAT THEY WERE DOIN' TO THE KID.
THE TRIAL... SHIPPIN' HIM OFF TO SOME RUSSIAN GULAG...
...I'M JUST SURPRISED IT'S YOU SUGGESTING THIS, NOT ME.
I KNOW, BUT...
...IF JAMES DOES SURVIVE...
IF WE MAKE IT THROUGH THIS...

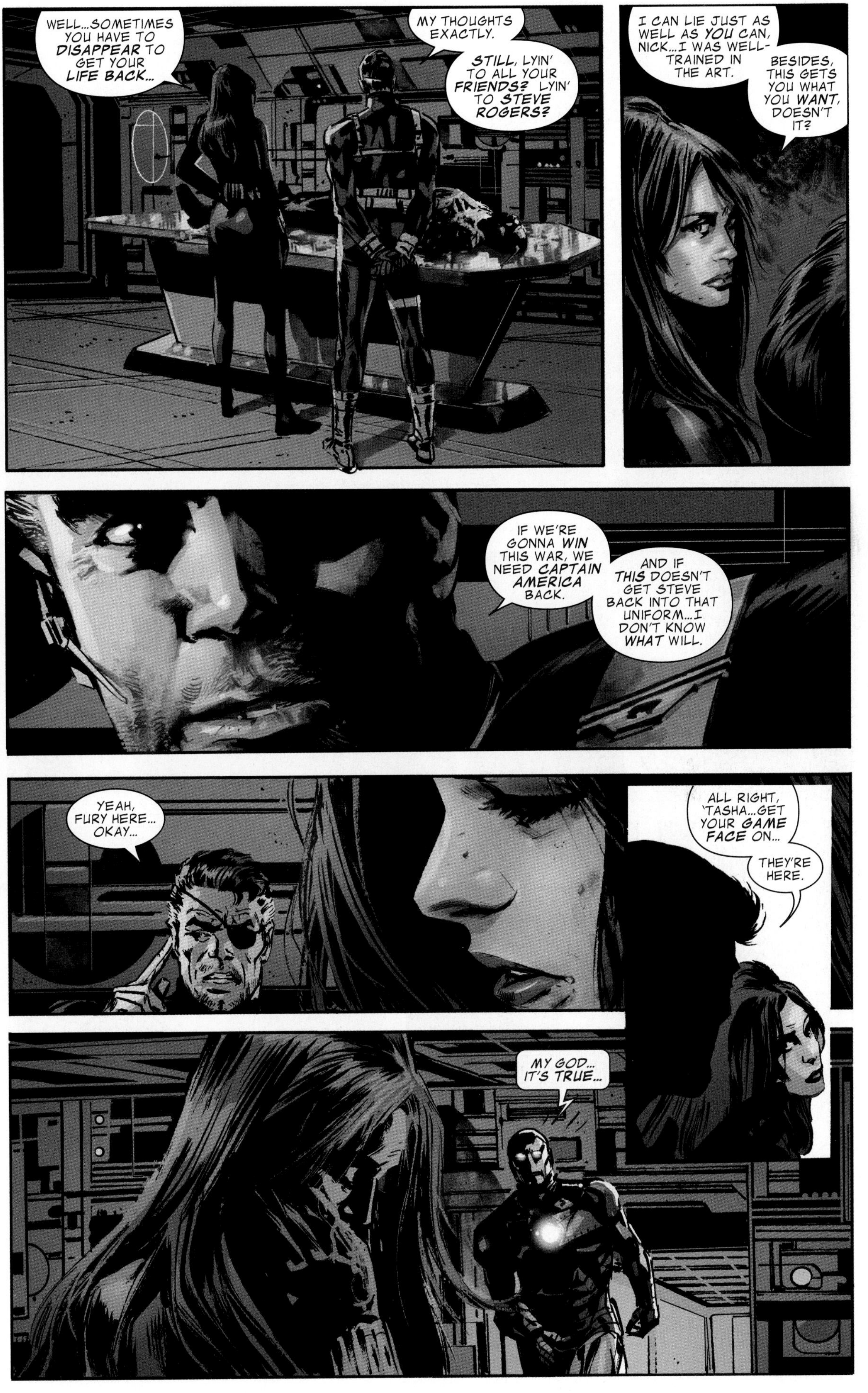

WELL...SOMETIMES YOU HAVE TO **DISAPPEAR** TO GET YOUR **LIFE BACK...**
MY THOUGHTS EXACTLY.
STILL, LYIN' TO ALL YOUR **FRIENDS?** LYIN' TO **STEVE ROGERS?**
I CAN LIE JUST AS WELL AS **YOU** CAN, NICK...I WAS WELL-TRAINED IN THE ART.
BESIDES, THIS GETS YOU WHAT YOU **WANT**, DOESN'T IT?
IF WE'RE GONNA **WIN** THIS WAR, WE NEED **CAPTAIN AMERICA** BACK.
AND IF **THIS** DOESN'T GET STEVE BACK INTO THAT UNIFORM...I DON'T KNOW **WHAT** WILL.
YEAH, FURY HERE... OKAY...
ALL RIGHT, 'TASHA...GET YOUR **GAME FACE** ON...
THEY'RE HERE.
MY GOD... IT'S **TRUE**...

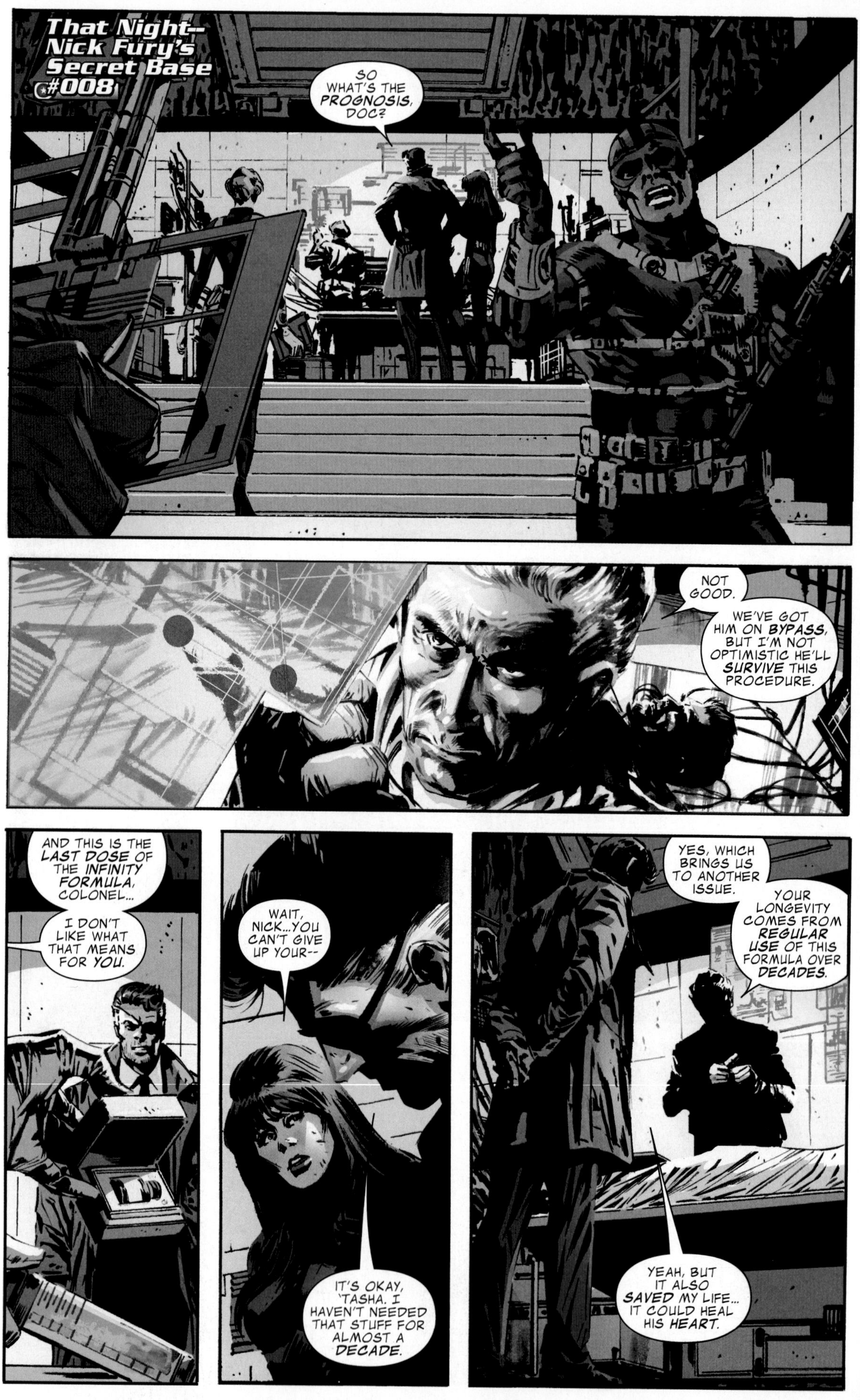
That Night--
Nick Fury's
Secret Base
#008
SO WHAT'S THE PROGNOSIS, DOC?
NOT GOOD.
WE'VE GOT HIM ON BYPASS, BUT I'M NOT OPTIMISTIC HE'LL SURVIVE THIS PROCEDURE.
AND THIS IS THE LAST DOSE OF THE INFINITY FORMULA, COLONEL...
I DON'T LIKE WHAT THAT MEANS FOR YOU.
WAIT, NICK...YOU CAN'T GIVE UP YOUR--
IT'S OKAY, 'TASHA. I HAVEN'T NEEDED THAT STUFF FOR ALMOST A DECADE.
YES, WHICH BRINGS US TO ANOTHER ISSUE.
YOUR LONGEVITY COMES FROM REGULAR USE OF THIS FORMULA OVER DECADES.
YEAH, BUT IT ALSO SAVED MY LIFE... IT COULD HEAL HIS HEART.

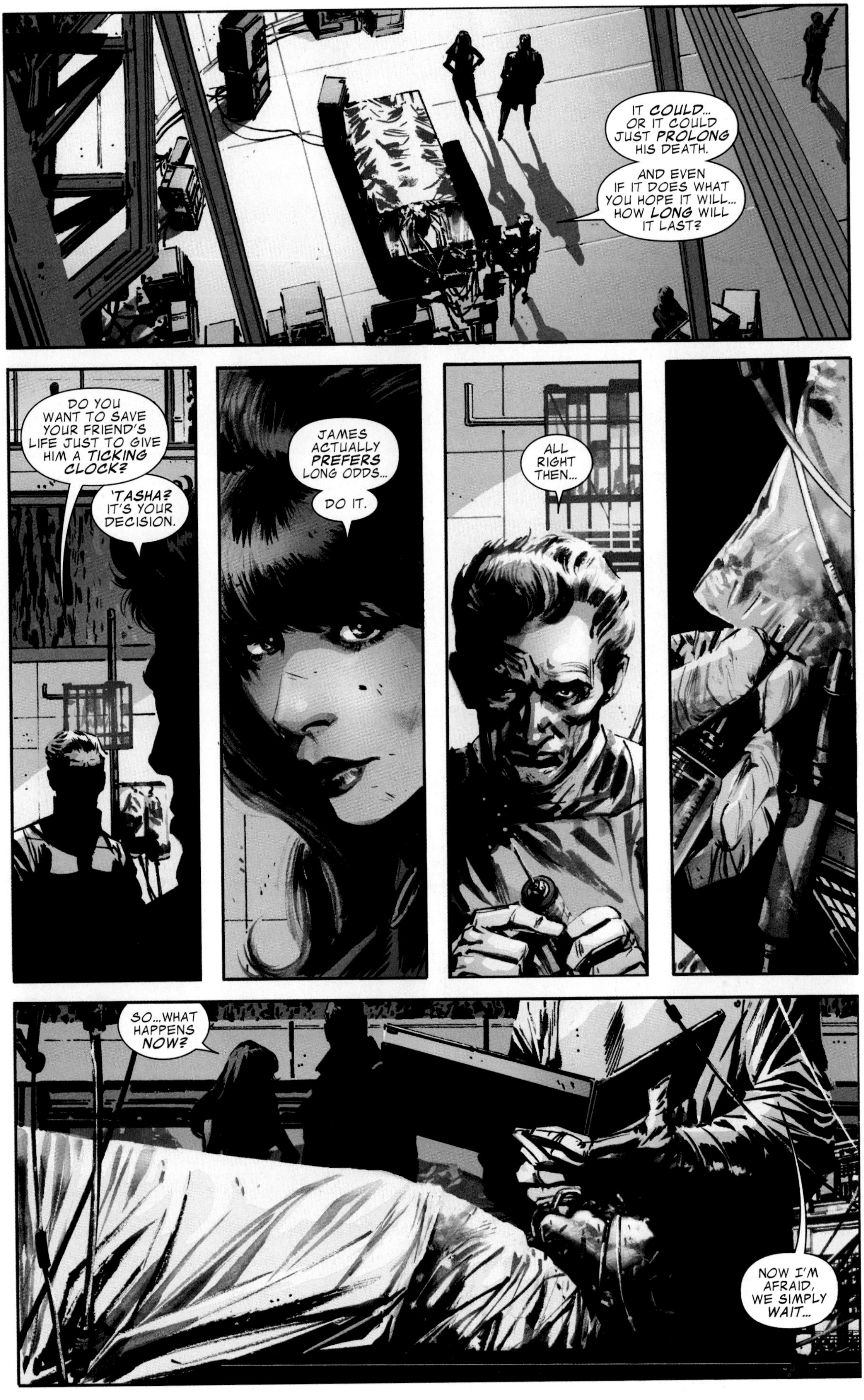
IT COULD... OR IT COULD JUST PROLONG HIS DEATH.
AND EVEN IF IT DOES WHAT YOU HOPE IT WILL... HOW LONG WILL IT LAST?
DO YOU WANT TO SAVE YOUR FRIEND'S LIFE JUST TO GIVE HIM A TICKING CLOCK?
'TASHA? IT'S YOUR DECISION.
JAMES ACTUALLY PREFERS LONG ODDS...
DO IT.
ALL RIGHT THEN...
SO...WHAT HAPPENS NOW?
NOW I'M AFRAID, WE SIMPLY WAIT...

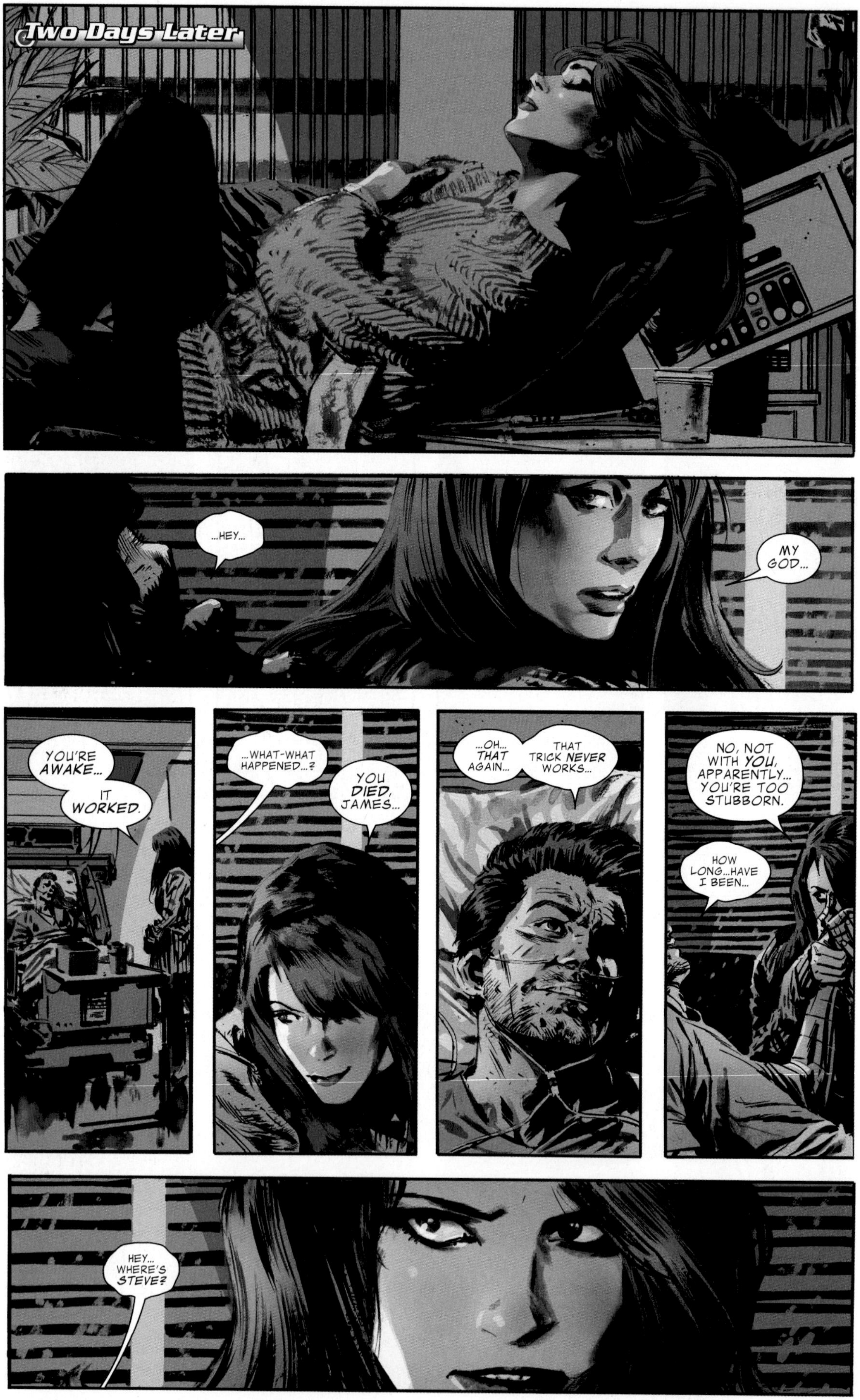
Two Days Later
...HEY...
MY GOD...
YOU'RE AWAKE...
IT WORKED.
...WHAT-WHAT HAPPENED...?
YOU DIED, JAMES...
...OH... THAT AGAIN...
THAT TRICK NEVER WORKS...
NO, NOT WITH YOU, APPARENTLY... YOU'RE TOO STUBBORN.
HOW LONG...HAVE I BEEN...
HEY... WHERE'S STEVE?

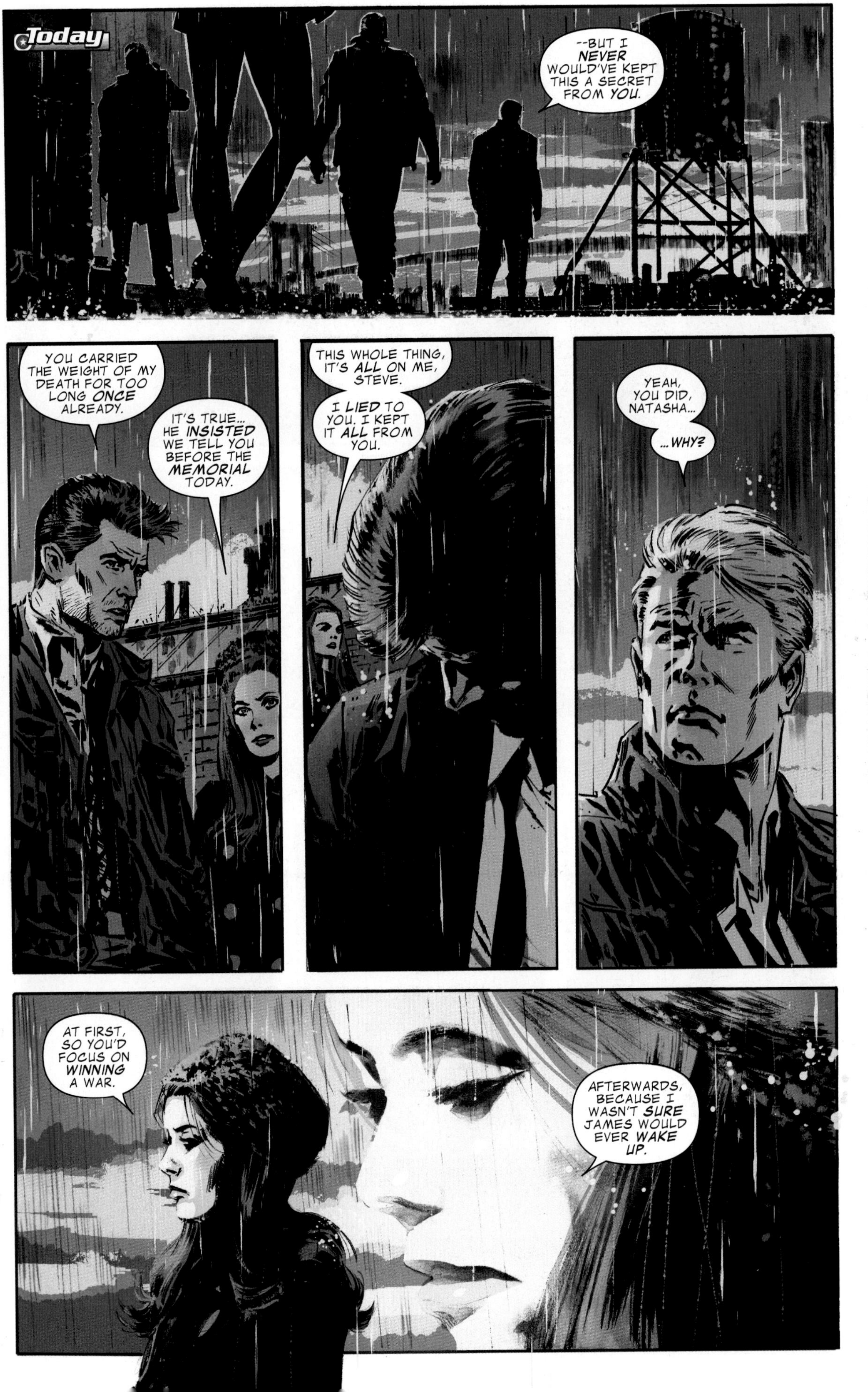
Today
--BUT I NEVER WOULD'VE KEPT THIS A SECRET FROM YOU.
YOU CARRIED THE WEIGHT OF MY DEATH FOR TOO LONG ONCE ALREADY.
IT'S TRUE... HE INSISTED WE TELL YOU BEFORE THE MEMORIAL TODAY.
THIS WHOLE THING, IT'S ALL ON ME, STEVE.
I LIED TO YOU. I KEPT IT ALL FROM YOU.
YEAH, YOU DID, NATASHA...
...WHY?
AT FIRST, SO YOU'D FOCUS ON WINNING A WAR.
AFTERWARDS, BECAUSE I WASN'T SURE JAMES WOULD EVER WAKE UP.

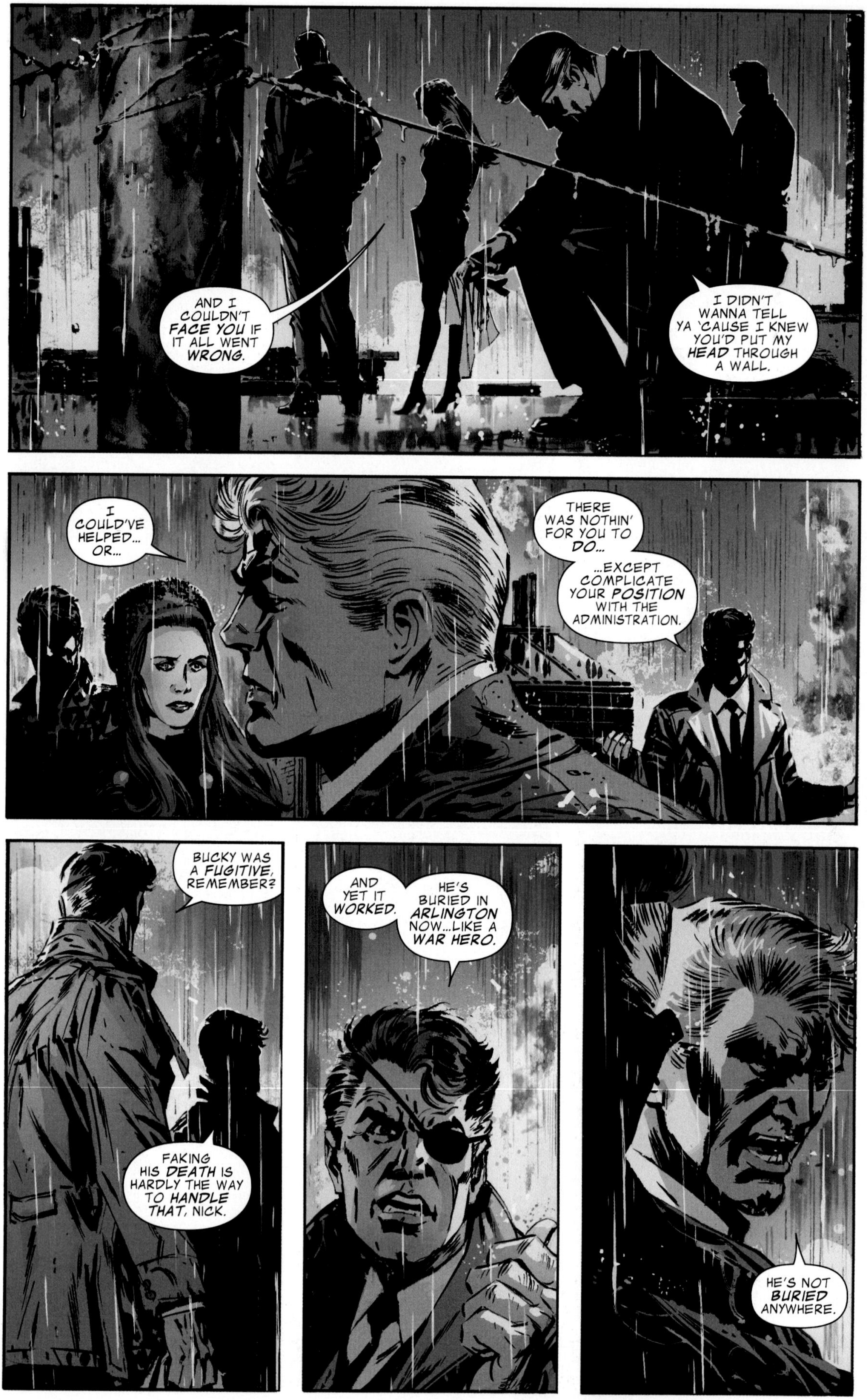

AND I COULDN'T FACE YOU IF IT ALL WENT WRONG.
I DIDN'T WANNA TELL YA 'CAUSE I KNEW YOU'D PUT MY HEAD THROUGH A WALL.
I COULD'VE HELPED... OR...
THERE WAS NOTHIN' FOR YOU TO DO...
...EXCEPT COMPLICATE YOUR POSITION WITH THE ADMINISTRATION.
BUCKY WAS A FUGITIVE, REMEMBER?
FAKING HIS DEATH IS HARDLY THE WAY TO HANDLE THAT, NICK.
AND YET IT WORKED.
HE'S BURIED IN ARLINGTON NOW...LIKE A WAR HERO.
HE'S NOT BURIED ANYWHERE.

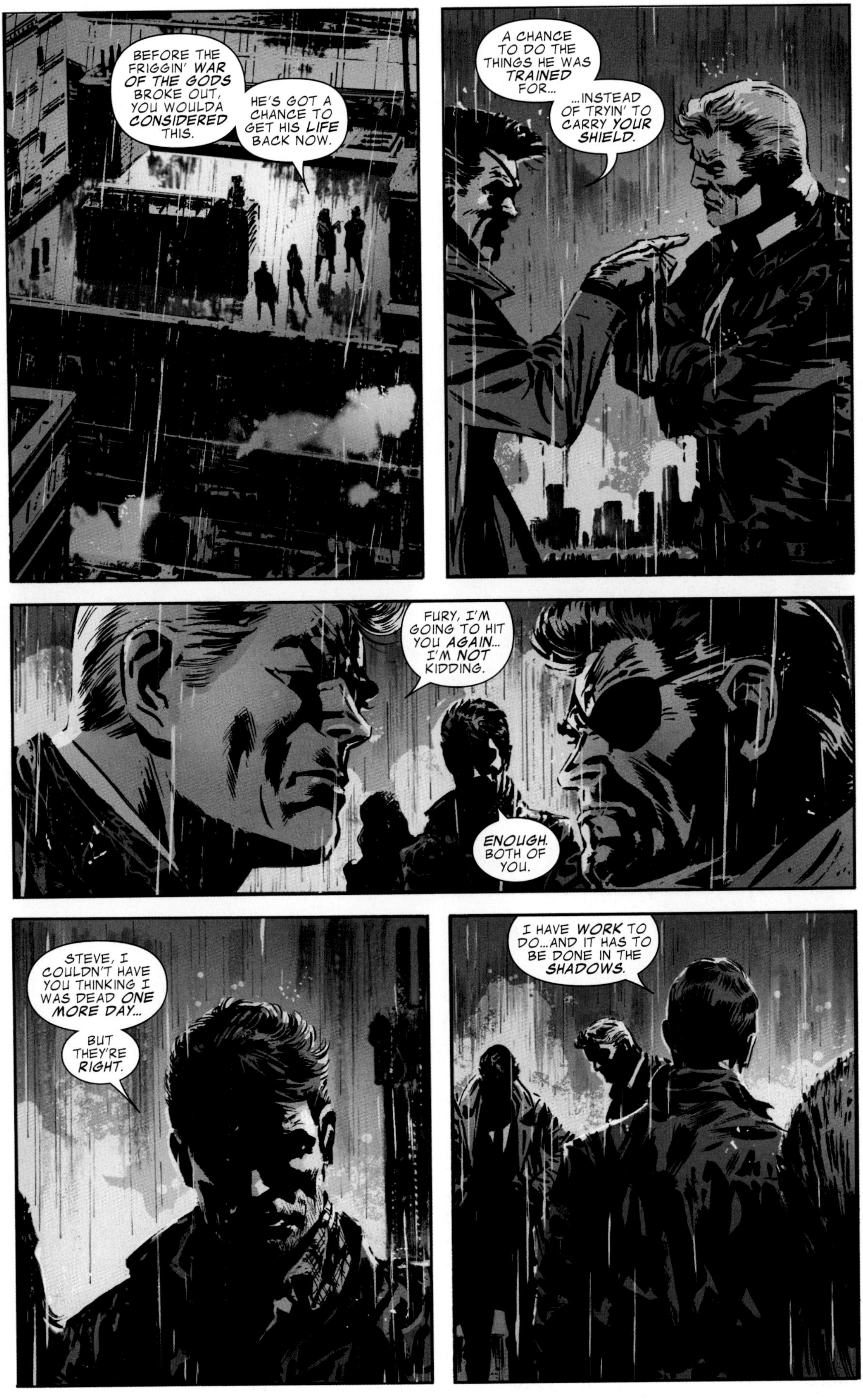
BEFORE THE FRIGGIN' WAR OF THE GODS BROKE OUT, YOU WOULDA CONSIDERED THIS.
HE'S GOT A CHANCE TO GET HIS LIFE BACK NOW.
A CHANCE TO DO THE THINGS HE WAS TRAINED FOR...
...INSTEAD OF TRYIN' TO CARRY YOUR SHIELD.
FURY, I'M GOING TO HIT YOU AGAIN... I'M NOT KIDDING.
ENOUGH. BOTH OF YOU.
STEVE, I COULDN'T HAVE YOU THINKING I WAS DEAD ONE MORE DAY...
BUT THEY'RE RIGHT.
I HAVE WORK TO DO...AND IT HAS TO BE DONE IN THE SHADOWS.

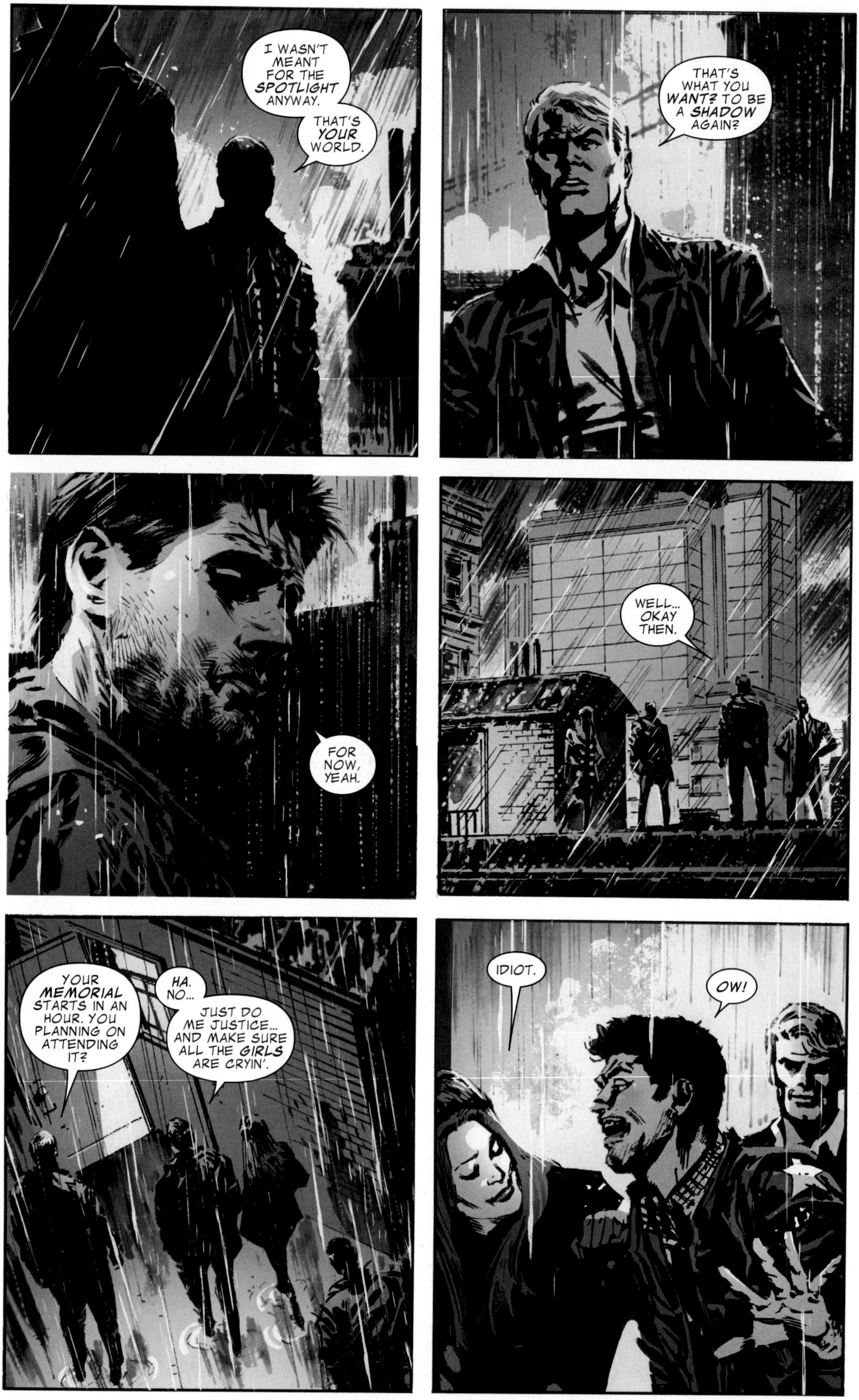
I WASN'T MEANT FOR THE SPOTLIGHT ANYWAY.
THAT'S YOUR WORLD.
THAT'S WHAT YOU WANT? TO BE A SHADOW AGAIN?
FOR NOW, YEAH.
WELL... OKAY THEN.
YOUR MEMORIAL STARTS IN AN HOUR. YOU PLANNING ON ATTENDING IT?
HA. NO...
JUST DO ME JUSTICE... AND MAKE SURE ALL THE GIRLS ARE CRYIN'.
IDIOT.
OW!

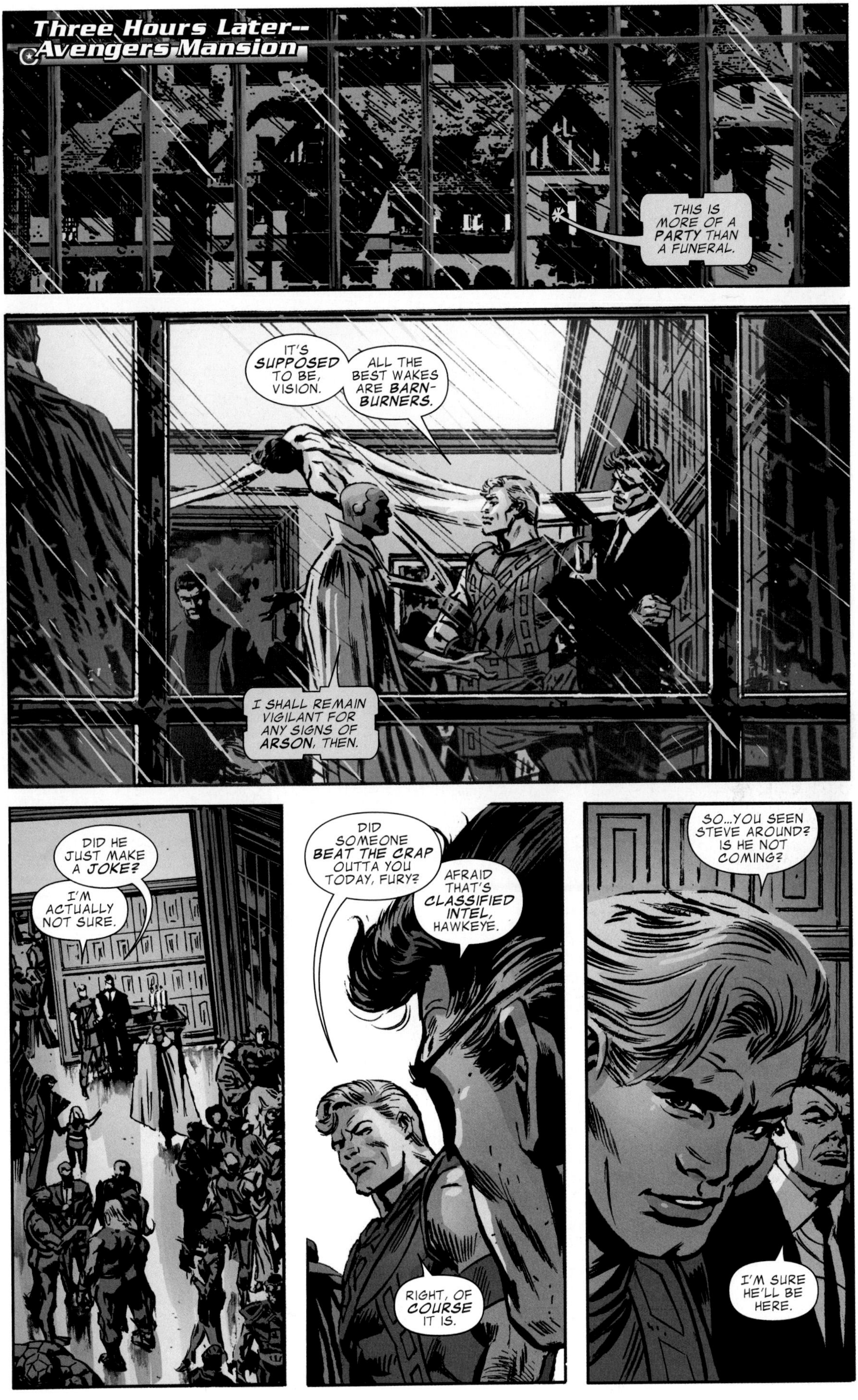
Three Hours Later--
Avengers Mansion
THIS IS MORE OF A PARTY THAN A FUNERAL.
IT'S SUPPOSED TO BE, VISION.
ALL THE BEST WAKES ARE BARN-BURNERS.
I SHALL REMAIN VIGILANT FOR ANY SIGNS OF ARSON, THEN.
DID HE JUST MAKE A JOKE?
I'M ACTUALLY NOT SURE.
DID SOMEONE BEAT THE CRAP OUTTA YOU TODAY, FURY?
AFRAID THAT'S CLASSIFIED INTEL, HAWKEYE.
RIGHT, OF COURSE IT IS.
SO...YOU SEEN STEVE AROUND? IS HE NOT COMING?
I'M SURE HE'LL BE HERE.

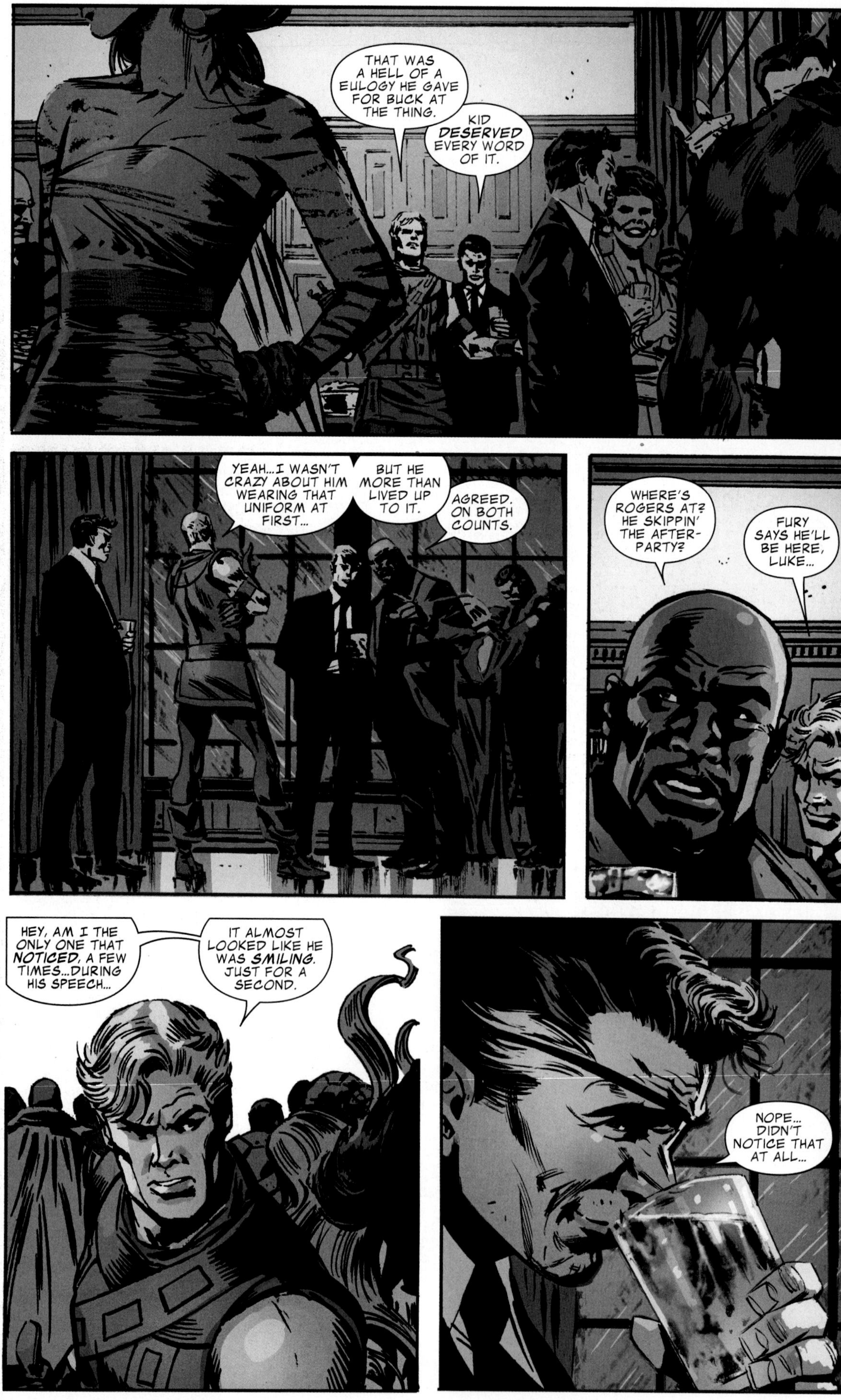
THAT WAS A HELL OF A EULOGY HE GAVE FOR BUCK AT THE THING.
KID DESERVED EVERY WORD OF IT.
YEAH...I WASN'T CRAZY ABOUT HIM WEARING THAT UNIFORM AT FIRST...
BUT HE MORE THAN LIVED UP TO IT.
AGREED. ON BOTH COUNTS.
WHERE'S ROGERS AT? HE SKIPPIN' THE AFTER-PARTY?
FURY SAYS HE'LL BE HERE, LUKE...
HEY, AM I THE ONLY ONE THAT NOTICED, A FEW TIMES...DURING HIS SPEECH...
IT ALMOST LOOKED LIKE HE WAS SMILING. JUST FOR A SECOND.
NOPE... DIDN'T NOTICE THAT AT ALL...

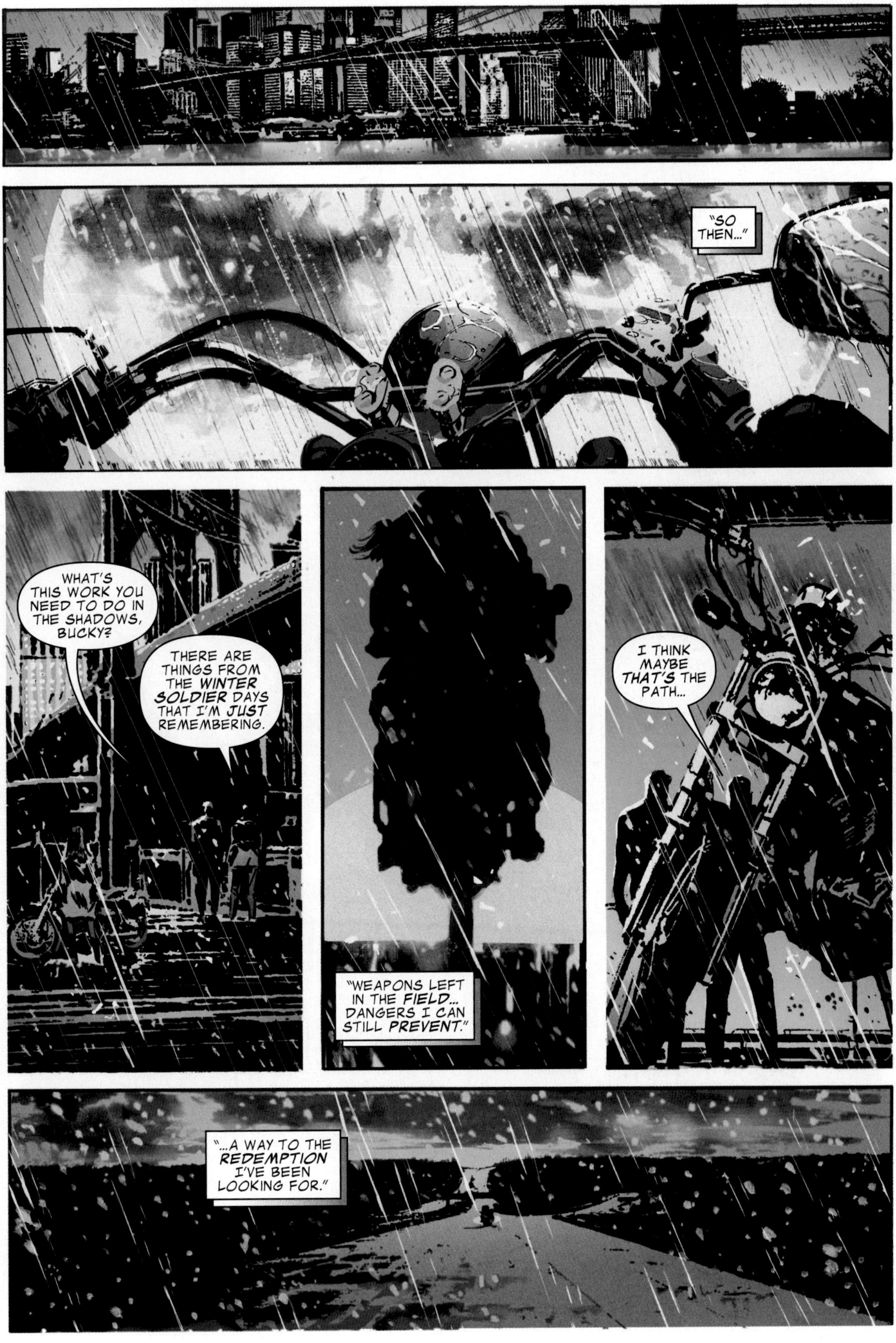
"SO THEN..."
WHAT'S THIS WORK YOU NEED TO DO IN THE SHADOWS, BUCKY?
THERE ARE THINGS FROM THE WINTER SOLDIER DAYS THAT I'M JUST REMEMBERING.
"WEAPONS LEFT IN THE FIELD... DANGERS I CAN STILL PREVENT."
I THINK MAYBE THAT'S THE PATH...
"...A WAY TO THE REDEMPTION I'VE BEEN LOOKING FOR."

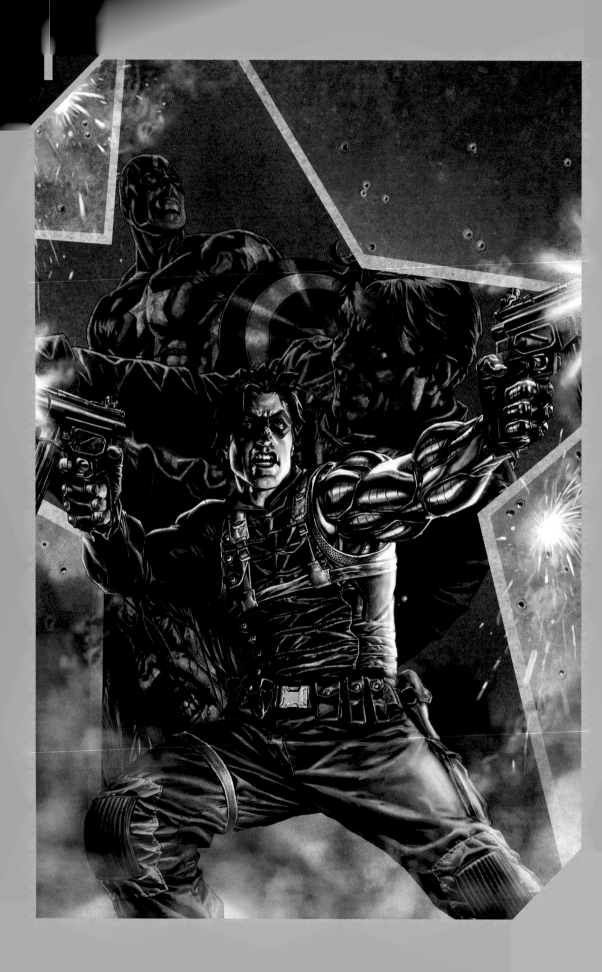

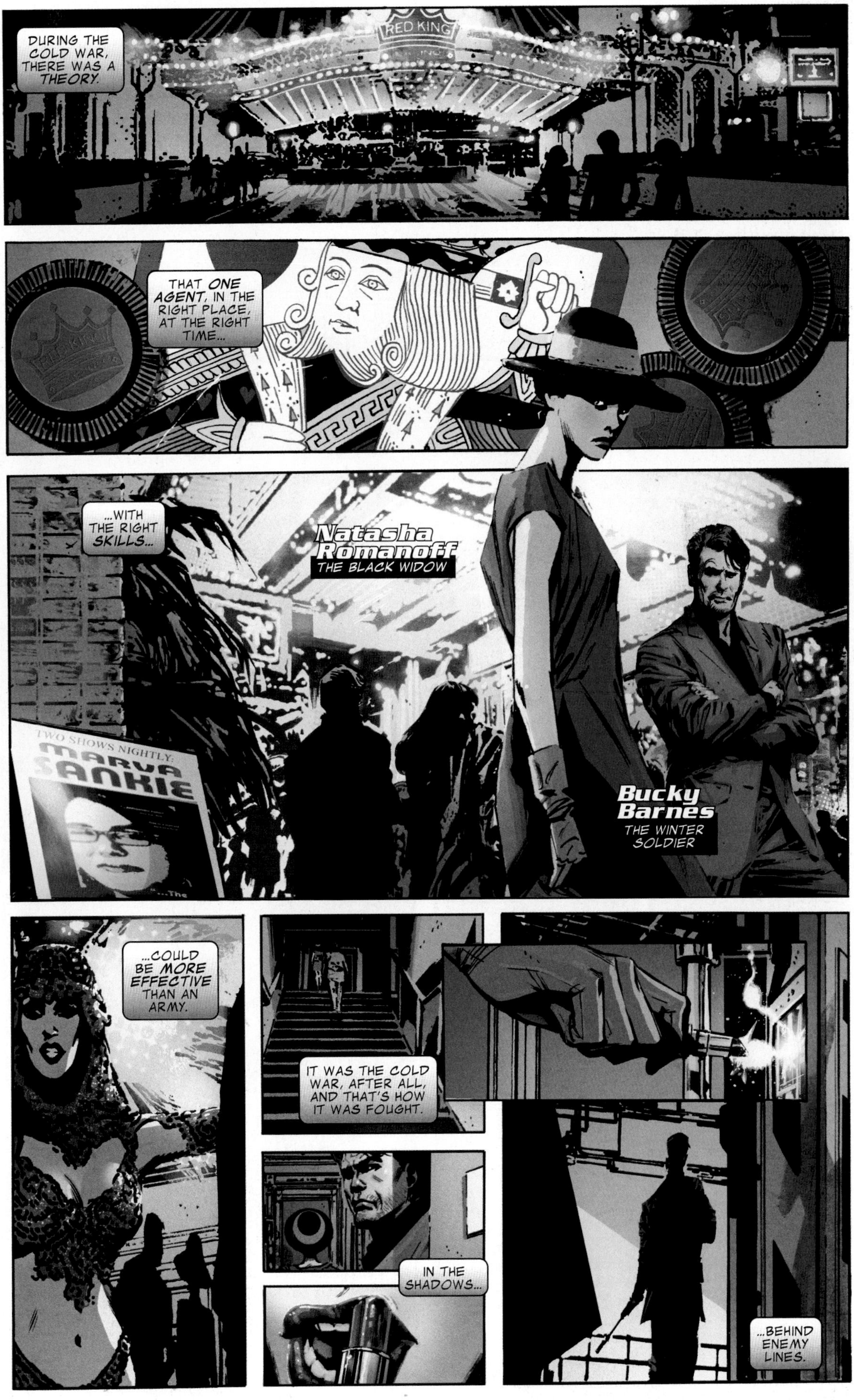
DURING THE COLD WAR, THERE WAS A THEORY.
RED KING
THAT ONE AGENT, IN THE RIGHT PLACE, AT THE RIGHT TIME...
...WITH THE RIGHT SKILLS...
Natasha Romanoff
THE BLACK WIDOW
TWO SHOWS NIGHTLY:
MARVA SANKIE
Bucky Barnes
THE WINTER SOLDIER
...COULD BE MORE EFFECTIVE THAN AN ARMY.
IT WAS THE COLD WAR, AFTER ALL, AND THAT'S HOW IT WAS FOUGHT.
IN THE SHADOWS...
...BEHIND ENEMY LINES.

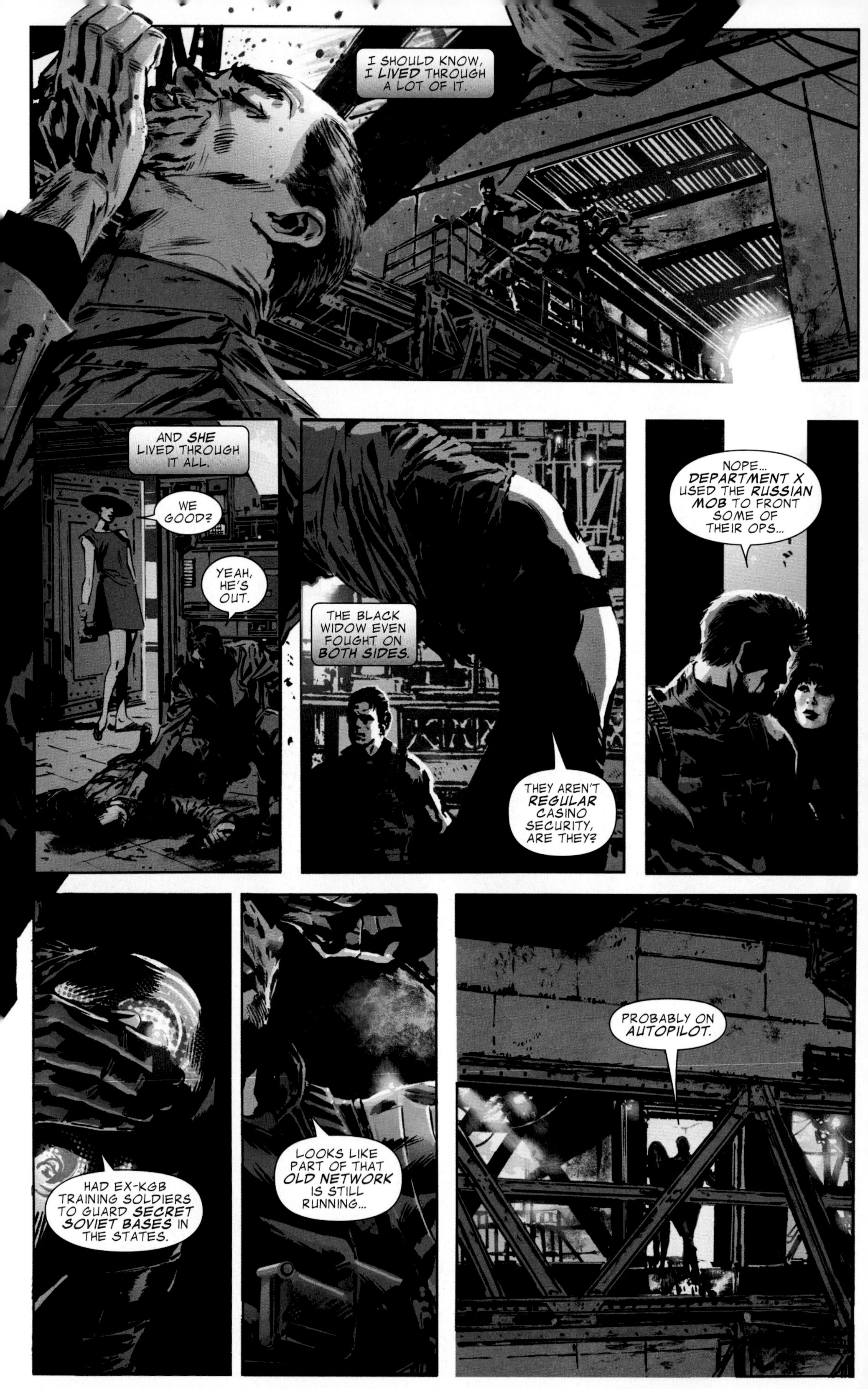
I SHOULD KNOW, I LIVED THROUGH A LOT OF IT.
AND SHE LIVED THROUGH IT ALL.
WE GOOD?
YEAH, HE'S OUT.
THE BLACK WIDOW EVEN FOUGHT ON BOTH SIDES.
THEY AREN'T REGULAR CASINO SECURITY, ARE THEY?
NOPE... DEPARTMENT X USED THE RUSSIAN MOB TO FRONT SOME OF THEIR OPS...
HAD EX-KGB TRAINING SOLDIERS TO GUARD SECRET SOVIET BASES IN THE STATES.
LOOKS LIKE PART OF THAT OLD NETWORK IS STILL RUNNING...
PROBABLY ON AUTOPILOT.

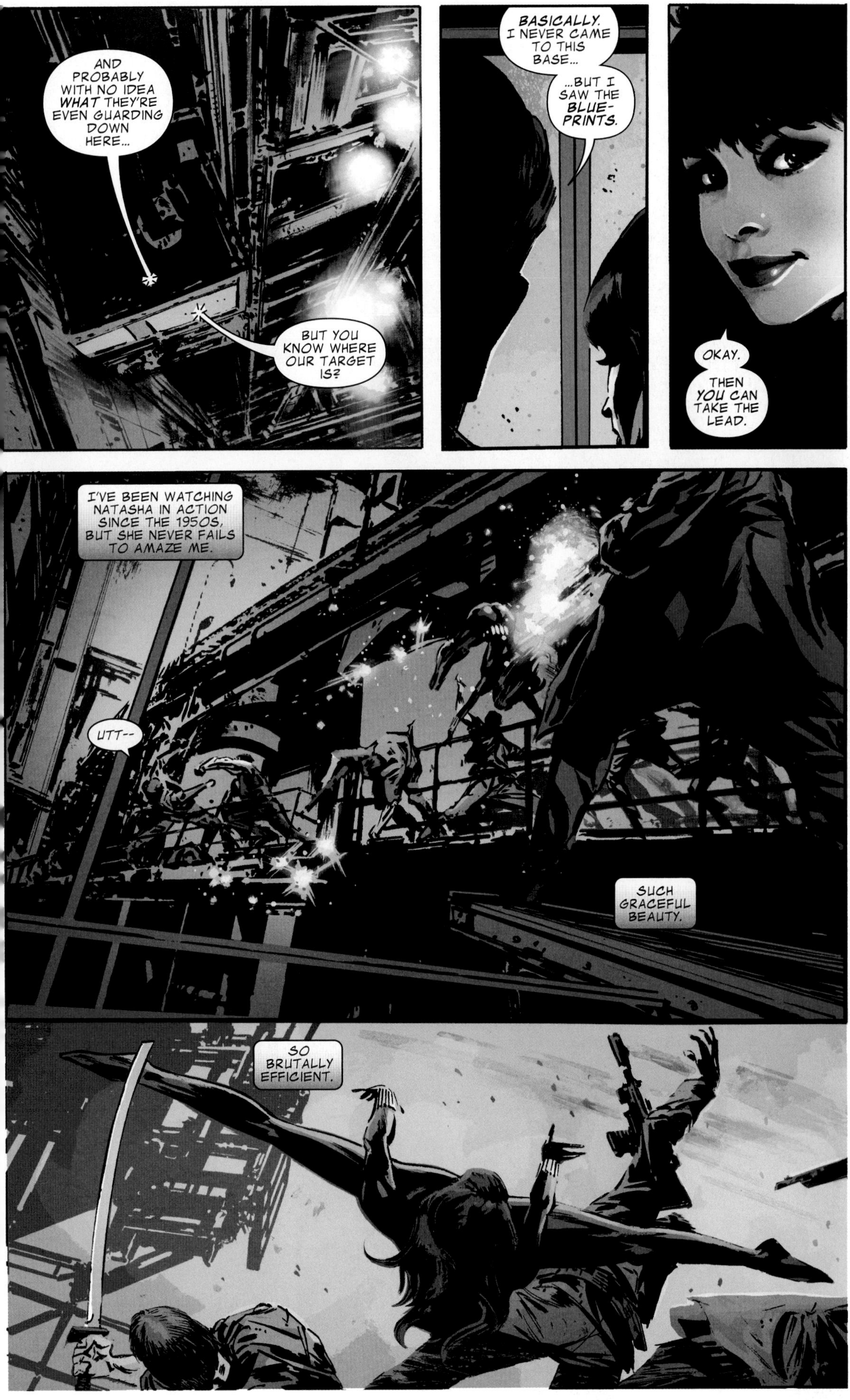
AND PROBABLY WITH NO IDEA WHAT THEY'RE EVEN GUARDING DOWN HERE...
BUT YOU KNOW WHERE OUR TARGET IS?
BASICALLY. I NEVER CAME TO THIS BASE...
...BUT I SAW THE BLUE-PRINTS.
OKAY.
THEN YOU CAN TAKE THE LEAD.
I'VE BEEN WATCHING NATASHA IN ACTION SINCE THE 1950S, BUT SHE NEVER FAILS TO AMAZE ME.
UTT--
SUCH GRACEFUL BEAUTY.
SO BRUTALLY EFFICIENT.

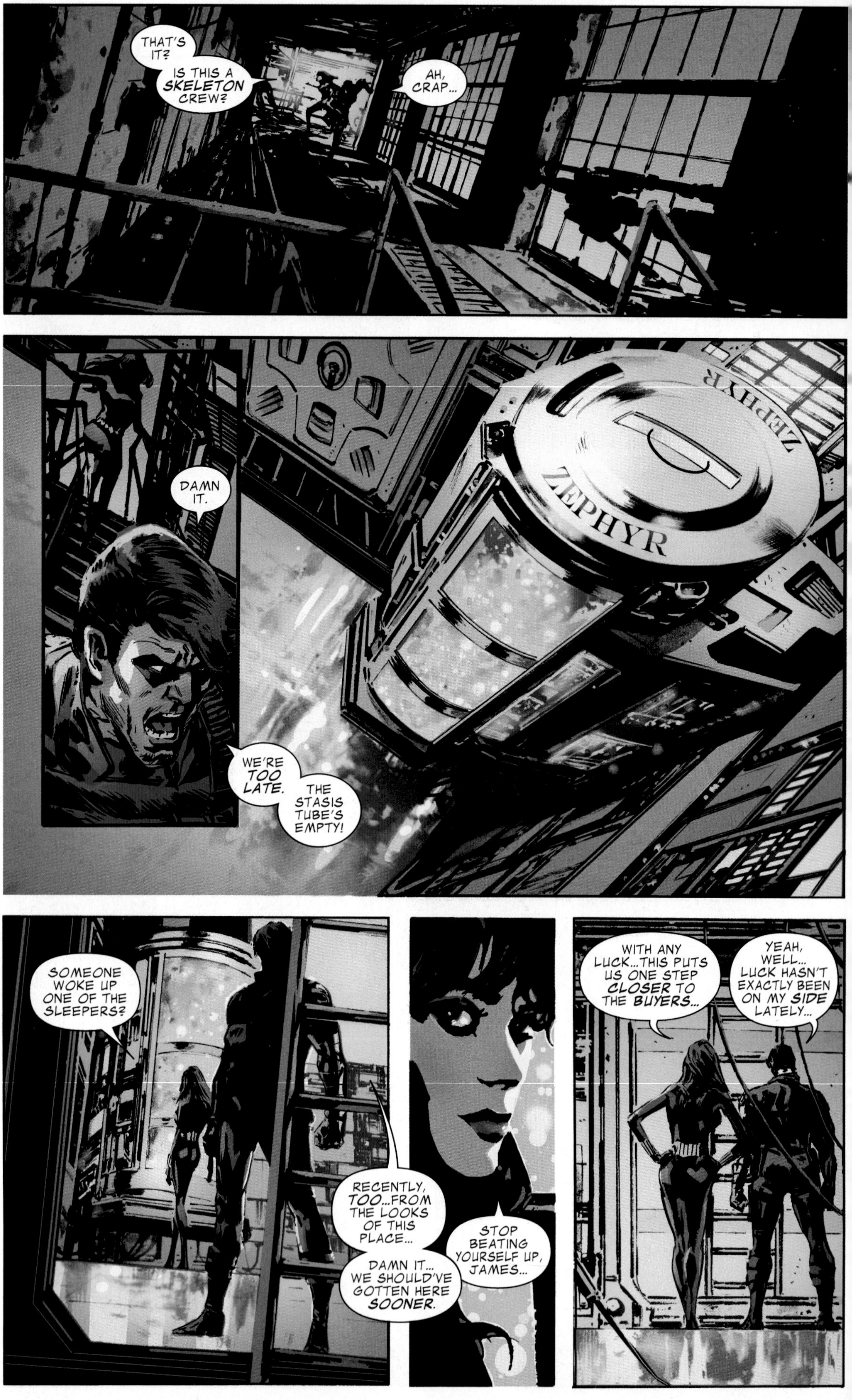
THAT'S IT?
IS THIS A SKELETON CREW?
AH, CRAP...
DAMN IT.
ZEPHYR
WE'RE TOO LATE.
THE STASIS TUBE'S EMPTY!
SOMEONE WOKE UP ONE OF THE SLEEPERS?
RECENTLY, TOO...FROM THE LOOKS OF THIS PLACE...
DAMN IT... WE SHOULD'VE GOTTEN HERE SOONER.
STOP BEATING YOURSELF UP, JAMES...
WITH ANY LUCK...THIS PUTS US ONE STEP CLOSER TO THE BUYERS...
YEAH, WELL... LUCK HASN'T EXACTLY BEEN ON MY SIDE LATELY...

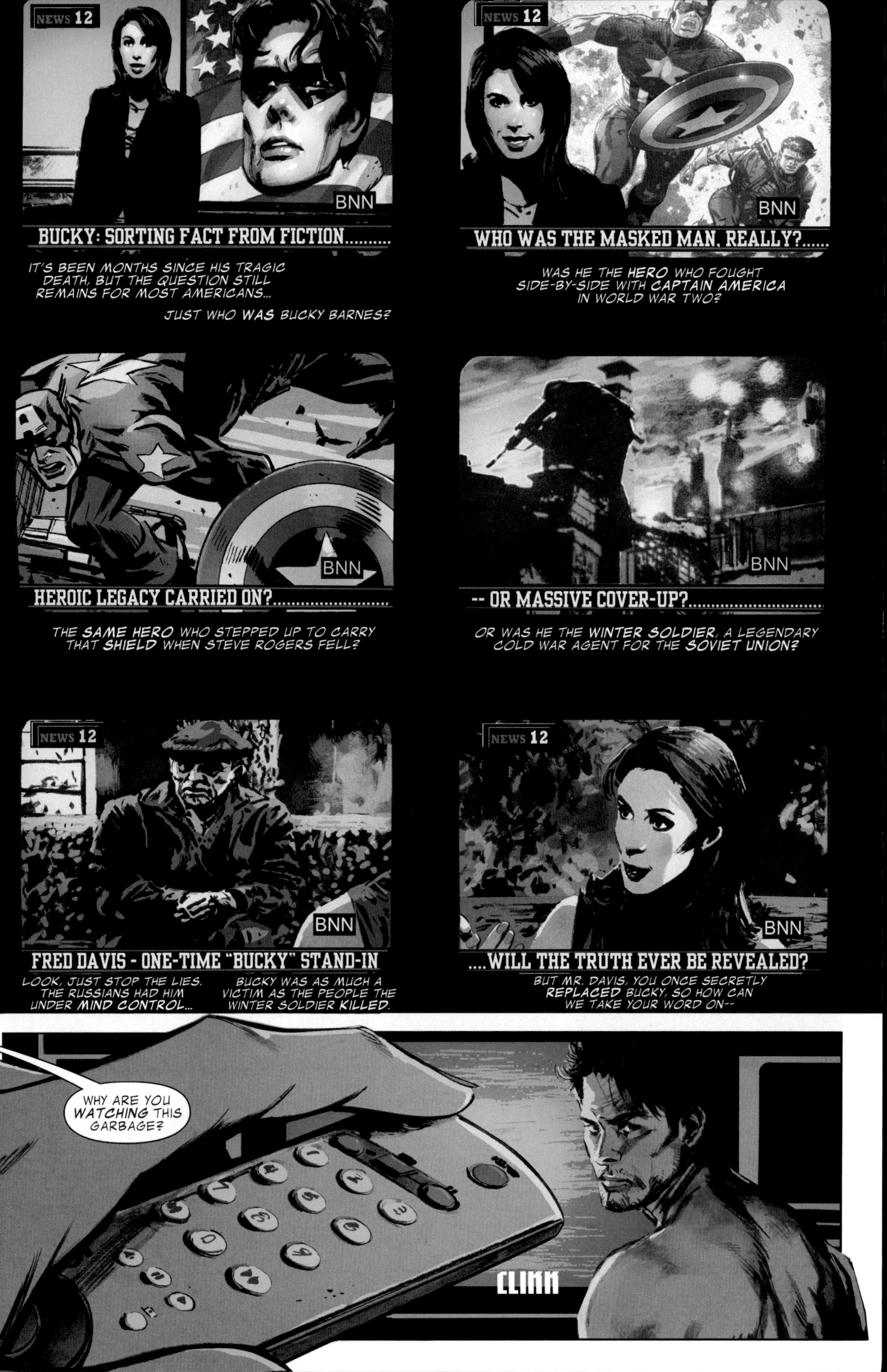
NEWS 12
BNN
BUCKY: SORTING FACT FROM FICTION..........
IT'S BEEN MONTHS SINCE HIS TRAGIC DEATH, BUT THE QUESTION STILL REMAINS FOR MOST AMERICANS...
JUST WHO WAS BUCKY BARNES?
NEWS 12
BNN
WHO WAS THE MASKED MAN, REALLY?......
WAS HE THE HERO WHO FOUGHT SIDE-BY-SIDE WITH CAPTAIN AMERICA IN WORLD WAR TWO?
BNN
HEROIC LEGACY CARRIED ON?........................
THE SAME HERO WHO STEPPED UP TO CARRY THAT SHIELD WHEN STEVE ROGERS FELL?
BNN
-- OR MASSIVE COVER-UP?..............................
OR WAS HE THE WINTER SOLDIER, A LEGENDARY COLD WAR AGENT FOR THE SOVIET UNION?
NEWS 12
BNN
FRED DAVIS - ONE-TIME "BUCKY" STAND-IN
LOOK, JUST STOP THE LIES. THE RUSSIANS HAD HIM UNDER MIND CONTROL...
BUCKY WAS AS MUCH A VICTIM AS THE PEOPLE THE WINTER SOLDIER KILLED.
NEWS 12
BNN
....WILL THE TRUTH EVER BE REVEALED?
BUT MR. DAVIS, YOU ONCE SECRETLY REPLACED BUCKY, SO HOW CAN WE TAKE YOUR WORD ON--
WHY ARE YOU WATCHING THIS GARBAGE?
CLINK

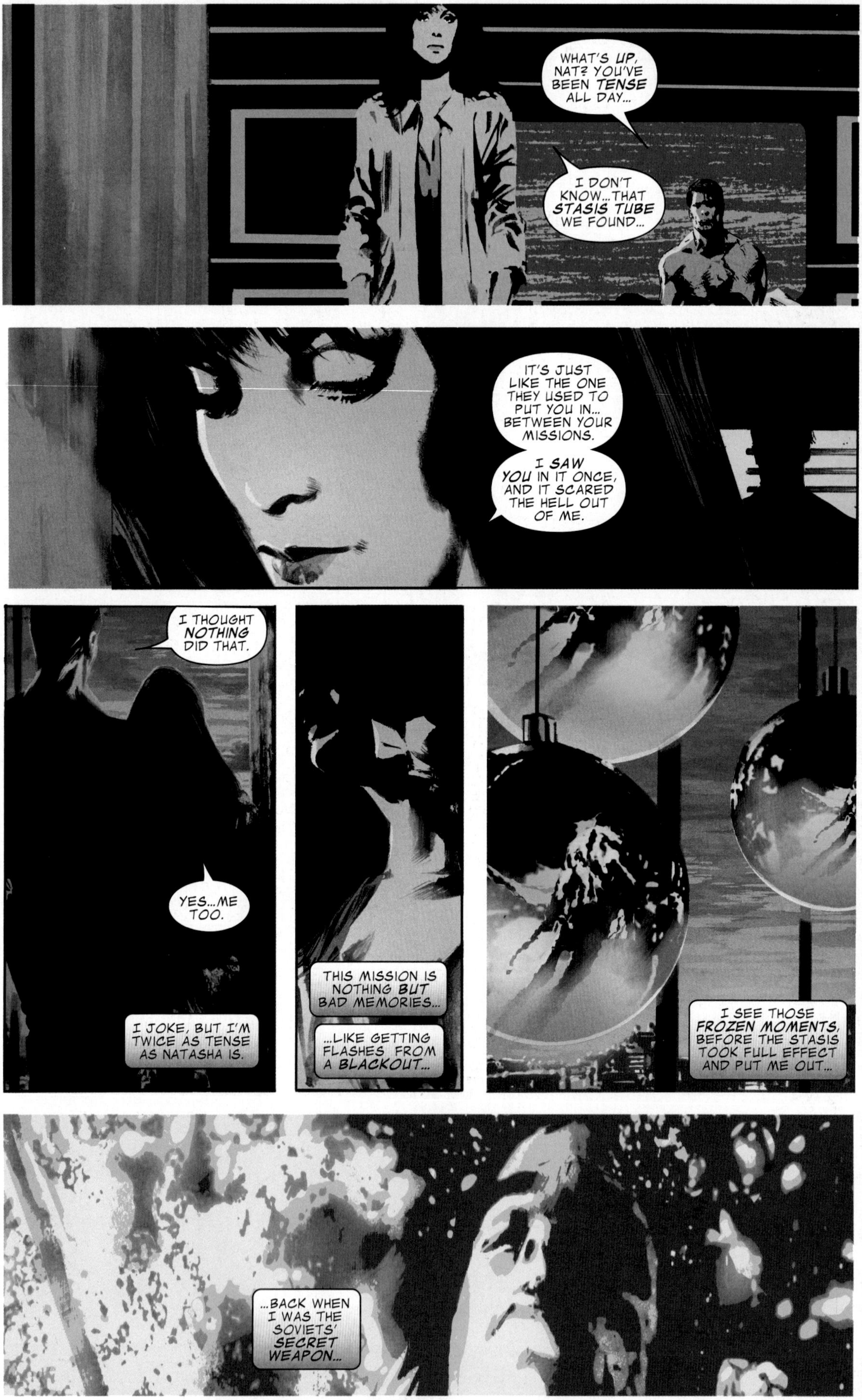
WHAT'S UP, NAT? YOU'VE BEEN TENSE ALL DAY...
I DON'T KNOW...THAT STASIS TUBE WE FOUND...
IT'S JUST LIKE THE ONE THEY USED TO PUT YOU IN... BETWEEN YOUR MISSIONS.
I SAW YOU IN IT ONCE, AND IT SCARED THE HELL OUT OF ME.
I THOUGHT NOTHING DID THAT.
YES...ME TOO.
I JOKE, BUT I'M TWICE AS TENSE AS NATASHA IS.
THIS MISSION IS NOTHING BUT BAD MEMORIES...
...LIKE GETTING FLASHES FROM A BLACKOUT...
I SEE THOSE FROZEN MOMENTS, BEFORE THE STASIS TOOK FULL EFFECT AND PUT ME OUT...
...BACK WHEN I WAS THE SOVIETS' SECRET WEAPON...

I SEE MYSELF TRAINING OTHER SOLDIERS-- TO KILL WITH PRECISION AND SKILL...

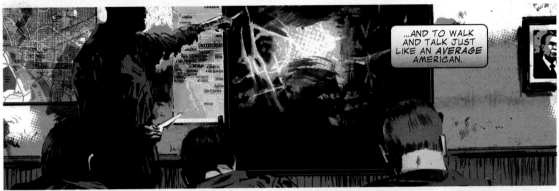

...AND TO WALK AND TALK JUST LIKE AN *AVERAGE* AMERICAN.

I WASN'T REALLY *ME* THEN, MY OLD PAL FRED DAVIS GOT THAT RIGHT...

BUT I STILL REMEMBER IT ALL, EITHER WAY.

I SEE THE THREE *SLEEPERS* IN TUBES LIKE THE ONE I SLEPT AWAY *DECADES* INSIDE OF...

READY TO BE SHIPPED TO *AMERICA,* WHERE THEY WOULD WAIT TO BE AWAKENED.

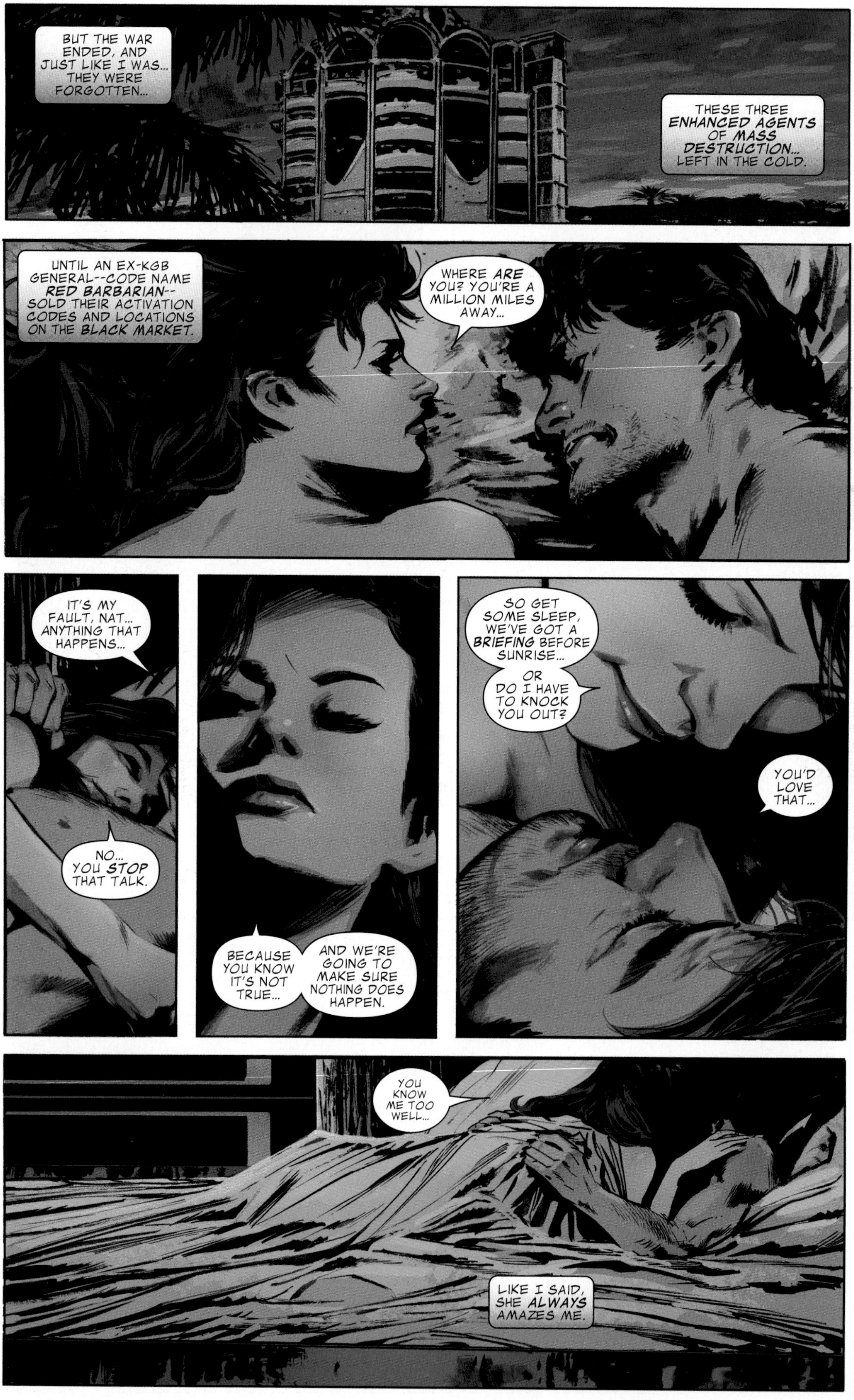

BUT THE WAR ENDED, AND JUST LIKE I WAS... THEY WERE FORGOTTEN...
THESE THREE ENHANCED AGENTS OF MASS DESTRUCTION... LEFT IN THE COLD.
UNTIL AN EX-KGB GENERAL--CODE NAME RED BARBARIAN--SOLD THEIR ACTIVATION CODES AND LOCATIONS ON THE BLACK MARKET.
WHERE ARE YOU? YOU'RE A MILLION MILES AWAY...
IT'S MY FAULT, NAT... ANYTHING THAT HAPPENS...
NO... YOU STOP THAT TALK.
BECAUSE YOU KNOW IT'S NOT TRUE...
AND WE'RE GOING TO MAKE SURE NOTHING DOES HAPPEN.
SO GET SOME SLEEP, WE'VE GOT A BRIEFING BEFORE SUNRISE...
OR DO I HAVE TO KNOCK YOU OUT?
YOU'D LOVE THAT...
YOU KNOW ME TOO WELL...
LIKE I SAID, SHE ALWAYS AMAZES ME.

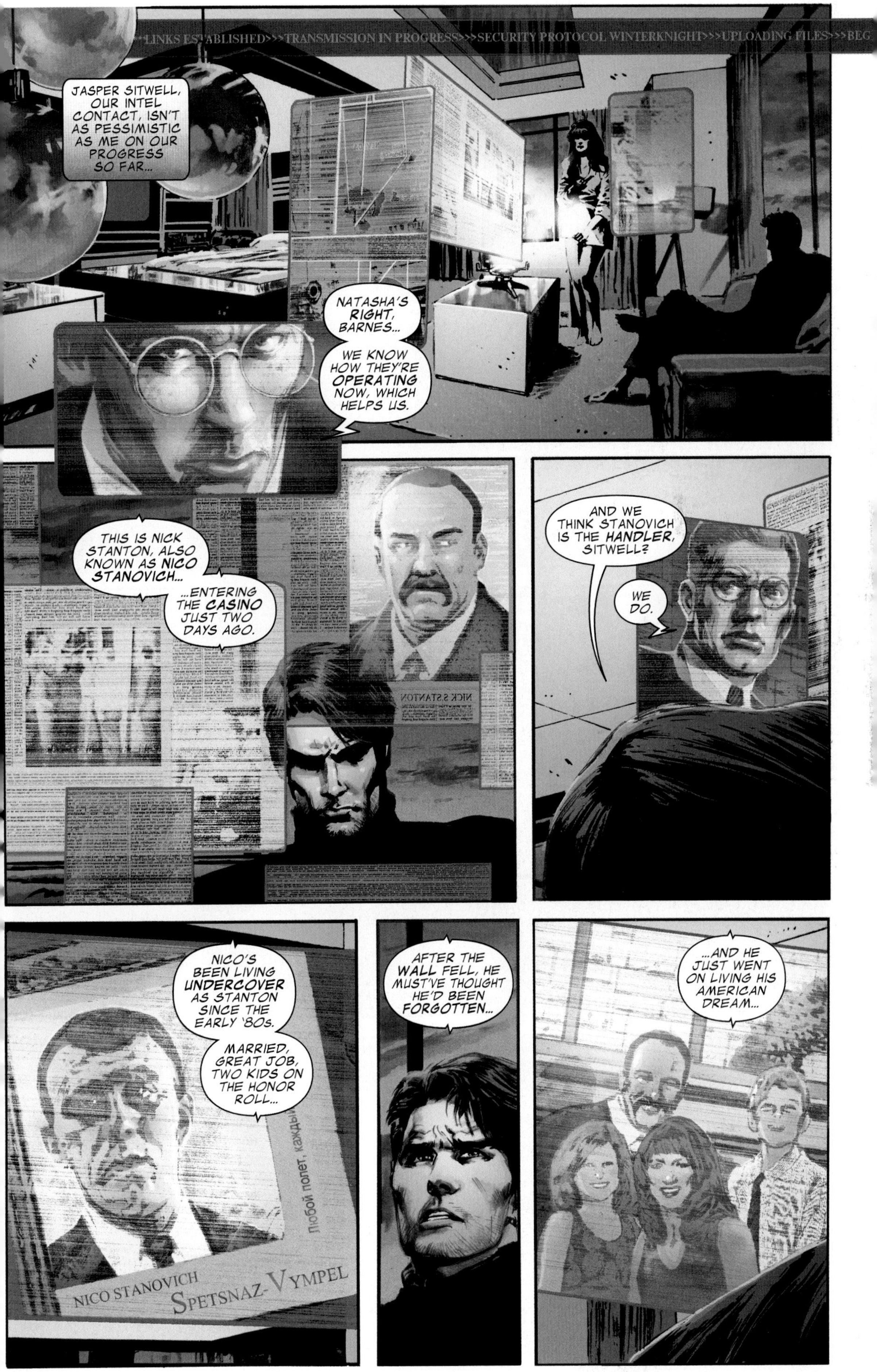
**LINKS ESTABLISHED>>>TRANSMISSION IN PROGRESS>>>SECURITY PROTOCOL WINTERKNIGHT>>>UPLOADING FILES>>>BEG
JASPER SITWELL, OUR INTEL CONTACT, ISN'T AS PESSIMISTIC AS ME ON OUR PROGRESS SO FAR...
NATASHA'S RIGHT, BARNES...
WE KNOW HOW THEY'RE OPERATING NOW, WHICH HELPS US.
THIS IS NICK STANTON, ALSO KNOWN AS NICO STANOVICH...
...ENTERING THE CASINO JUST TWO DAYS AGO.
NICK STANTON
AND WE THINK STANOVICH IS THE HANDLER, SITWELL?
WE DO.
NICO'S BEEN LIVING UNDERCOVER AS STANTON SINCE THE EARLY '80s.
MARRIED, GREAT JOB, TWO KIDS ON THE HONOR ROLL...
Любой полет, каждый
NICO STANOVICH
SPETSNAZ-VYMPEL
AFTER THE WALL FELL, HE MUST'VE THOUGHT HE'D BEEN FORGOTTEN...
...AND HE JUST WENT ON LIVING HIS AMERICAN DREAM...

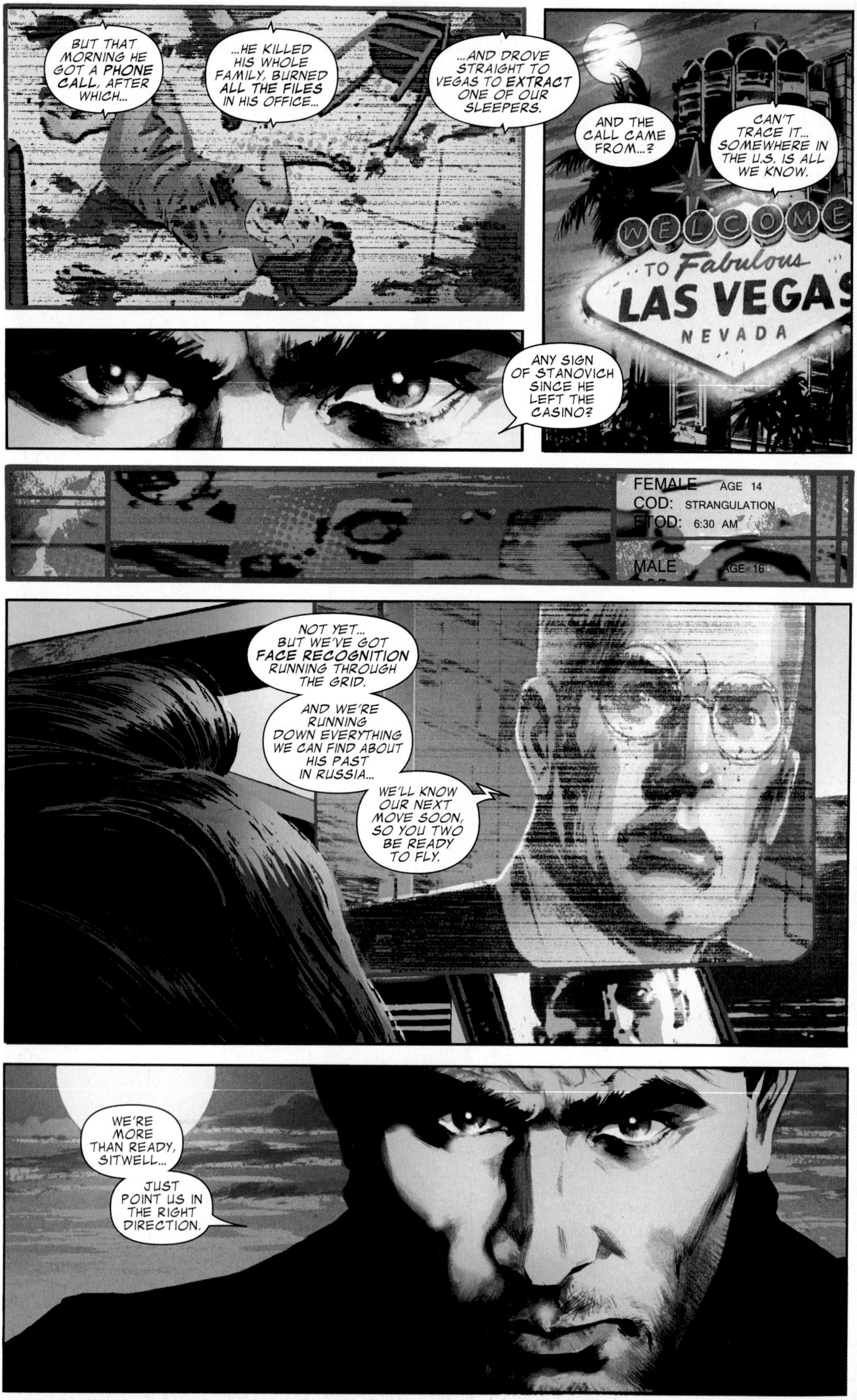
BUT THAT MORNING HE GOT A PHONE CALL, AFTER WHICH...
...HE KILLED HIS WHOLE FAMILY, BURNED ALL THE FILES IN HIS OFFICE...
...AND DROVE STRAIGHT TO VEGAS TO EXTRACT ONE OF OUR SLEEPERS.
AND THE CALL CAME FROM...?
CAN'T TRACE IT... SOMEWHERE IN THE U.S. IS ALL WE KNOW.
WELCOME
TO Fabulous
LAS VEGAS
NEVADA
ANY SIGN OF STANOVICH SINCE HE LEFT THE CASINO?
FEMALE AGE 14
COD: STRANGULATION
ETOD: 6:30 AM
MALE AGE 16
NOT YET... BUT WE'VE GOT FACE RECOGNITION RUNNING THROUGH THE GRID.
AND WE'RE RUNNING DOWN EVERYTHING WE CAN FIND ABOUT HIS PAST IN RUSSIA...
WE'LL KNOW OUR NEXT MOVE SOON, SO YOU TWO BE READY TO FLY.
WE'RE MORE THAN READY, SITWELL...
JUST POINT US IN THE RIGHT DIRECTION.

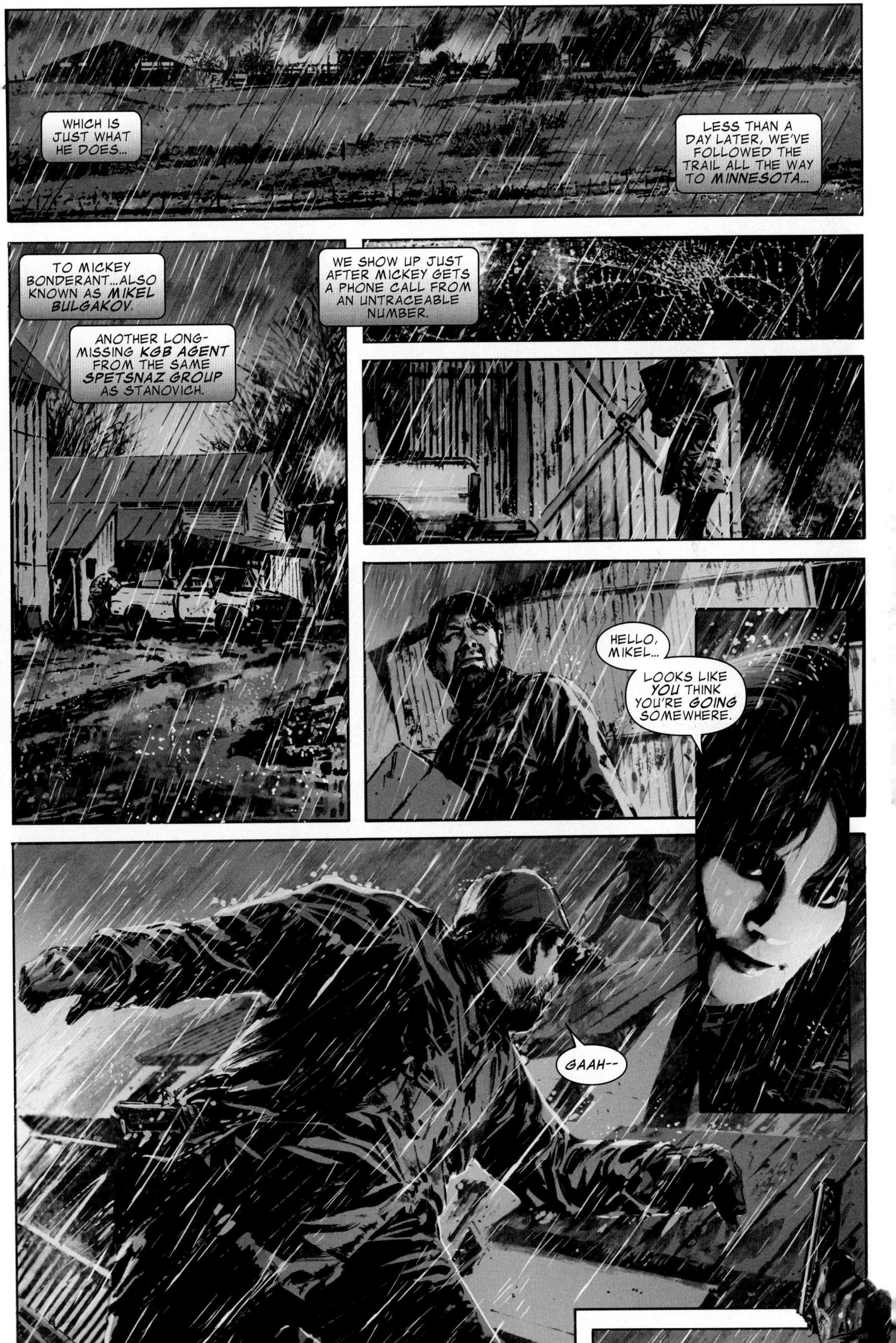

WHICH IS JUST WHAT HE DOES...
LESS THAN A DAY LATER, WE'VE FOLLOWED THE TRAIL ALL THE WAY TO MINNESOTA...
TO MICKEY BONDERANT...ALSO KNOWN AS MIKEL BULGAKOV.
ANOTHER LONG-MISSING KGB AGENT FROM THE SAME SPETSNAZ GROUP AS STANOVICH.
WE SHOW UP JUST AFTER MICKEY GETS A PHONE CALL FROM AN UNTRACEABLE NUMBER.
HELLO, MIKEL...
LOOKS LIKE YOU THINK YOU'RE GOING SOMEWHERE.
GAAH--

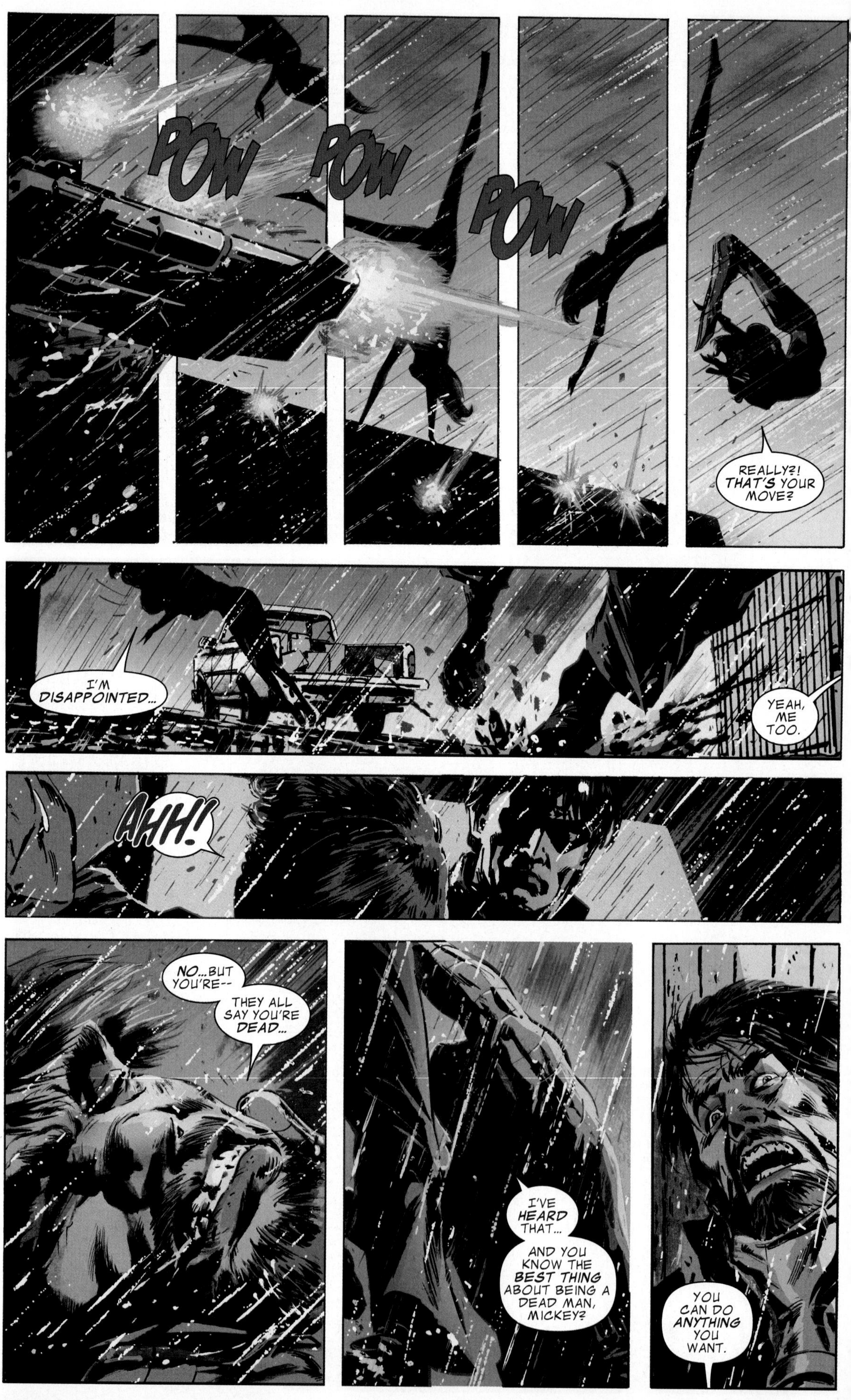

POW
POW
POW
REALLY?! THAT'S YOUR MOVE?
I'M DISAPPOINTED...
YEAH, ME TOO.
AHH!
NO...BUT YOU'RE--
THEY ALL SAY YOU'RE DEAD...
I'VE HEARD THAT...
AND YOU KNOW THE BEST THING ABOUT BEING A DEAD MAN, MICKEY?
YOU CAN DO ANYTHING YOU WANT.

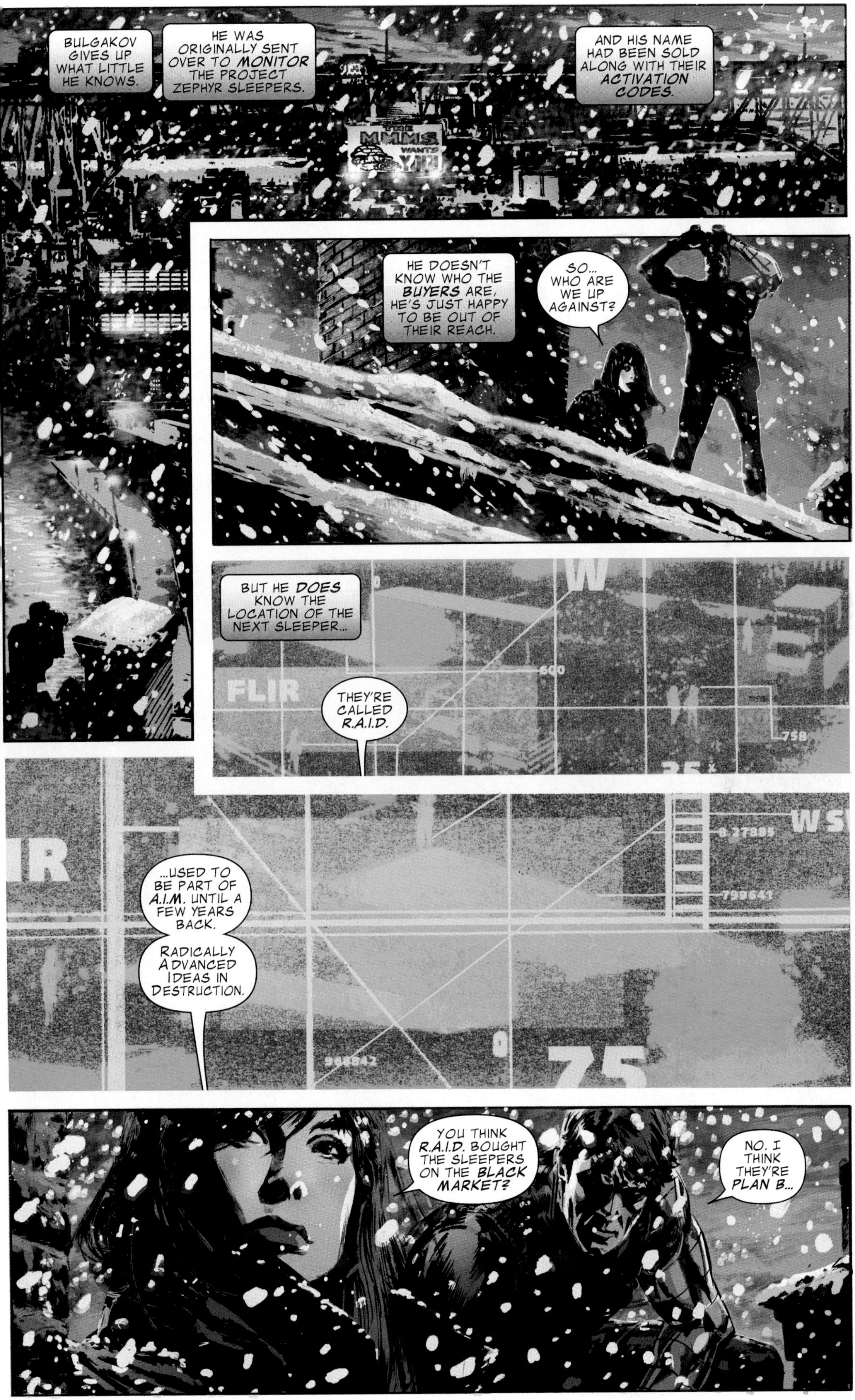

BULGAKOV GIVES UP WHAT LITTLE HE KNOWS.
HE WAS ORIGINALLY SENT OVER TO *MONITOR* THE PROJECT ZEPHYR SLEEPERS.
AND HIS NAME HAD BEEN SOLD ALONG WITH THEIR *ACTIVATION CODES.*
HE DOESN'T KNOW WHO THE *BUYERS* ARE, HE'S JUST HAPPY TO BE OUT OF THEIR REACH.
SO... WHO ARE WE UP AGAINST?
BUT HE *DOES* KNOW THE LOCATION OF THE NEXT SLEEPER...
FLIR
THEY'RE CALLED *R.A.I.D.*
...USED TO BE PART OF *A.I.M.* UNTIL A FEW YEARS BACK.
RADICALLY ADVANCED IDEAS IN DESTRUCTION.
YOU THINK *R.A.I.D.* BOUGHT THE SLEEPERS ON THE *BLACK MARKET?*
NO. I THINK THEY'RE *PLAN B...*

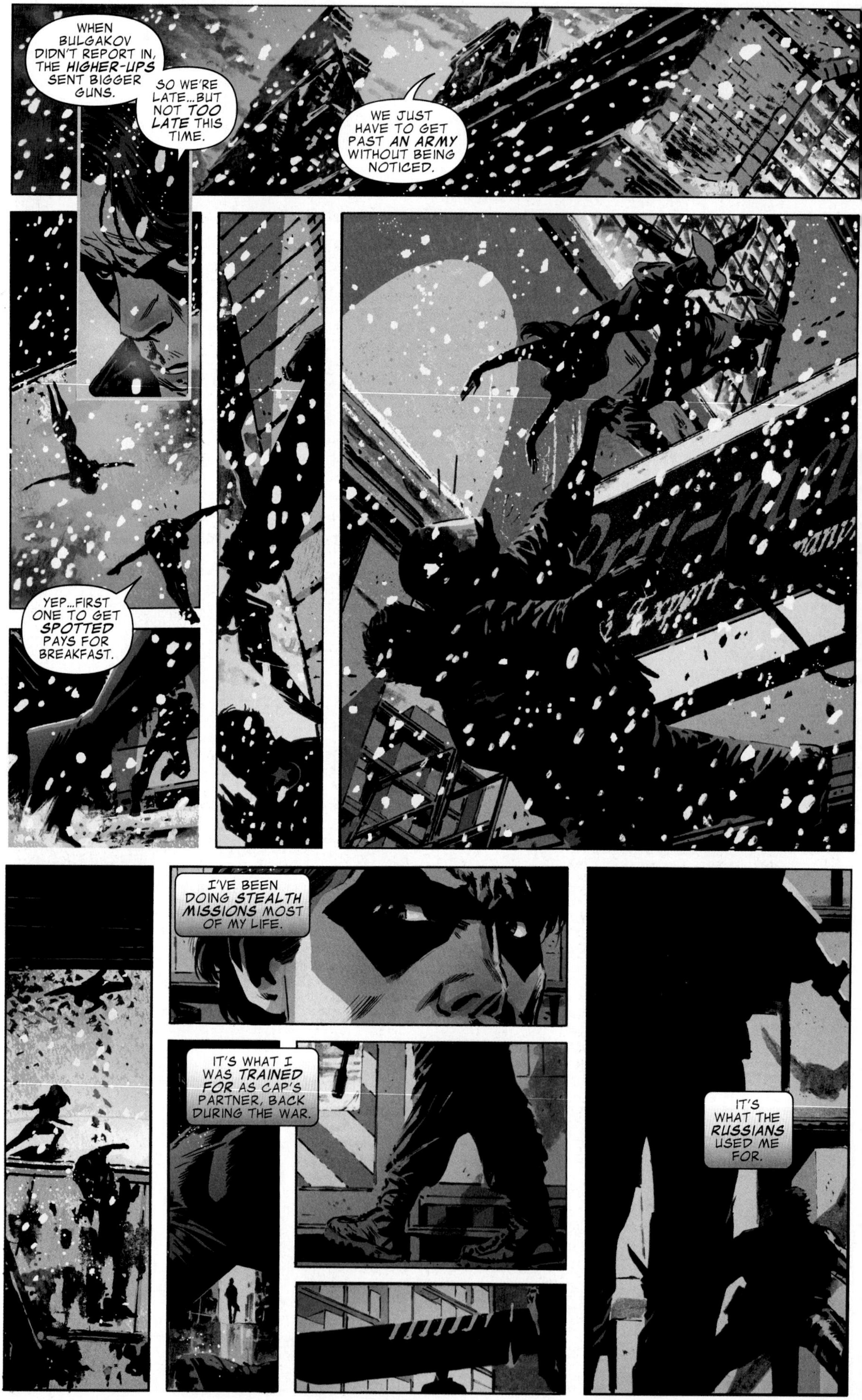
WHEN BULGAKOV DIDN'T REPORT IN, THE HIGHER-UPS SENT BIGGER GUNS.
SO WE'RE LATE...BUT NOT TOO LATE THIS TIME.
WE JUST HAVE TO GET PAST AN ARMY WITHOUT BEING NOTICED.
YEP...FIRST ONE TO GET SPOTTED PAYS FOR BREAKFAST.
I'VE BEEN DOING STEALTH MISSIONS MOST OF MY LIFE.
IT'S WHAT I WAS TRAINED FOR AS CAP'S PARTNER, BACK DURING THE WAR.
IT'S WHAT THE RUSSIANS USED ME FOR.

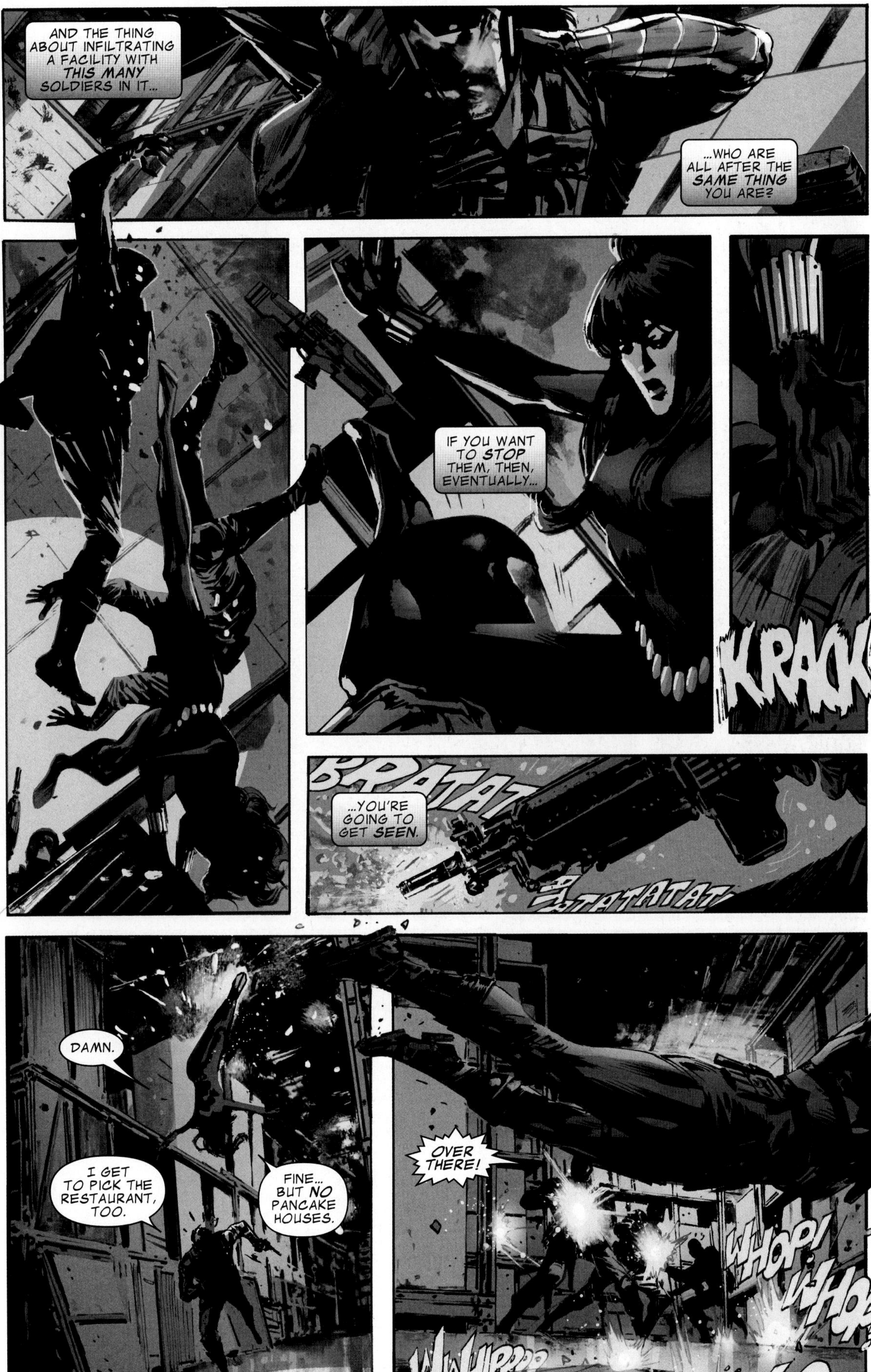
AND THE THING ABOUT INFILTRATING A FACILITY WITH THIS MANY SOLDIERS IN IT...
...WHO ARE ALL AFTER THE SAME THING YOU ARE?
IF YOU WANT TO STOP THEM, THEN, EVENTUALLY...
KRACK
...YOU'RE GOING TO GET SEEN.
DAMN.
I GET TO PICK THE RESTAURANT, TOO.
FINE... BUT NO PANCAKE HOUSES.
OVER THERE!
WHOP!
WHOP!
WHHIPPP
K-TOW

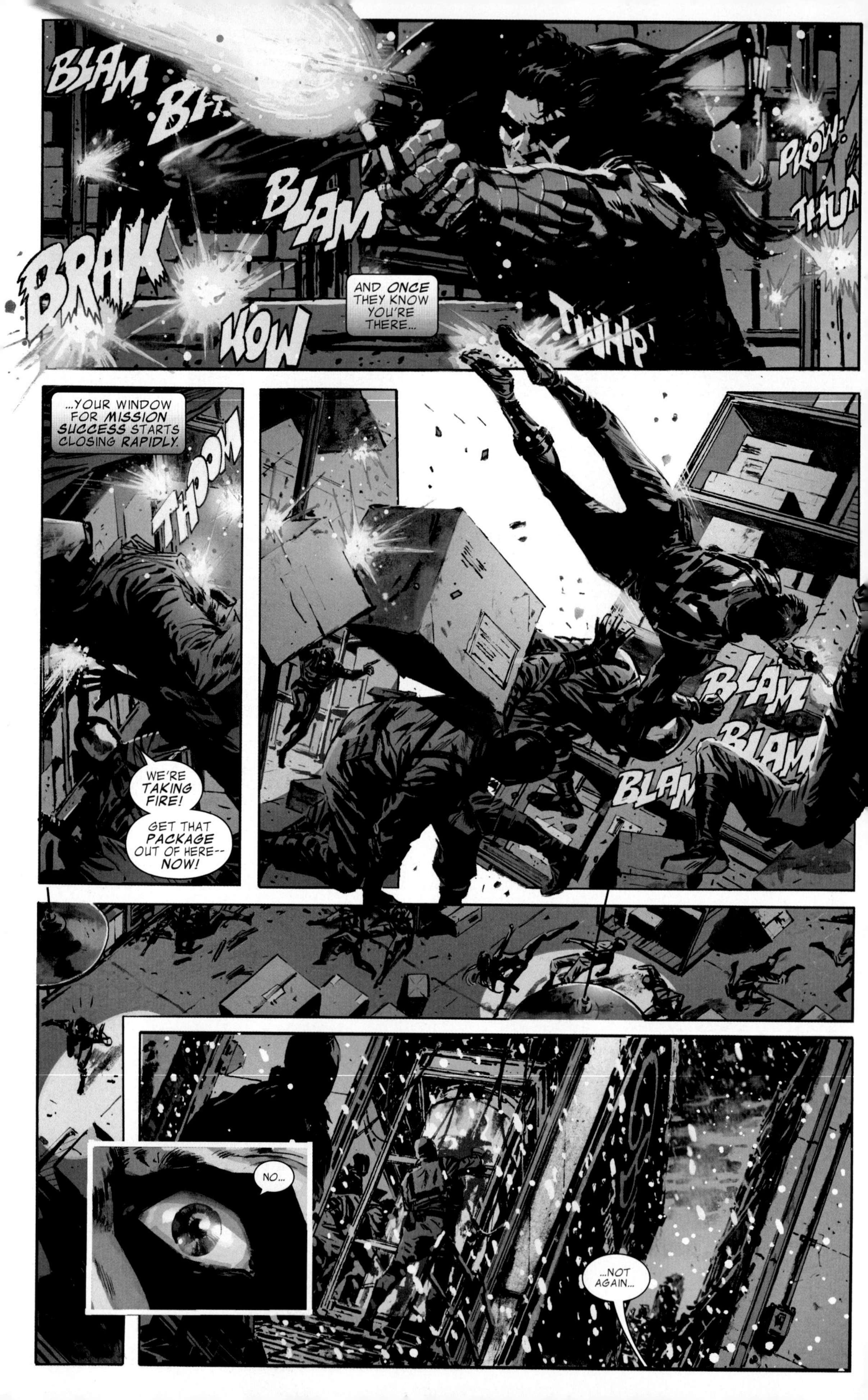
BLAM
BLAM
BRAK
KOW
AND ONCE THEY KNOW YOU'RE THERE...
THWIP!
PKOW!
...YOUR WINDOW FOR MISSION SUCCESS STARTS CLOSING RAPIDLY.
THOOM
WE'RE TAKING FIRE!
GET THAT PACKAGE OUT OF HERE-- NOW!
BLAM
NO...
...NOT AGAIN...

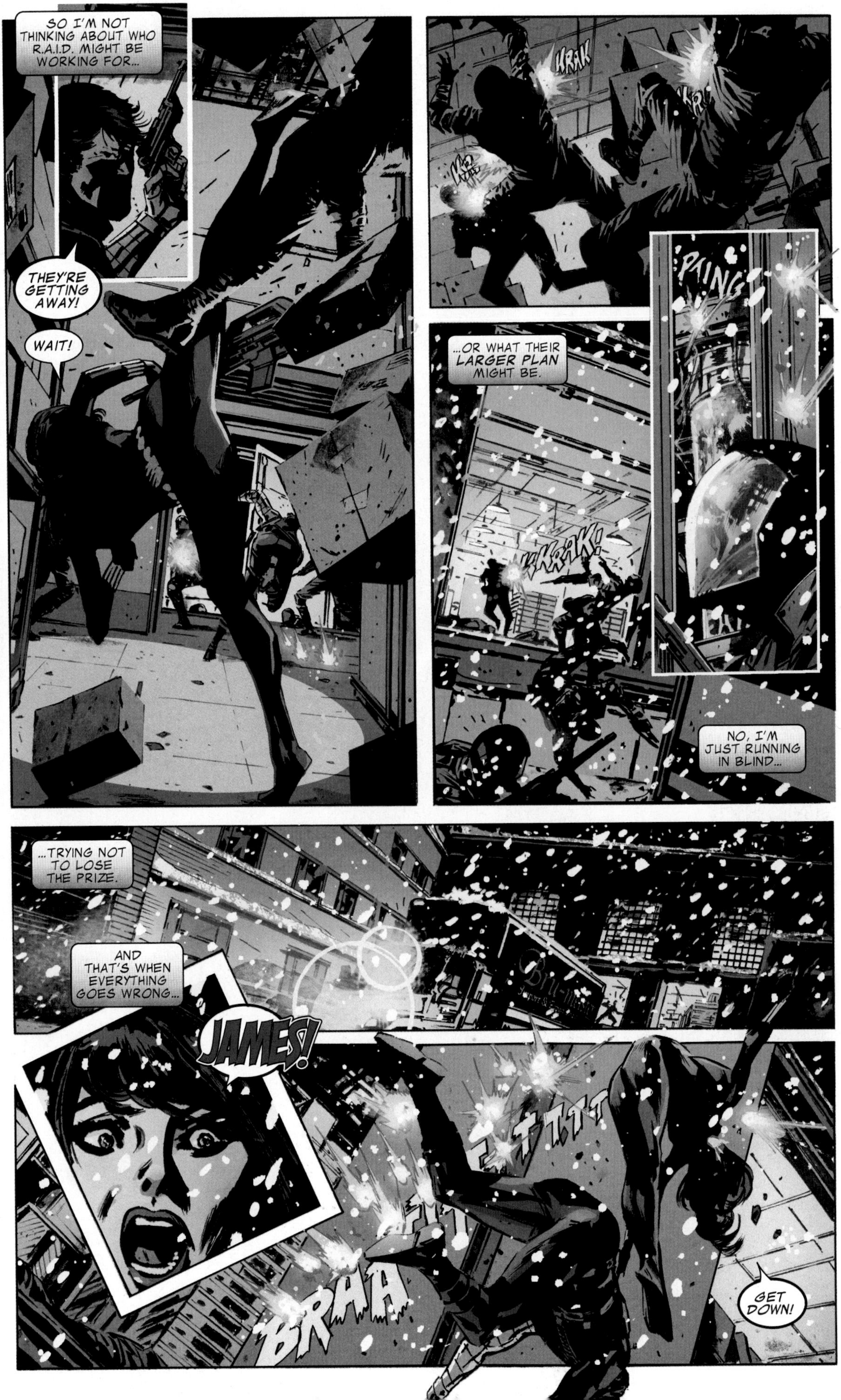
SO I'M NOT THINKING ABOUT WHO R.A.I.D. MIGHT BE WORKING FOR...
THEY'RE GETTING AWAY!
WAIT!
HRAK
...OR WHAT THEIR LARGER PLAN MIGHT BE.
PAING
KRAK!
NO, I'M JUST RUNNING IN BLIND...
...TRYING NOT TO LOSE THE PRIZE.
AND THAT'S WHEN EVERYTHING GOES WRONG...
JAMES!
BRAA
GET DOWN!

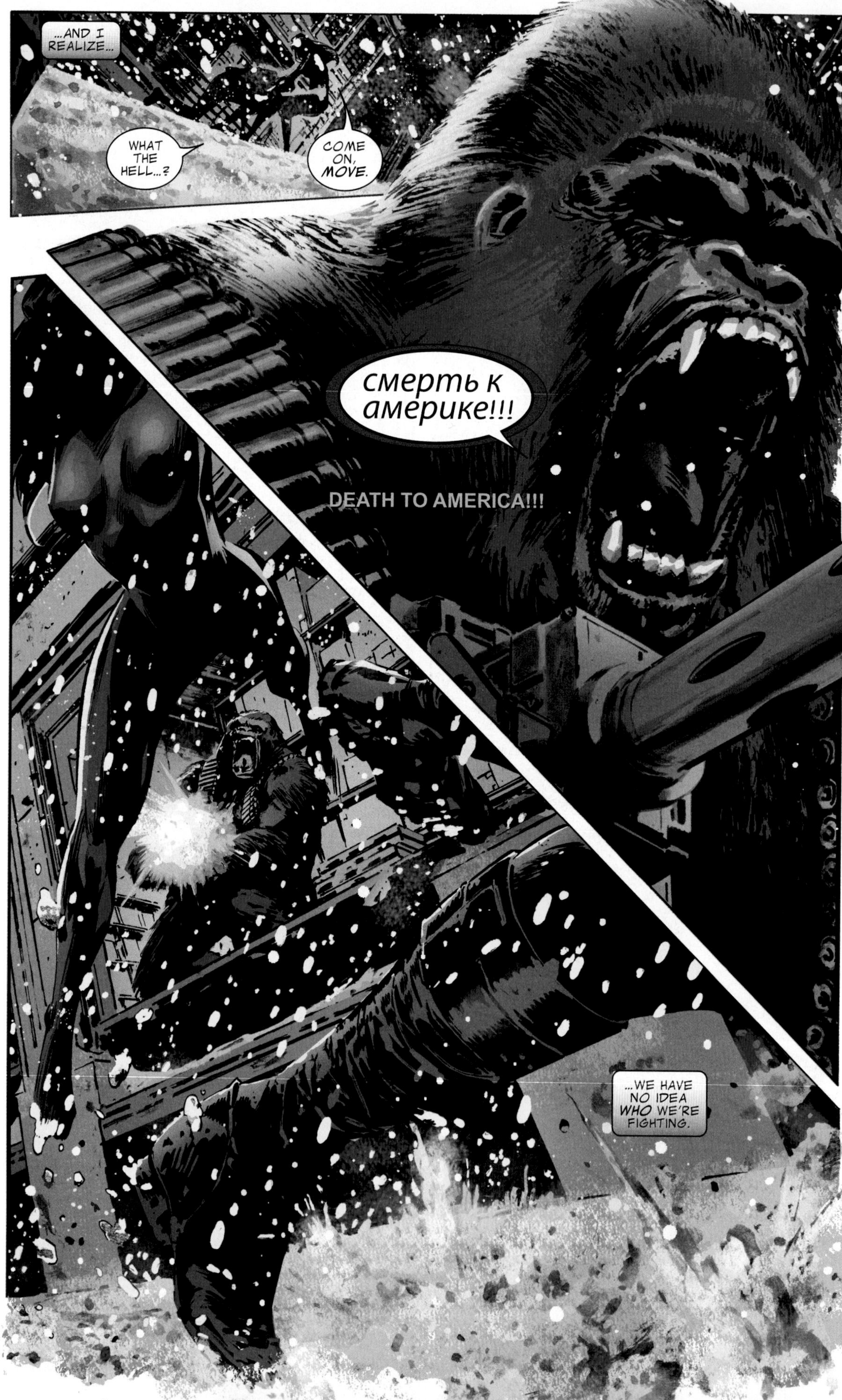
...AND I REALIZE...
WHAT THE HELL...?
COME ON, MOVE.
смерть к америке!!!
DEATH TO AMERICA!!!
...WE HAVE NO IDEA WHO WE'RE FIGHTING.

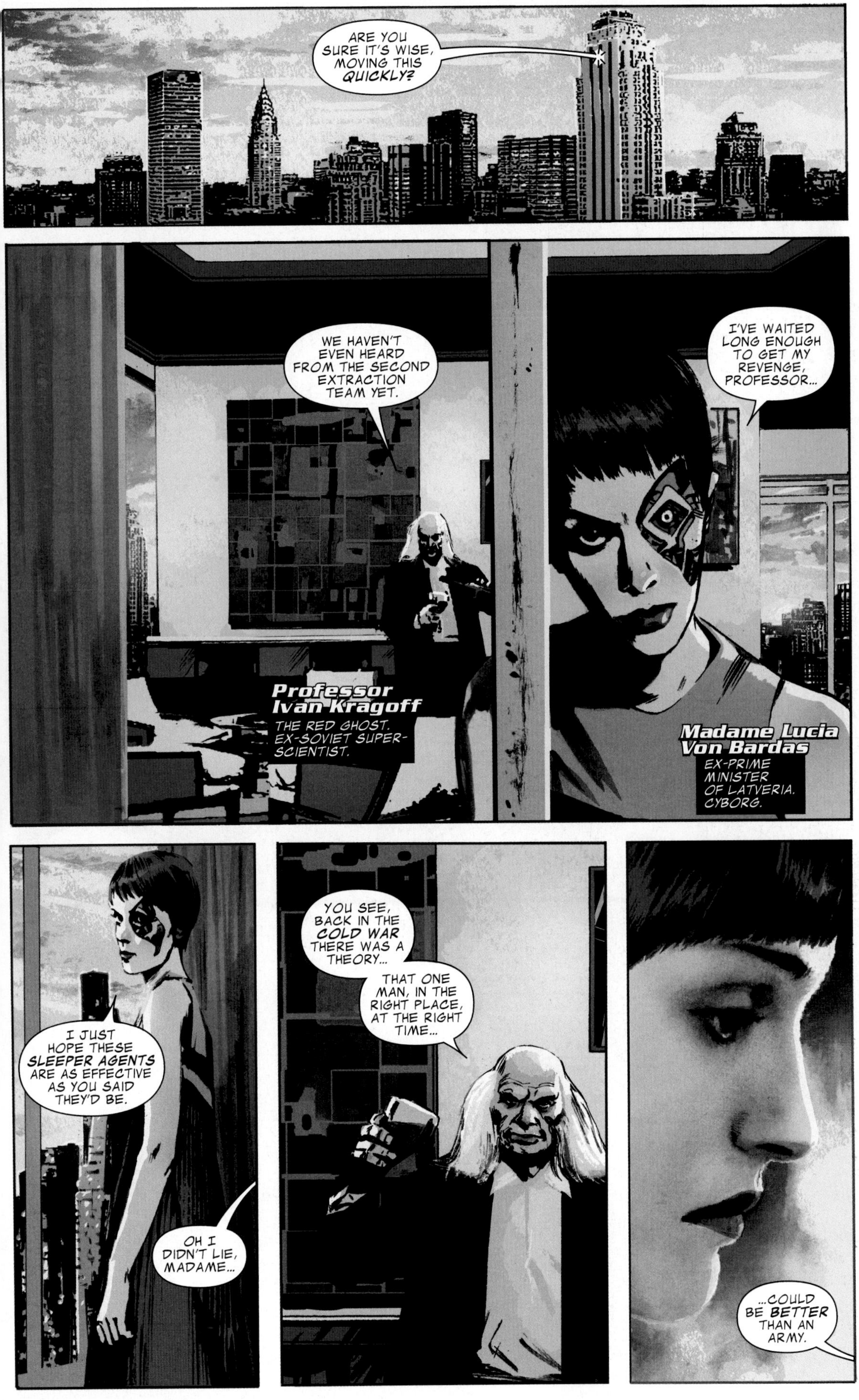
ARE YOU SURE IT'S WISE, MOVING THIS QUICKLY?
WE HAVEN'T EVEN HEARD FROM THE SECOND EXTRACTION TEAM YET.
I'VE WAITED LONG ENOUGH TO GET MY REVENGE, PROFESSOR...
Professor Ivan Kragoff
THE RED GHOST. EX-SOVIET SUPER-SCIENTIST.
Madame Lucia Von Bardas
EX-PRIME MINISTER OF LATVERIA. CYBORG.
I JUST HOPE THESE SLEEPER AGENTS ARE AS EFFECTIVE AS YOU SAID THEY'D BE.
OH I DIDN'T LIE, MADAME...
YOU SEE, BACK IN THE COLD WAR THERE WAS A THEORY...
THAT ONE MAN, IN THE RIGHT PLACE, AT THE RIGHT TIME...
...COULD BE BETTER THAN AN ARMY.

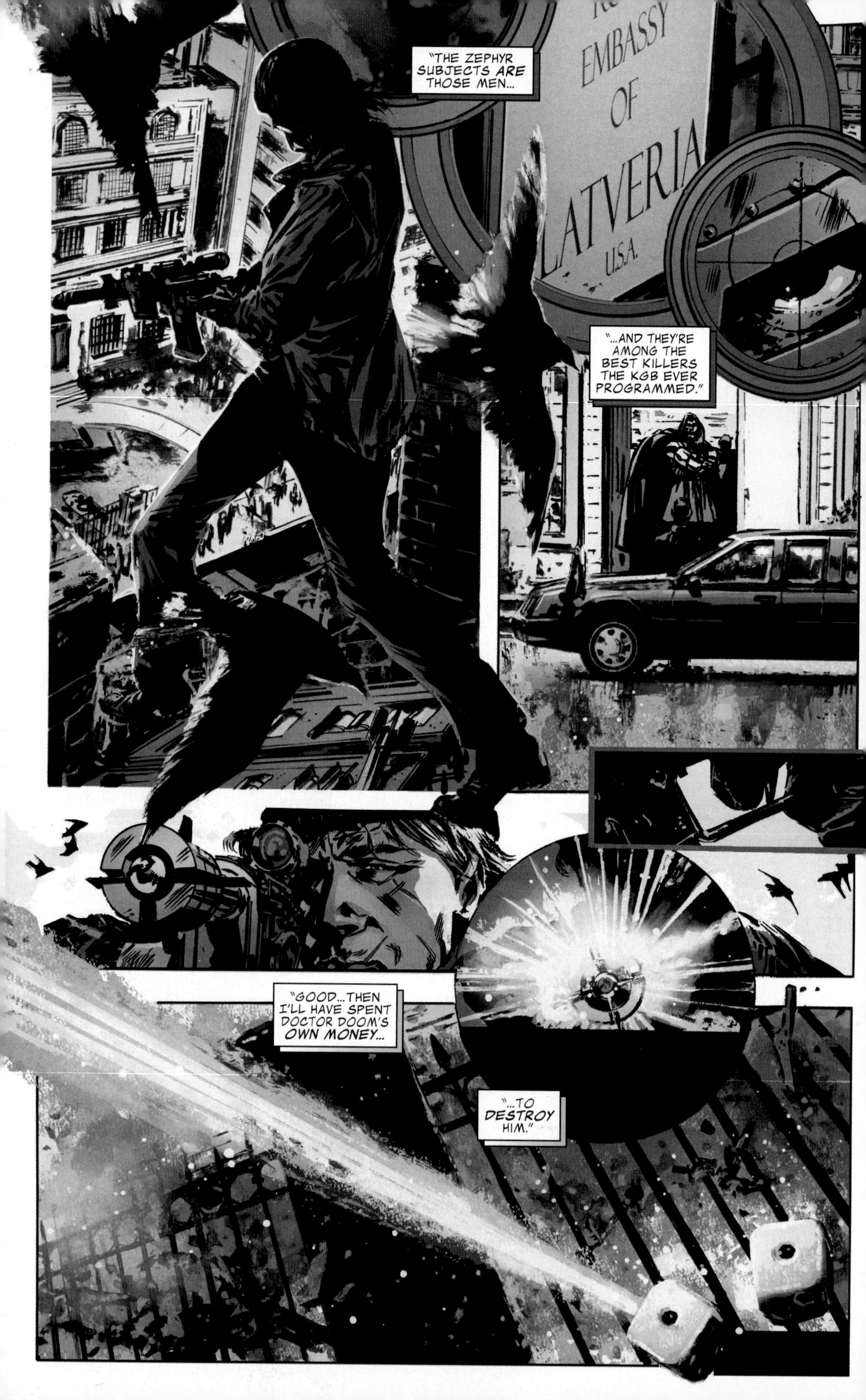
EMBASSY
OF
LATVERIA
U.S.A.
"THE ZEPHYR SUBJECTS *ARE* THOSE MEN...
"...AND THEY'RE AMONG THE BEST KILLERS THE KGB EVER PROGRAMMED."
"*GOOD*... THEN I'LL HAVE SPENT DOCTOR DOOM'S *OWN MONEY*...
"...TO *DESTROY* HIM."

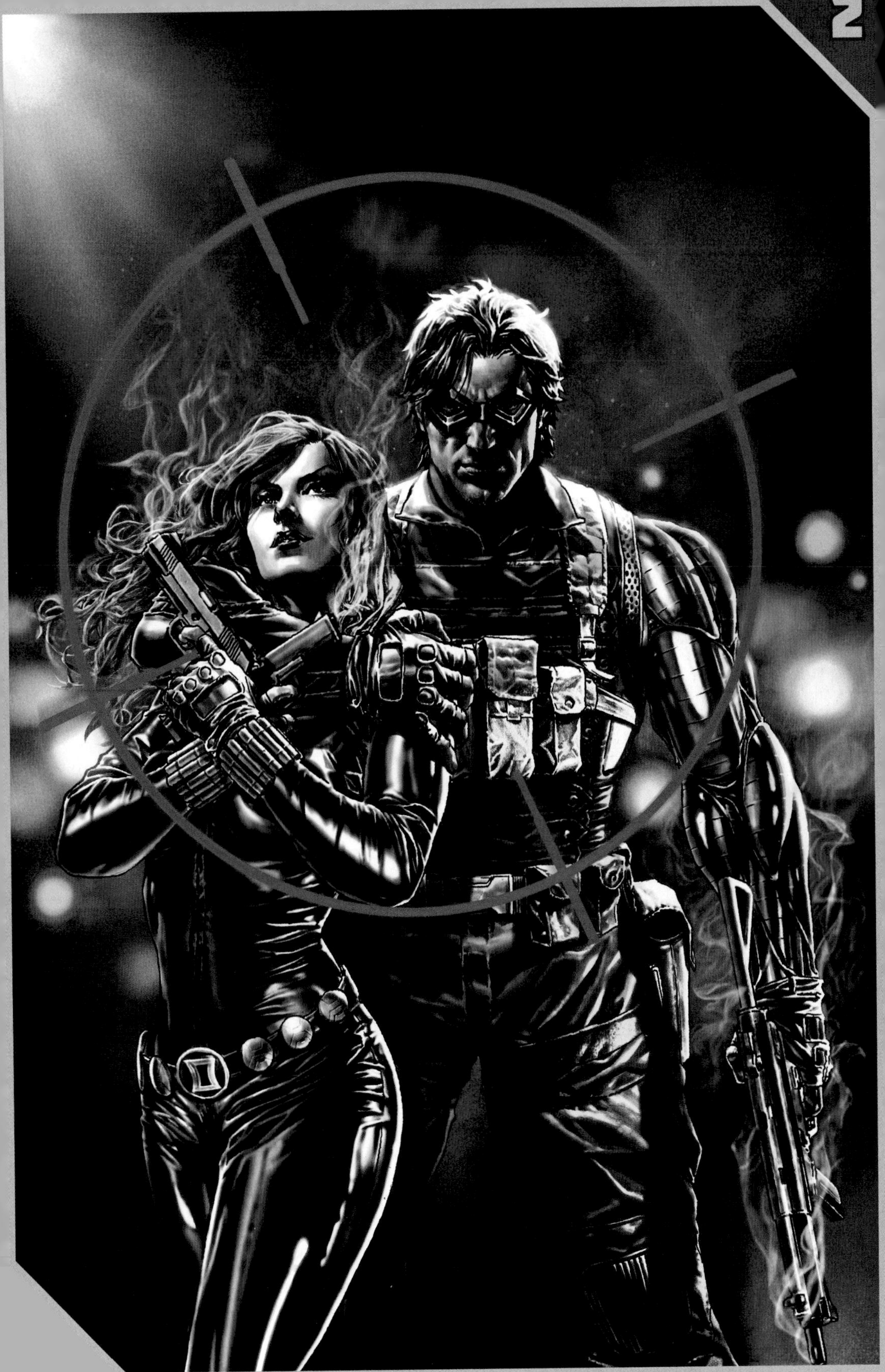

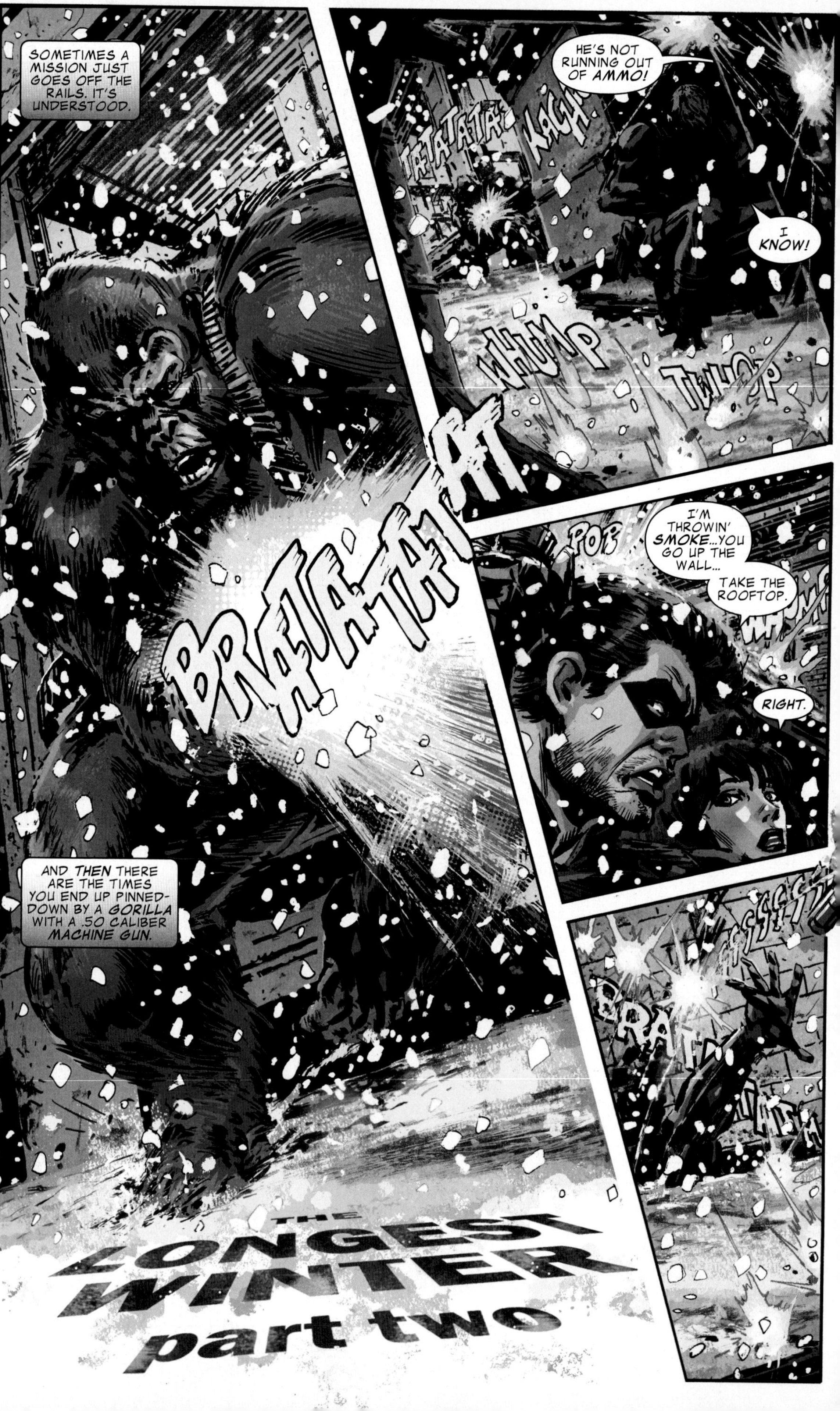

SOMETIMES A MISSION JUST GOES OFF THE RAILS. IT'S UNDERSTOOD.
AND THEN THERE ARE THE TIMES YOU END UP PINNED-DOWN BY A GORILLA WITH A .50 CALIBER MACHINE GUN.
BRATATATAT
THE LONGEST WINTER
part two
HE'S NOT RUNNING OUT OF AMMO!
TATATATA
KACHA
I KNOW!
WHUMP
TWHOP
POP
I'M THROWIN' SMOKE...YOU GO UP THE WALL...
TAKE THE ROOFTOP.
RIGHT.
BRAT

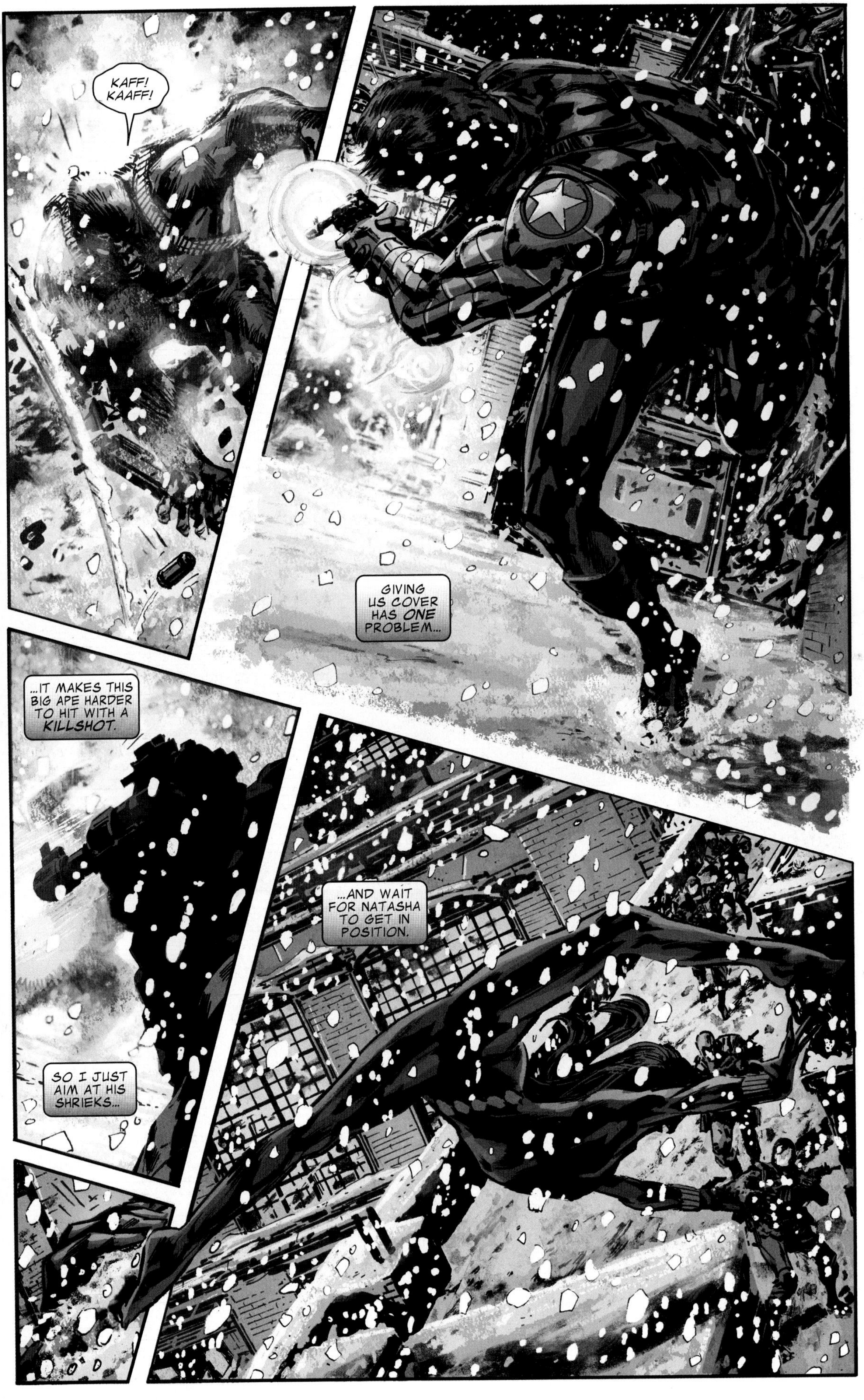
KAFF! KAAFF!
GIVING US COVER HAS ONE PROBLEM...
...IT MAKES THIS BIG APE HARDER TO HIT WITH A KILLSHOT.
SO I JUST AIM AT HIS SHRIEKS...
...AND WAIT FOR NATASHA TO GET IN POSITION.

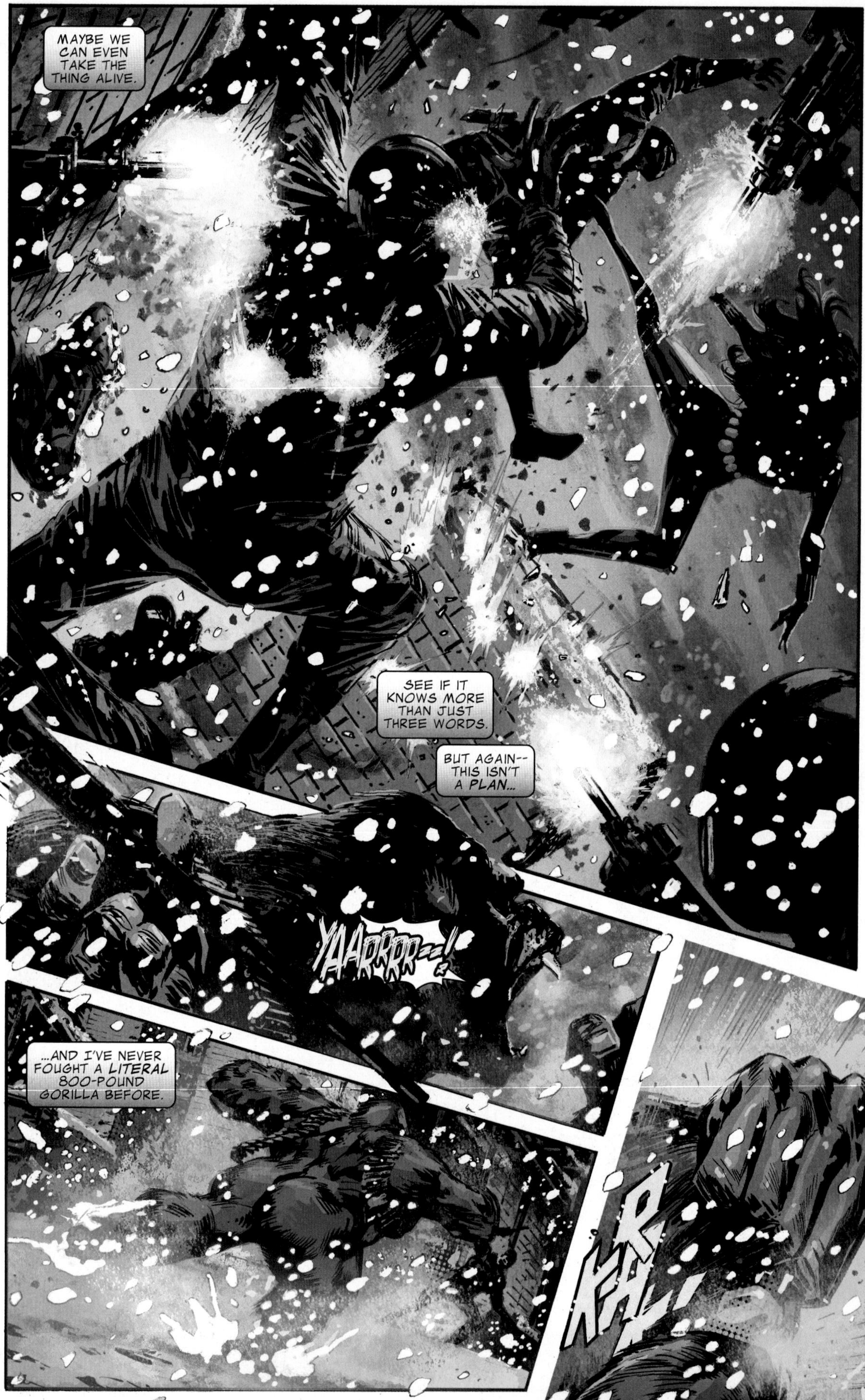
MAYBE WE CAN EVEN TAKE THE THING ALIVE.
SEE IF IT KNOWS MORE THAN JUST THREE WORDS.
BUT AGAIN-- THIS ISN'T A PLAN...
YAARRRR--!
...AND I'VE NEVER FOUGHT A LITERAL 800-POUND GORILLA BEFORE.

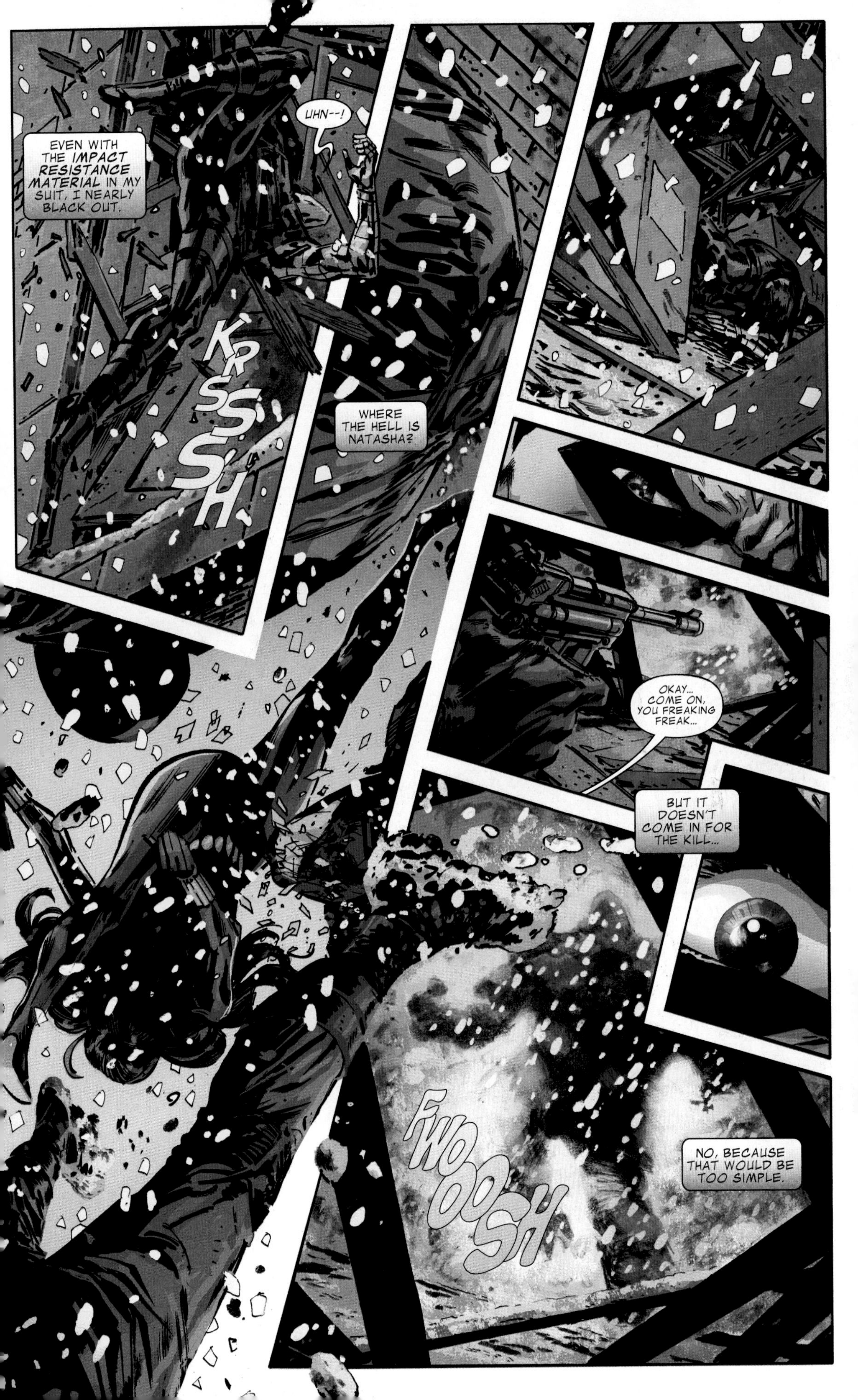
EVEN WITH THE IMPACT RESISTANCE MATERIAL IN MY SUIT, I NEARLY BLACK OUT.
UHN--!
KRSSSH
WHERE THE HELL IS NATASHA?
OKAY... COME ON, YOU FREAKING FREAK...
BUT IT DOESN'T COME IN FOR THE KILL...
FWOOOSH
NO, BECAUSE THAT WOULD BE TOO SIMPLE.

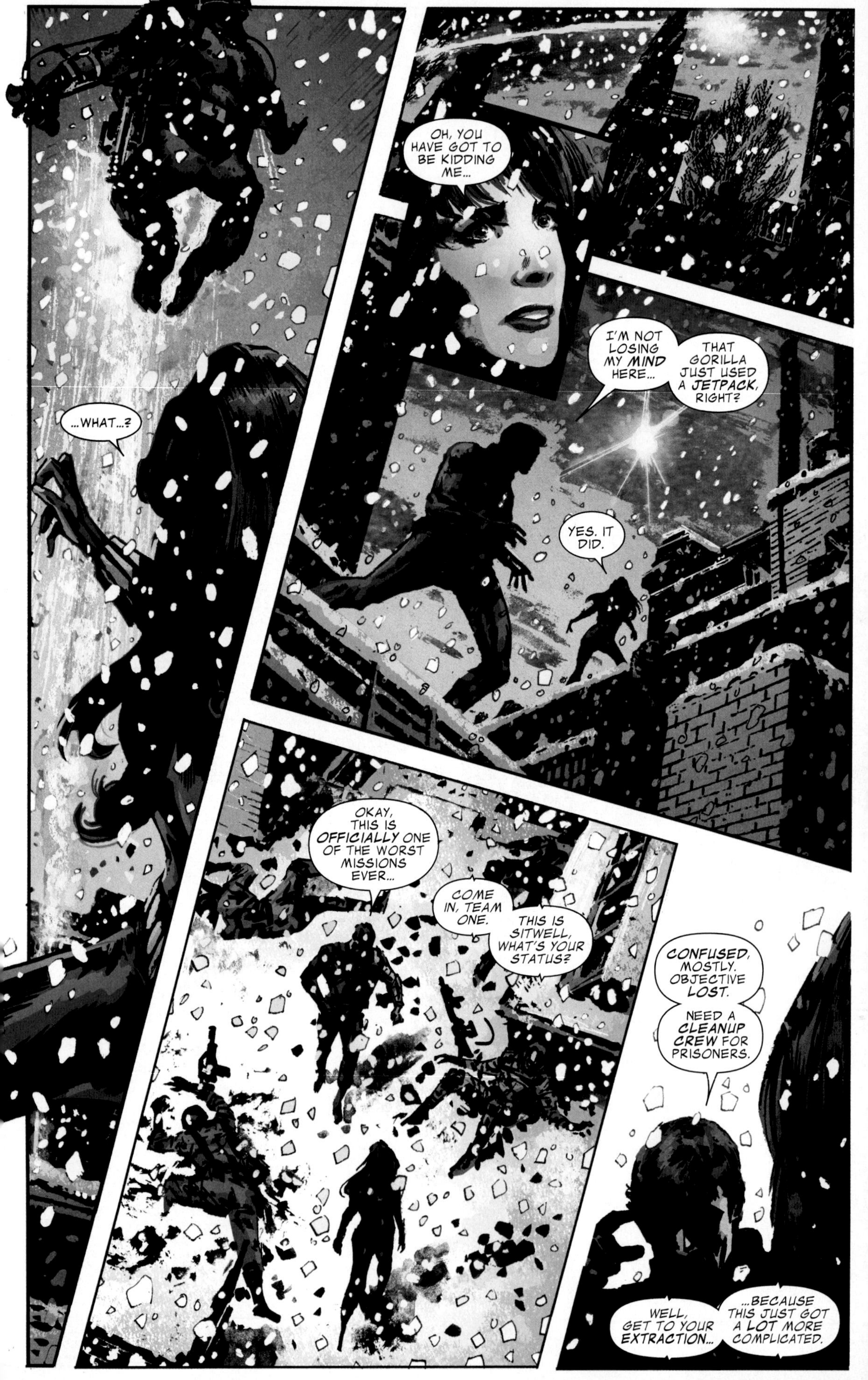

...WHAT...?
OH, YOU HAVE GOT TO BE KIDDING ME...
I'M NOT LOSING MY MIND HERE...
THAT GORILLA JUST USED A JETPACK, RIGHT?
YES. IT DID.
OKAY, THIS IS OFFICIALLY ONE OF THE WORST MISSIONS EVER...
COME IN, TEAM ONE.
THIS IS SITWELL, WHAT'S YOUR STATUS?
CONFUSED, MOSTLY. OBJECTIVE LOST.
NEED A CLEANUP CREW FOR PRISONERS.
WELL, GET TO YOUR EXTRACTION...
...BECAUSE THIS JUST GOT A LOT MORE COMPLICATED.

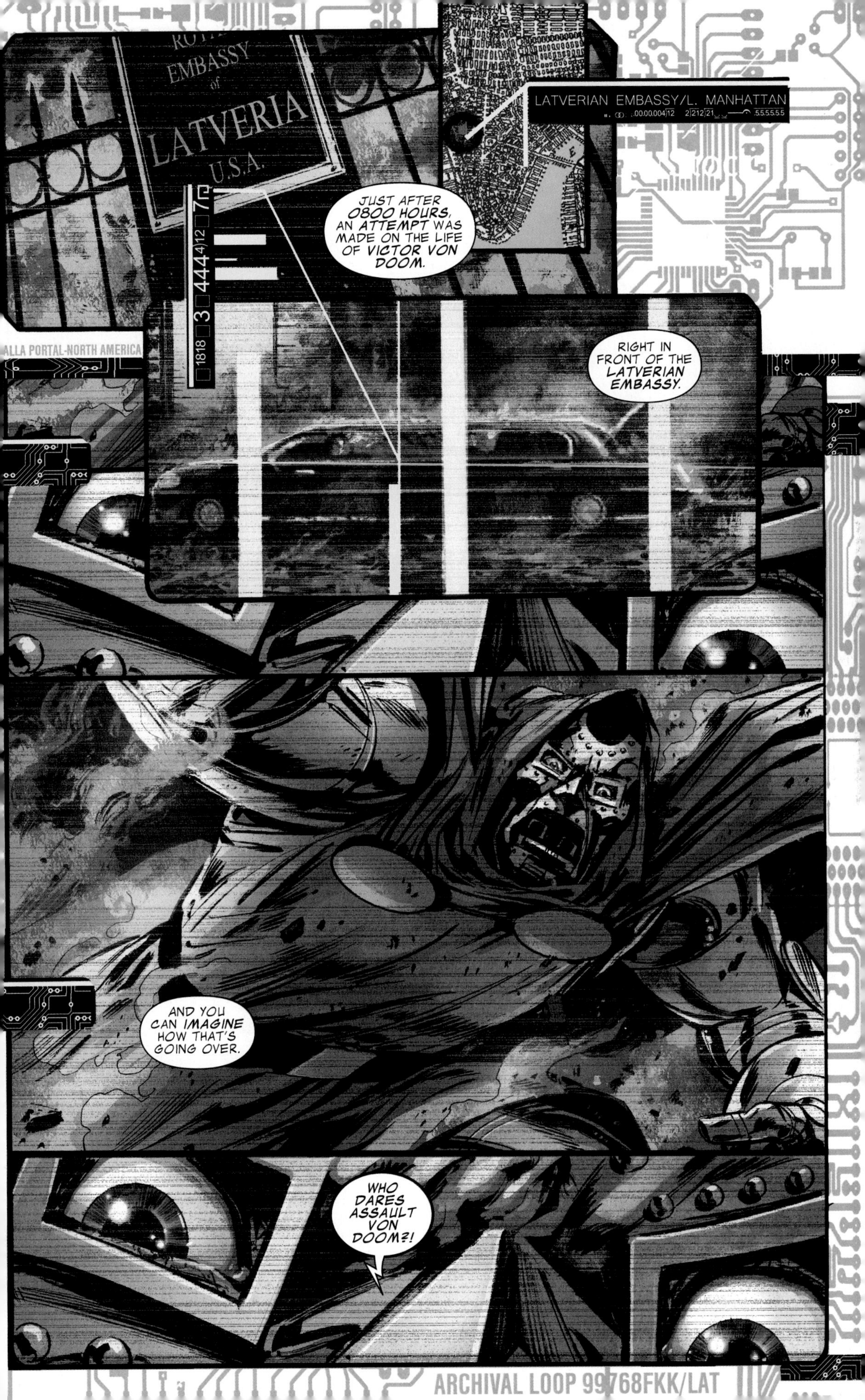
ROYAL EMBASSY of LATVERIA U.S.A.
LATVERIAN EMBASSY/L. MANHATTAN
JUST AFTER 0800 HOURS, AN ATTEMPT WAS MADE ON THE LIFE OF VICTOR VON DOOM.
ALLA PORTAL-NORTH AMERICA
RIGHT IN FRONT OF THE LATVERIAN EMBASSY.
AND YOU CAN IMAGINE HOW THAT'S GOING OVER.
WHO DARES ASSAULT VON DOOM?!
ARCHIVAL LOOP 99768FKK/LAT

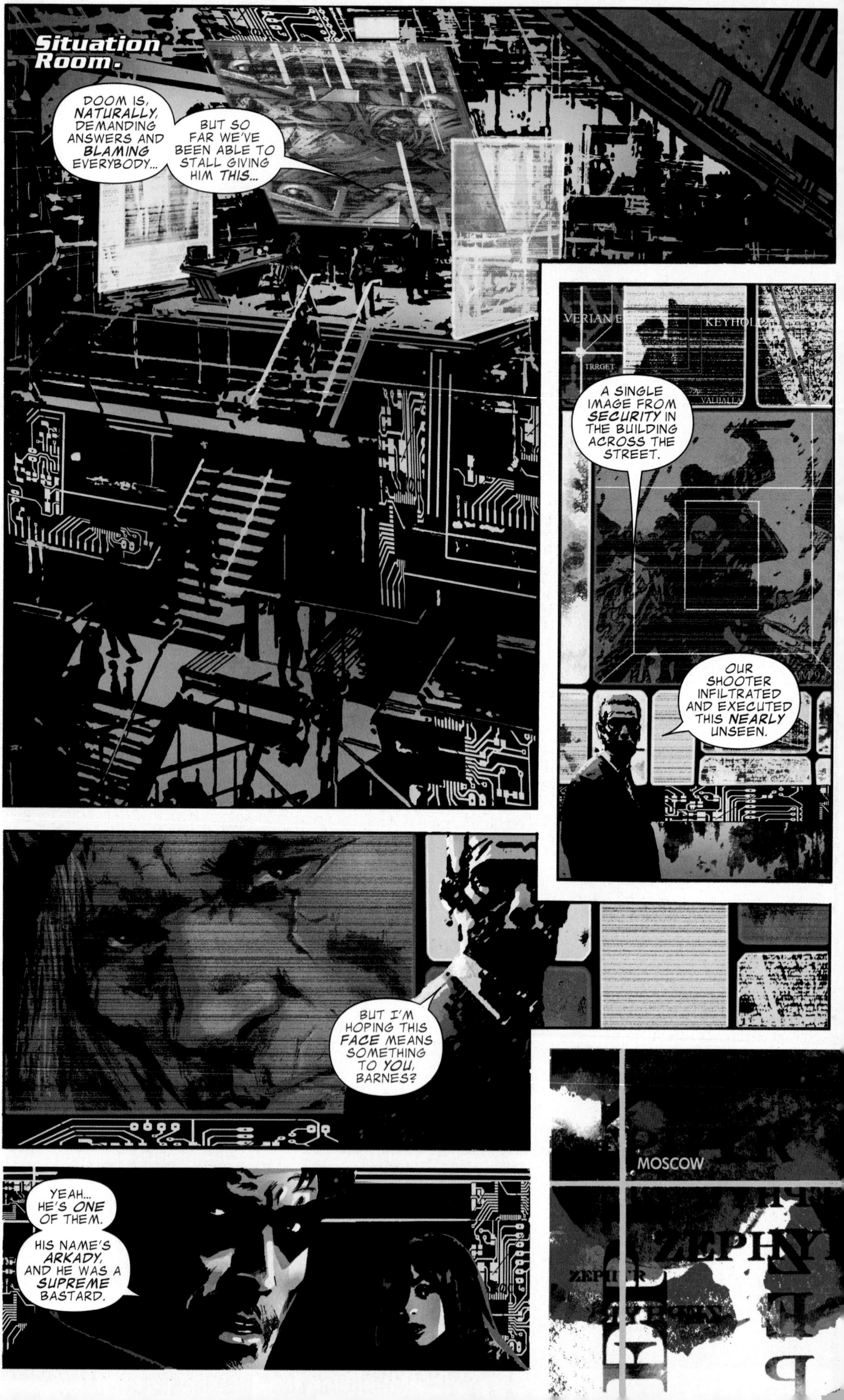
Situation Room.
DOOM IS, NATURALLY, DEMANDING ANSWERS AND BLAMING EVERYBODY...
BUT SO FAR WE'VE BEEN ABLE TO STALL GIVING HIM THIS...
A SINGLE IMAGE FROM SECURITY IN THE BUILDING ACROSS THE STREET.
OUR SHOOTER INFILTRATED AND EXECUTED THIS NEARLY UNSEEN.
BUT I'M HOPING THIS FACE MEANS SOMETHING TO YOU, BARNES?
YEAH... HE'S ONE OF THEM.
HIS NAME'S ARKADY, AND HE WAS A SUPREME BASTARD.
MOSCOW
ZEPHY

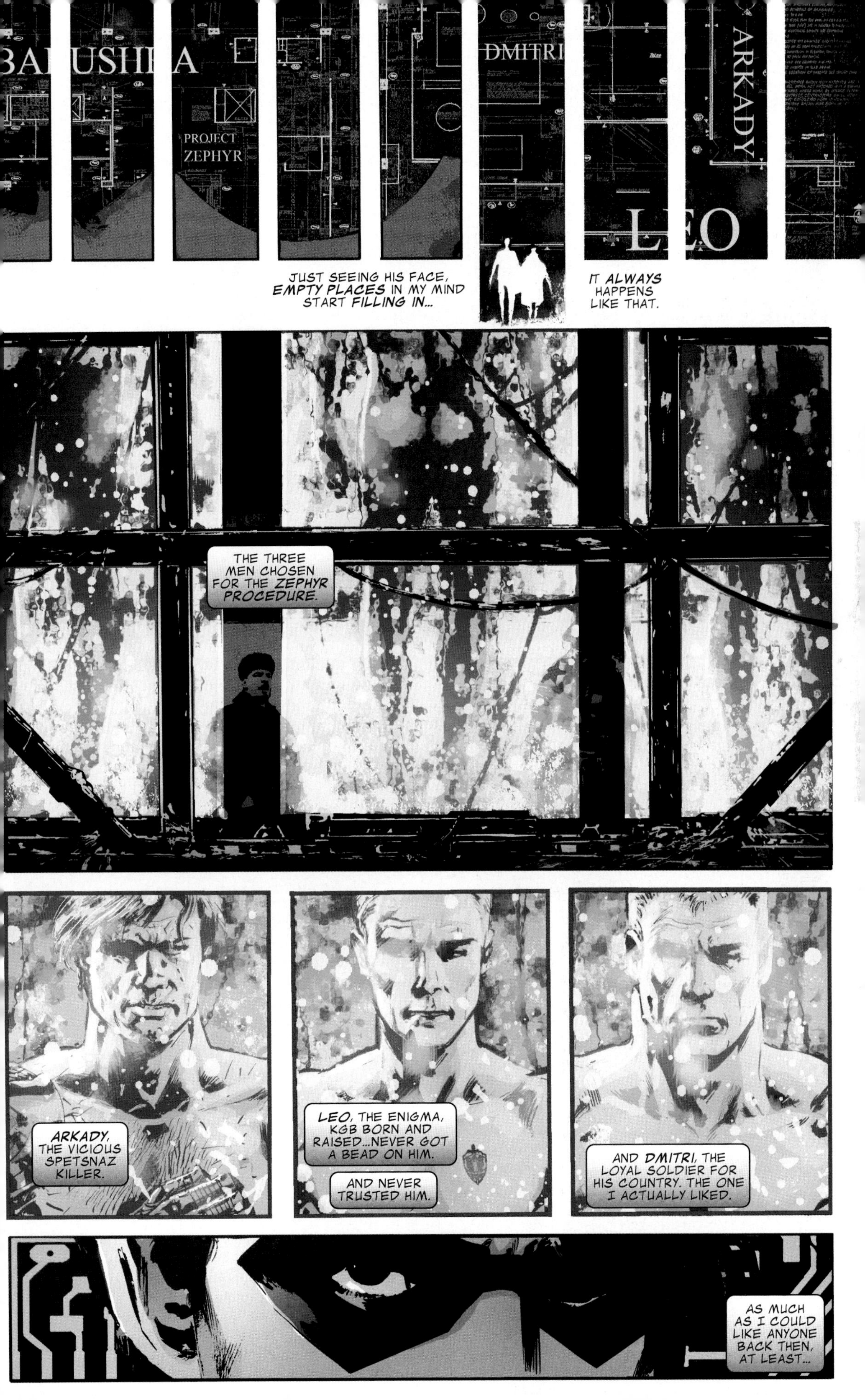
BABUSHKA
PROJECT ZEPHYR
DMITRI
ARKADY
LEO
JUST SEEING HIS FACE, EMPTY PLACES IN MY MIND START FILLING IN...
IT ALWAYS HAPPENS LIKE THAT.
THE THREE MEN CHOSEN FOR THE ZEPHYR PROCEDURE.
ARKADY, THE VICIOUS SPETSNAZ KILLER.
LEO, THE ENIGMA, KGB BORN AND RAISED...NEVER GOT A BEAD ON HIM.
AND NEVER TRUSTED HIM.
AND DMITRI, THE LOYAL SOLDIER FOR HIS COUNTRY. THE ONE I ACTUALLY LIKED.
AS MUCH AS I COULD LIKE ANYONE BACK THEN, AT LEAST...

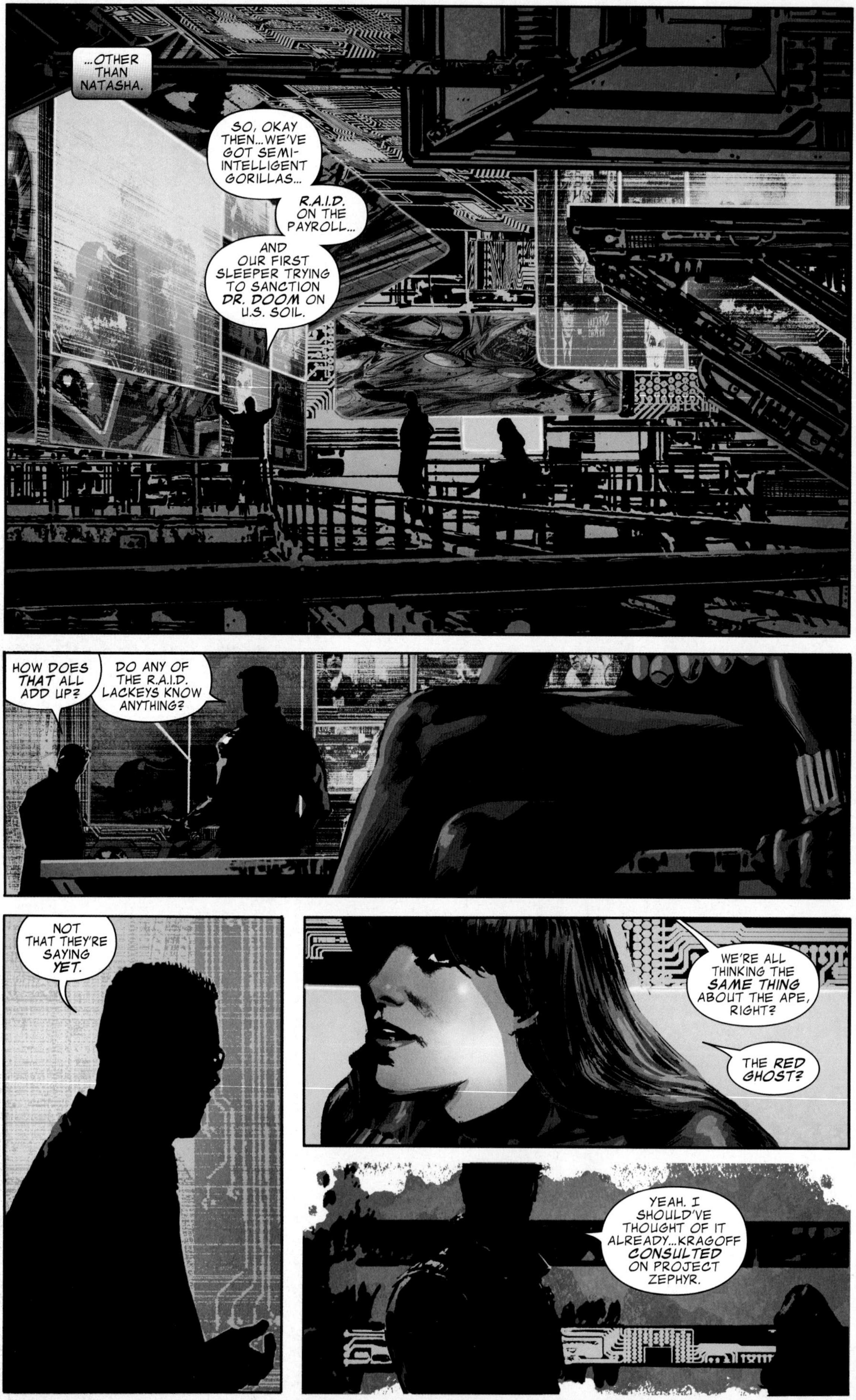
...OTHER THAN NATASHA.
SO, OKAY THEN...WE'VE GOT SEMI-INTELLIGENT GORILLAS...
R.A.I.D. ON THE PAYROLL...
AND OUR FIRST SLEEPER TRYING TO SANCTION DR. DOOM ON U.S. SOIL.
HOW DOES THAT ALL ADD UP?
DO ANY OF THE R.A.I.D. LACKEYS KNOW ANYTHING?
NOT THAT THEY'RE SAYING YET.
WE'RE ALL THINKING THE SAME THING ABOUT THE APE, RIGHT?
THE RED GHOST?
YEAH. I SHOULD'VE THOUGHT OF IT ALREADY...KRAGOFF CONSULTED ON PROJECT ZEPHYR.

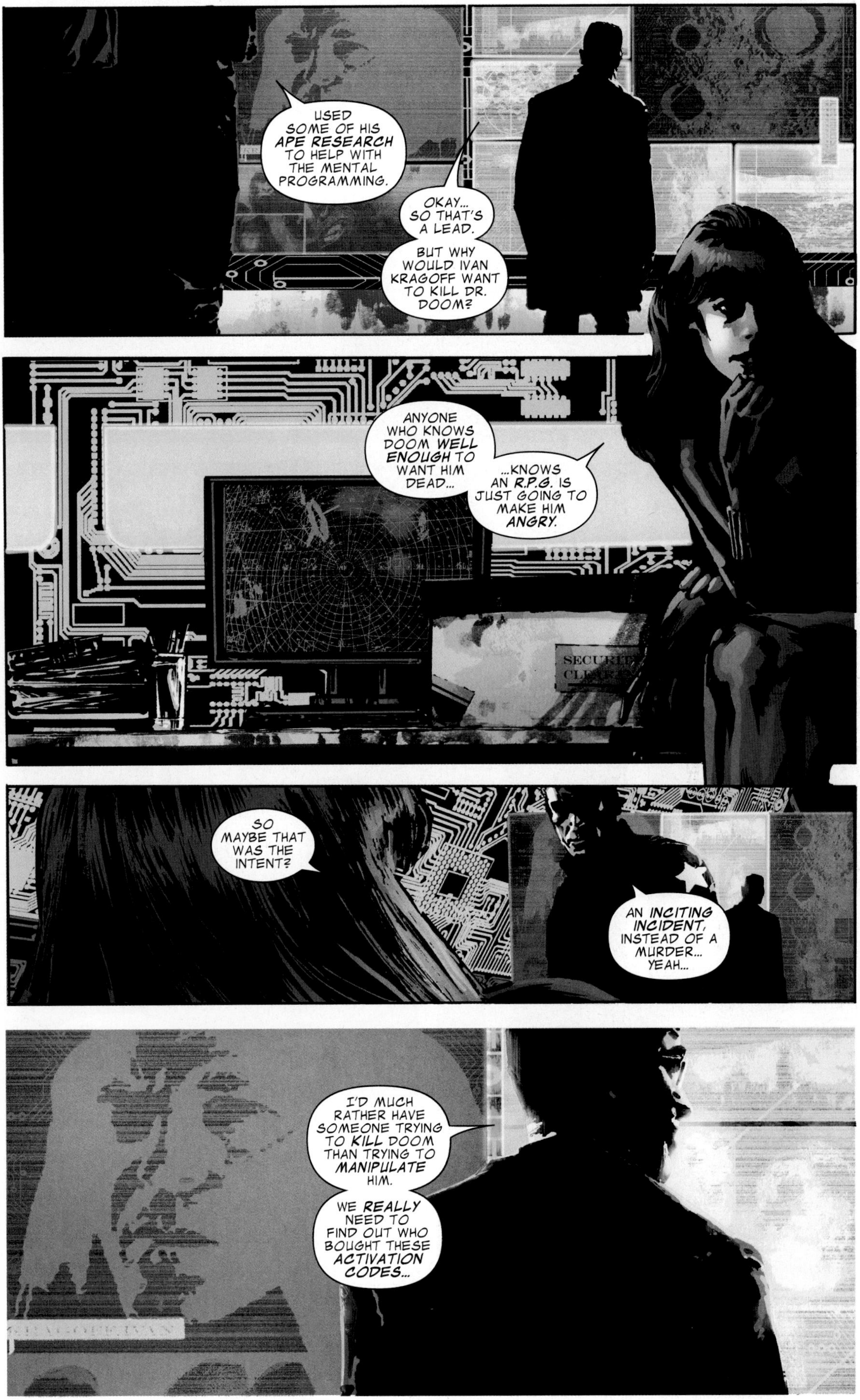
USED SOME OF HIS APE RESEARCH TO HELP WITH THE MENTAL PROGRAMMING.
OKAY... SO THAT'S A LEAD.
BUT WHY WOULD IVAN KRAGOFF WANT TO KILL DR. DOOM?
ANYONE WHO KNOWS DOOM WELL ENOUGH TO WANT HIM DEAD...
...KNOWS AN R.P.G. IS JUST GOING TO MAKE HIM ANGRY.
SO MAYBE THAT WAS THE INTENT?
AN INCITING INCIDENT, INSTEAD OF A MURDER... YEAH...
I'D MUCH RATHER HAVE SOMEONE TRYING TO KILL DOOM THAN TRYING TO MANIPULATE HIM.
WE REALLY NEED TO FIND OUT WHO BOUGHT THESE ACTIVATION CODES...

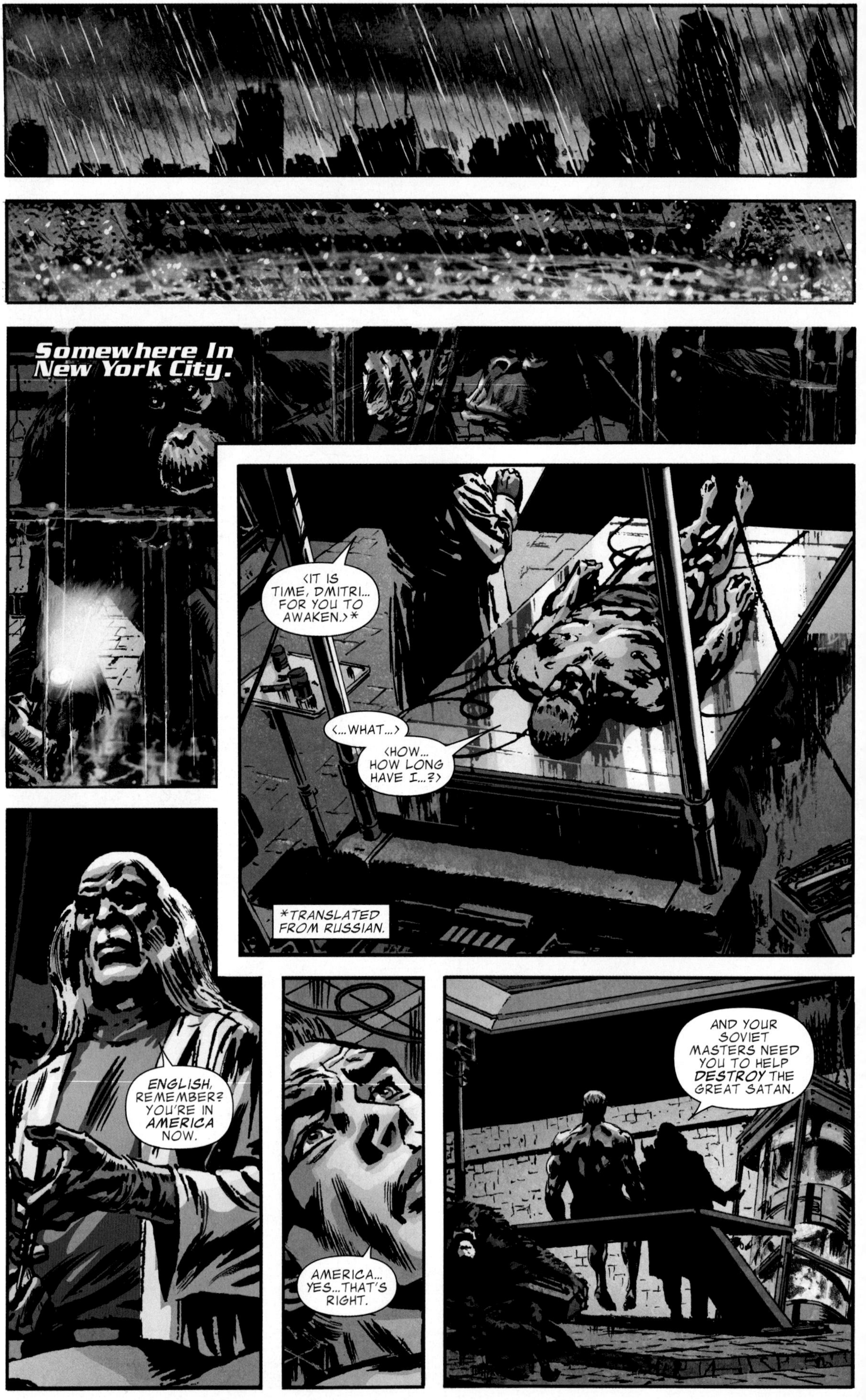

Somewhere In New York City.
<IT IS TIME, DMITRI... FOR YOU TO AWAKEN.>*
<...WHAT...>
<HOW... HOW LONG HAVE I...?>
*TRANSLATED FROM RUSSIAN.
ENGLISH, REMEMBER? YOU'RE IN AMERICA NOW.
AMERICA... YES...THAT'S RIGHT.
AND YOUR SOVIET MASTERS NEED YOU TO HELP DESTROY THE GREAT SATAN.

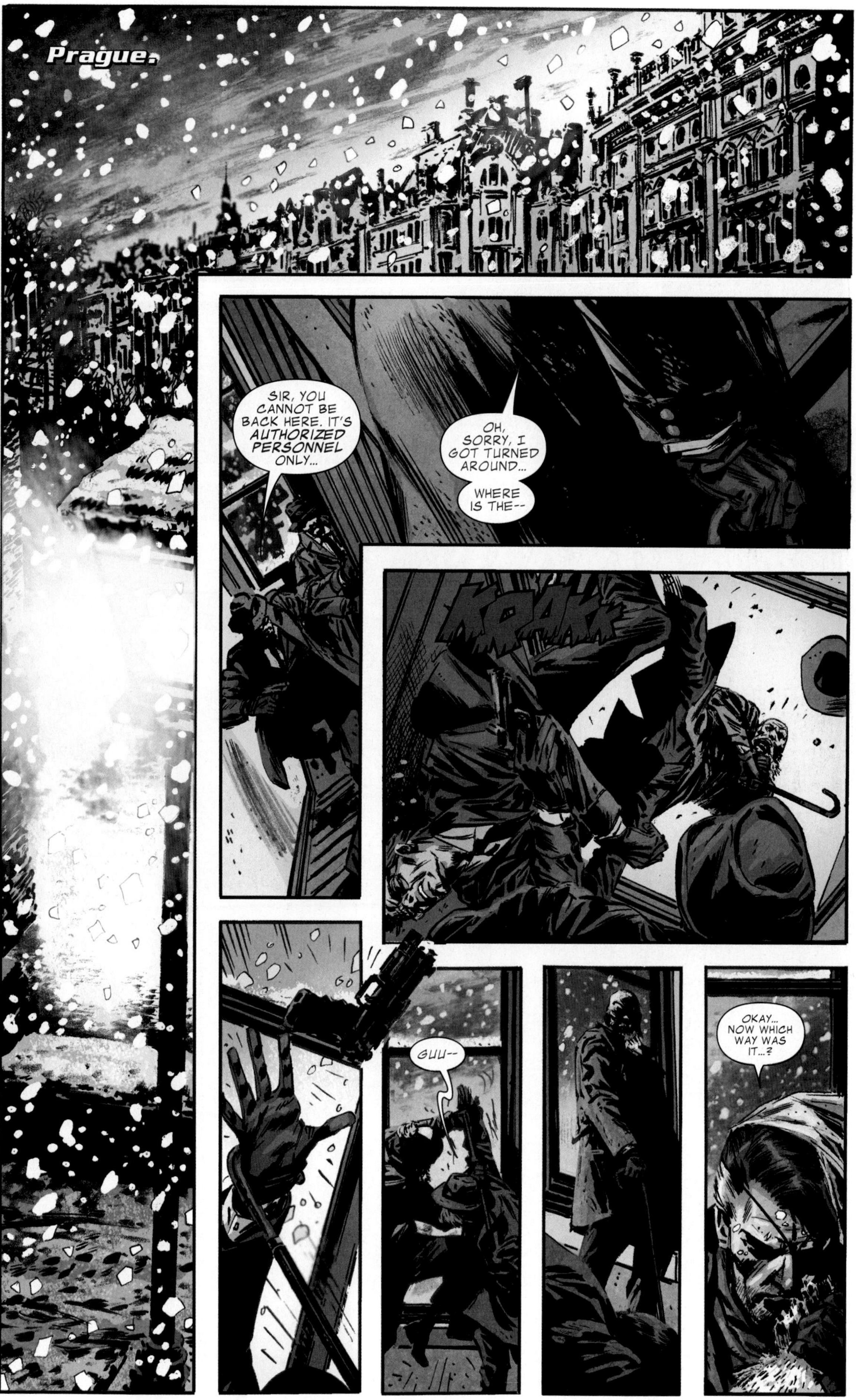
Prague.
SIR, YOU CANNOT BE BACK HERE. IT'S AUTHORIZED PERSONNEL ONLY...
OH, SORRY, I GOT TURNED AROUND...
WHERE IS THE--
GUU--
OKAY... NOW WHICH WAY WAS IT...?

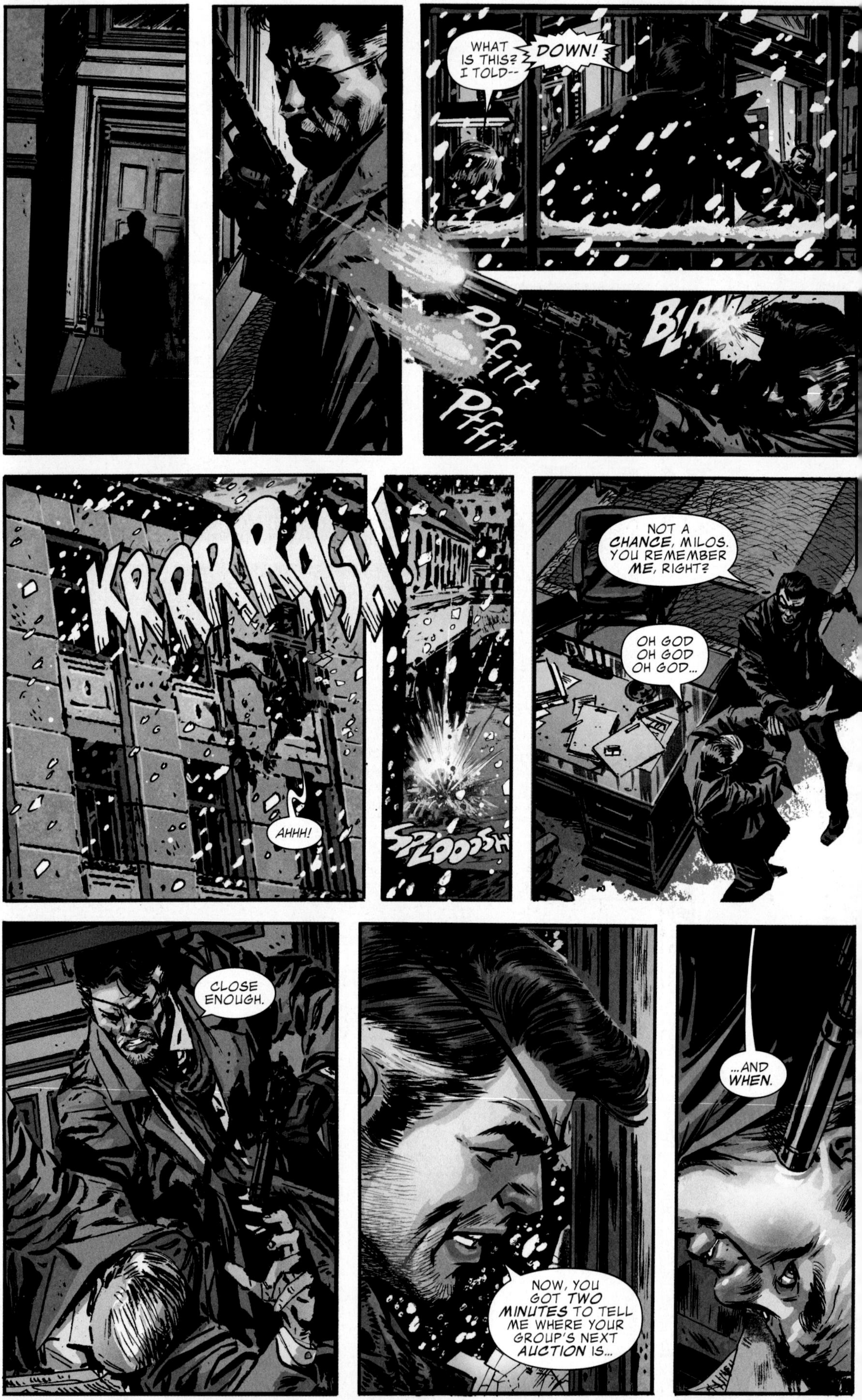

WHAT IS THIS? I TOLD--
DOWN!
PFFITT
PFFITT
BLAM
KRRRASH!
AHHH!
SPLOOOSH
NOT A CHANCE, MILOS. YOU REMEMBER ME, RIGHT?
OH GOD OH GOD OH GOD...
CLOSE ENOUGH.
NOW, YOU GOT TWO MINUTES TO TELL ME WHERE YOUR GROUP'S NEXT AUCTION IS...
...AND WHEN.

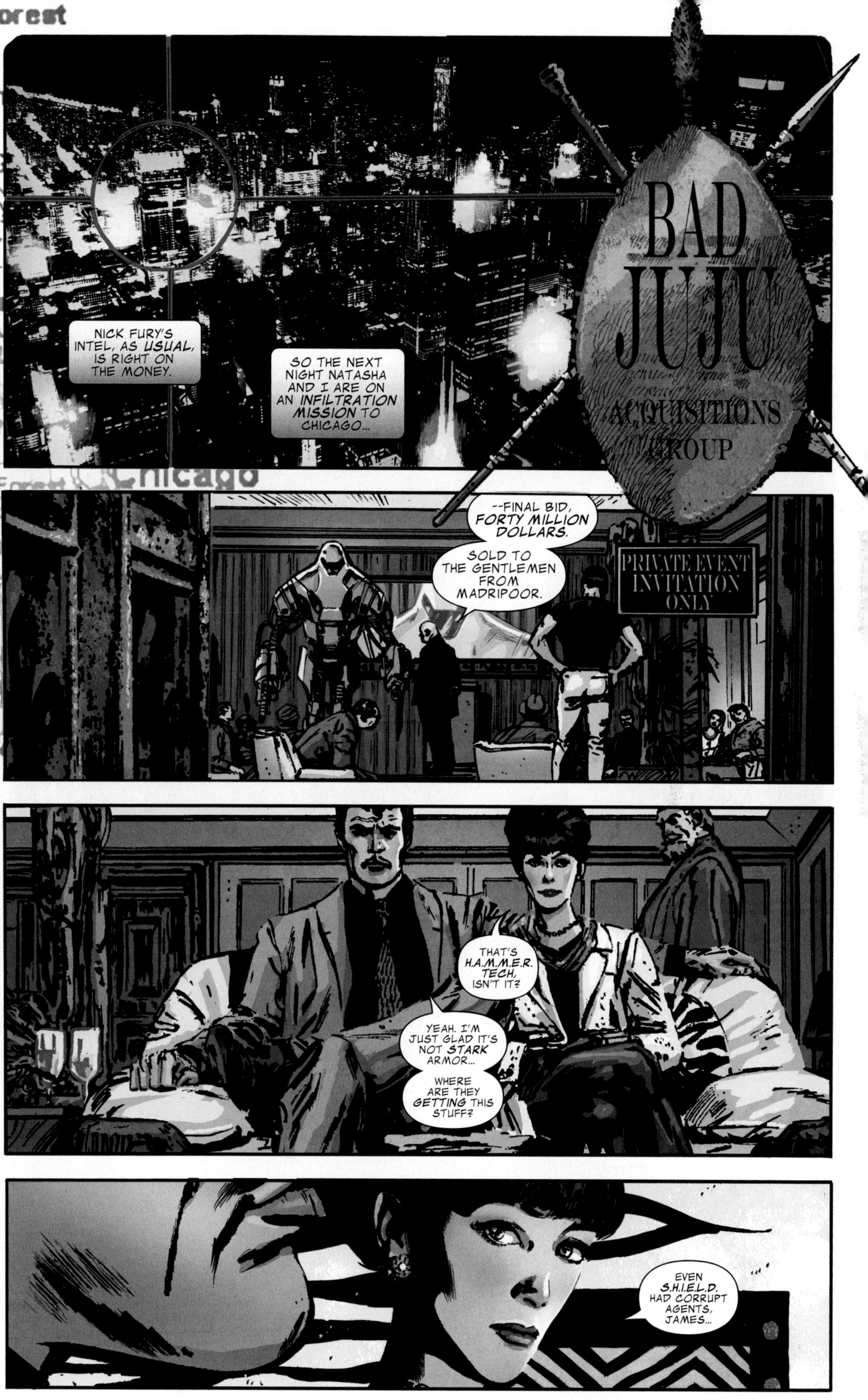
orest
BAD JUJU ACQUISITIONS GROUP
NICK FURY'S INTEL, AS USUAL, IS RIGHT ON THE MONEY.
SO THE NEXT NIGHT NATASHA AND I ARE ON AN INFILTRATION MISSION TO CHICAGO...
Chicago
--FINAL BID, FORTY MILLION DOLLARS.
SOLD TO THE GENTLEMEN FROM MADRIPOOR.
PRIVATE EVENT INVITATION ONLY
THAT'S H.A.M.M.E.R. TECH, ISN'T IT?
YEAH. I'M JUST GLAD IT'S NOT STARK ARMOR...
WHERE ARE THEY GETTING THIS STUFF?
EVEN S.H.I.E.L.D. HAD CORRUPT AGENTS, JAMES...

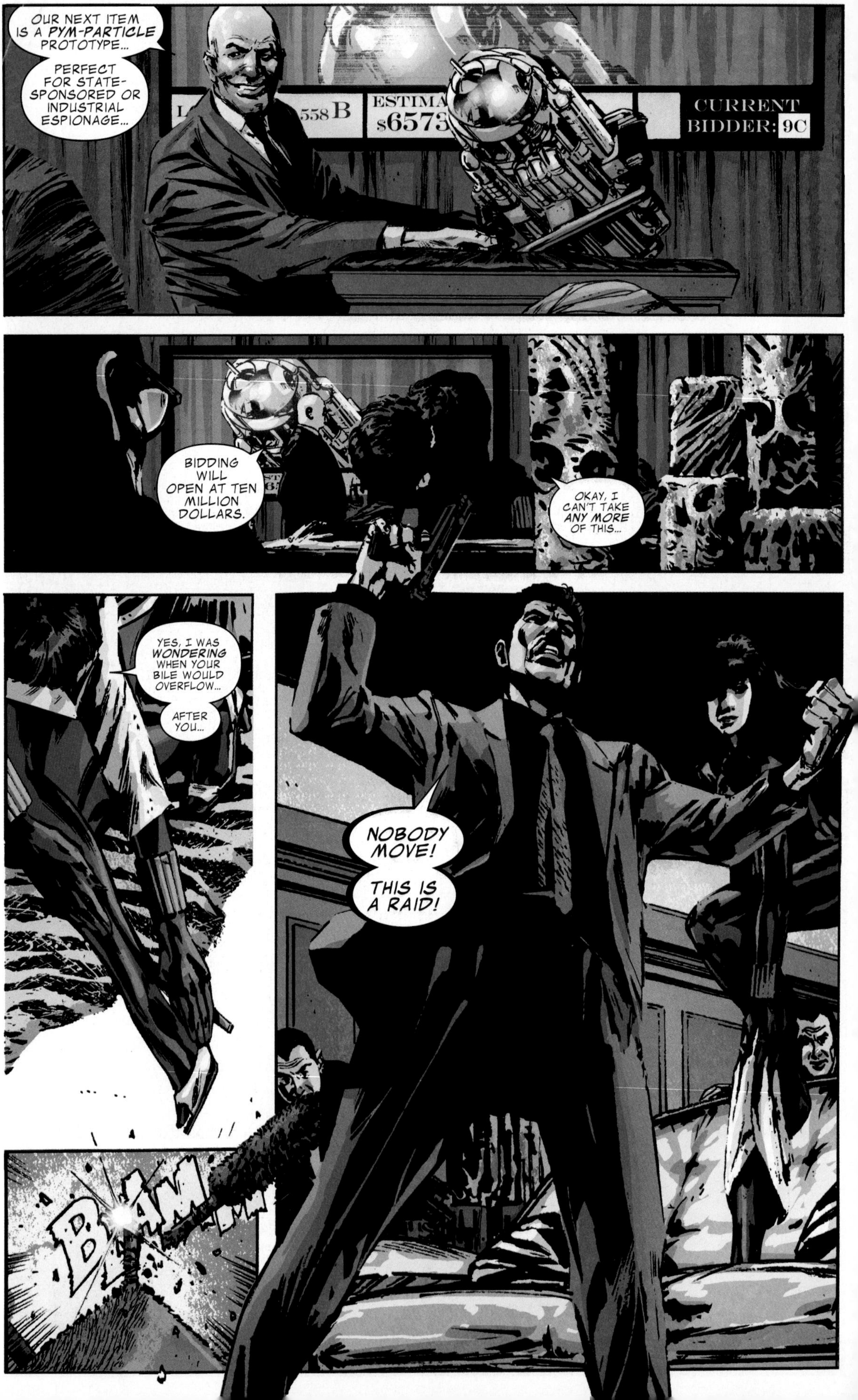
OUR NEXT ITEM IS A PYM-PARTICLE PROTOTYPE...
PERFECT FOR STATE-SPONSORED OR INDUSTRIAL ESPIONAGE...
558 B
ESTIMA
$6573
CURRENT BIDDER: 9C
BIDDING WILL OPEN AT TEN MILLION DOLLARS.
OKAY, I CAN'T TAKE ANY MORE OF THIS...
YES, I WAS WONDERING WHEN YOUR BILE WOULD OVERFLOW...
AFTER YOU...
...
NOBODY MOVE!
THIS IS A RAID!
BLAM

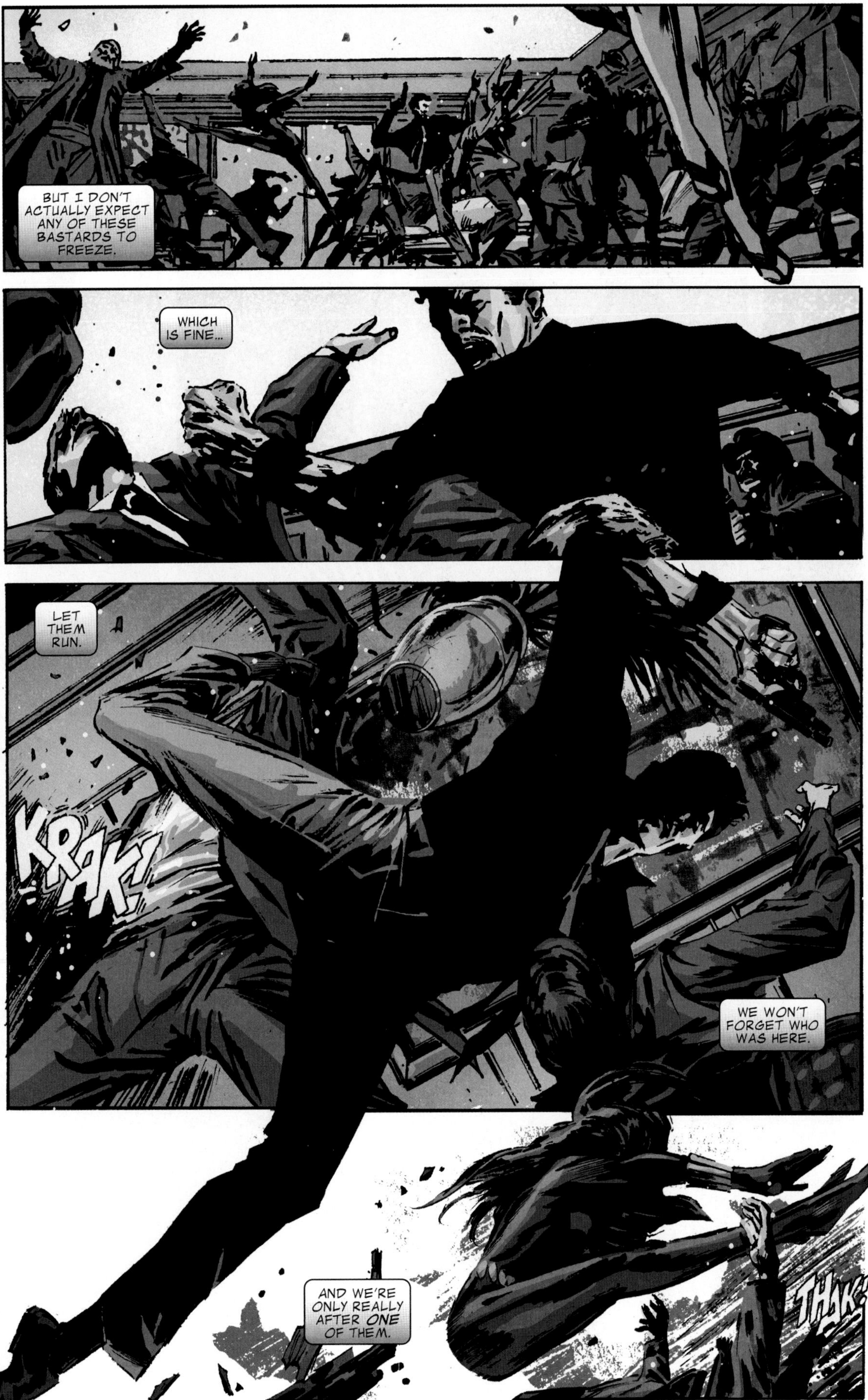
BUT I DON'T ACTUALLY EXPECT ANY OF THESE BASTARDS TO FREEZE.
WHICH IS FINE...
LET THEM RUN.
KRAK!
WE WON'T FORGET WHO WAS HERE.
AND WE'RE ONLY REALLY AFTER *ONE* OF THEM.
THAK!

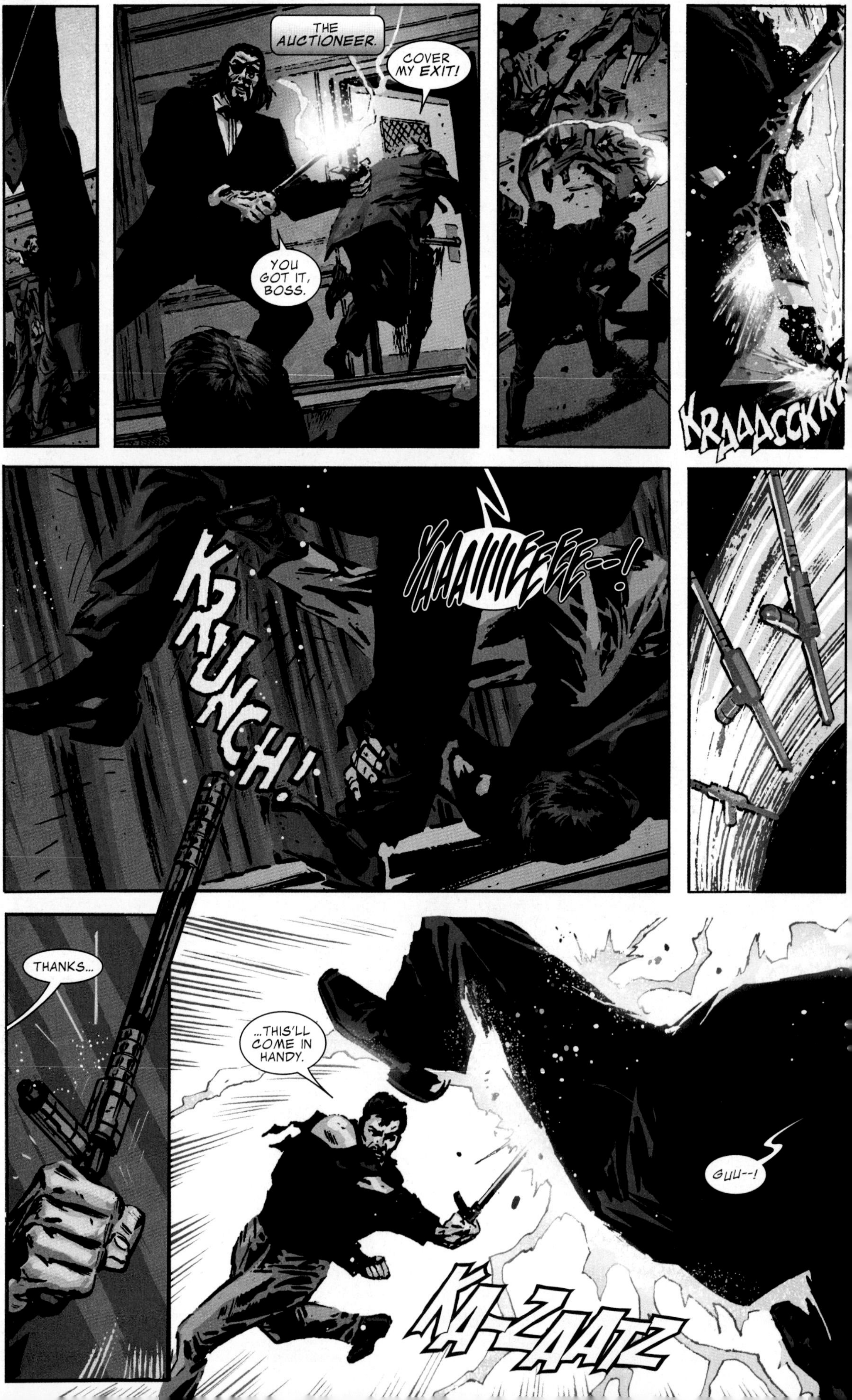
THE AUCTIONEER.
COVER MY EXIT!
YOU GOT IT, BOSS.
KRAAACCKKK
KRUNCH!
YAAAIIIEEEE--!
THANKS...
...THIS'LL COME IN HANDY.
GUU--!
KA-ZAATZ

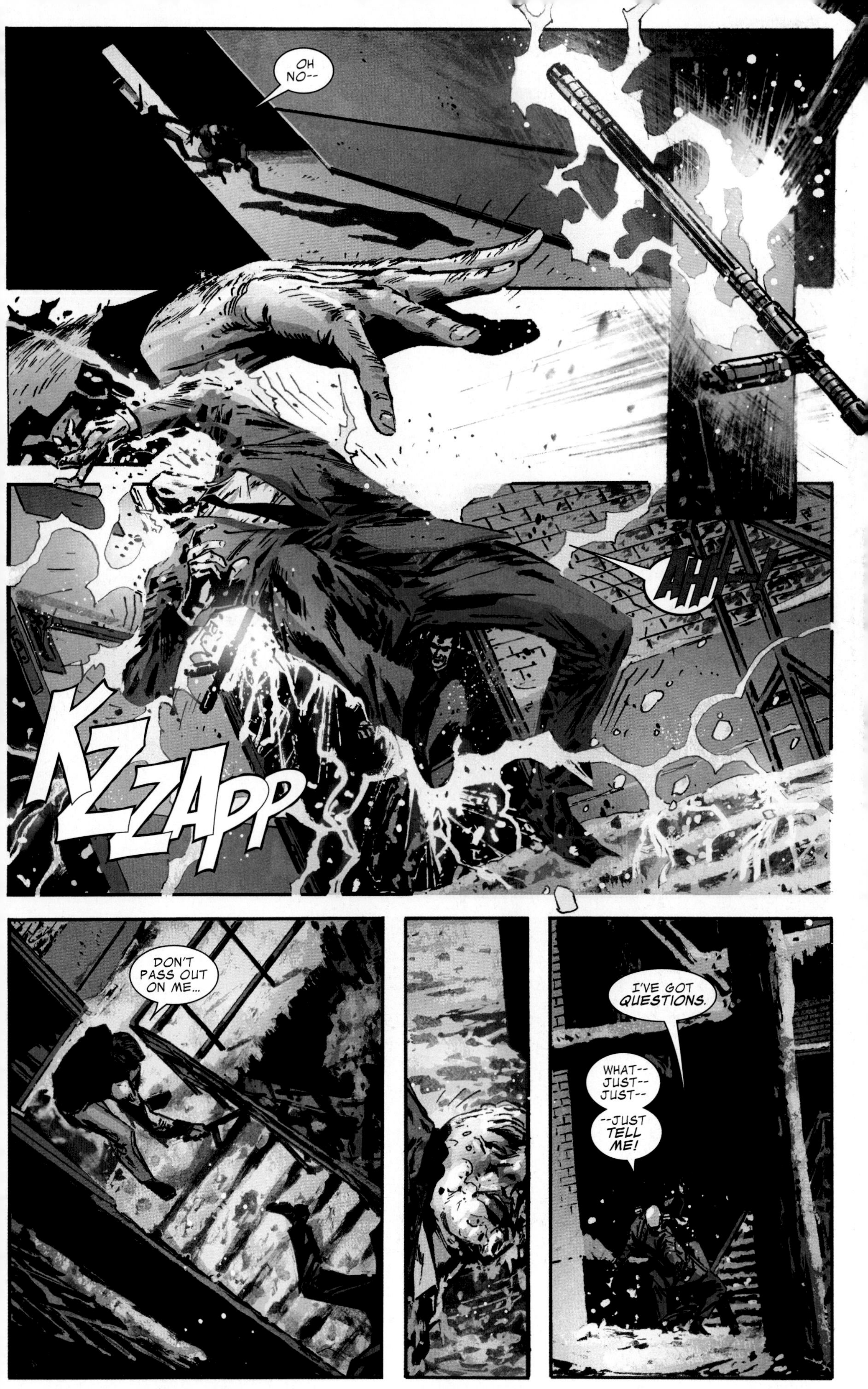
OH NO--
AHH
KZZAPP
DON'T PASS OUT ON ME...
I'VE GOT QUESTIONS.
WHAT-- JUST-- JUST--
--JUST TELL ME!

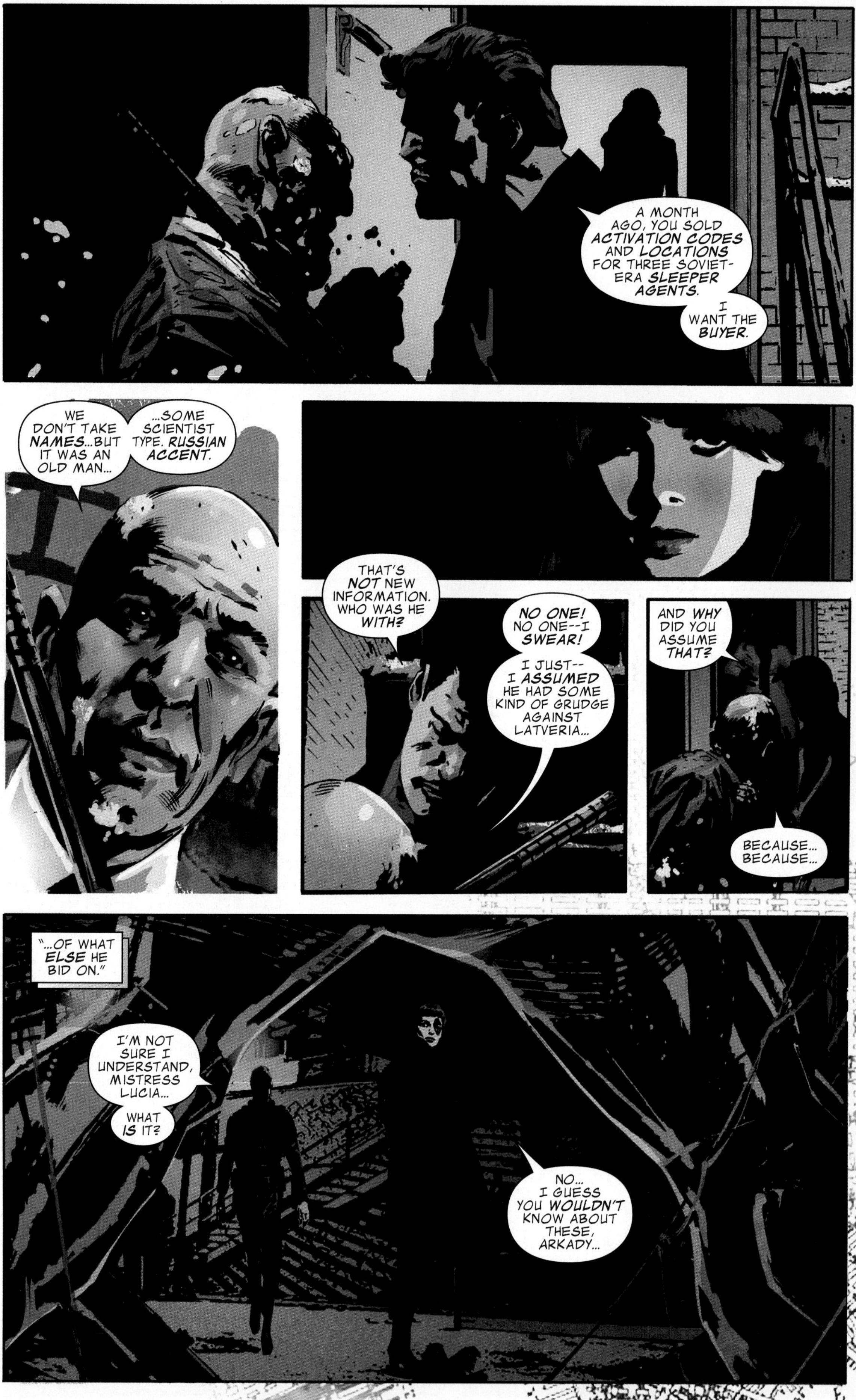
A MONTH AGO, YOU SOLD ACTIVATION CODES AND LOCATIONS FOR THREE SOVIET-ERA SLEEPER AGENTS.
I WANT THE BUYER.
WE DON'T TAKE NAMES...BUT IT WAS AN OLD MAN...
...SOME SCIENTIST TYPE. RUSSIAN ACCENT.
THAT'S NOT NEW INFORMATION. WHO WAS HE WITH?
NO ONE! NO ONE--I SWEAR!
I JUST--I ASSUMED HE HAD SOME KIND OF GRUDGE AGAINST LATVERIA...
AND WHY DID YOU ASSUME THAT?
BECAUSE... BECAUSE...
"...OF WHAT ELSE HE BID ON."
I'M NOT SURE I UNDERSTAND, MISTRESS LUCIA...
WHAT IS IT?
NO... I GUESS YOU WOULDN'T KNOW ABOUT THESE, ARKADY...

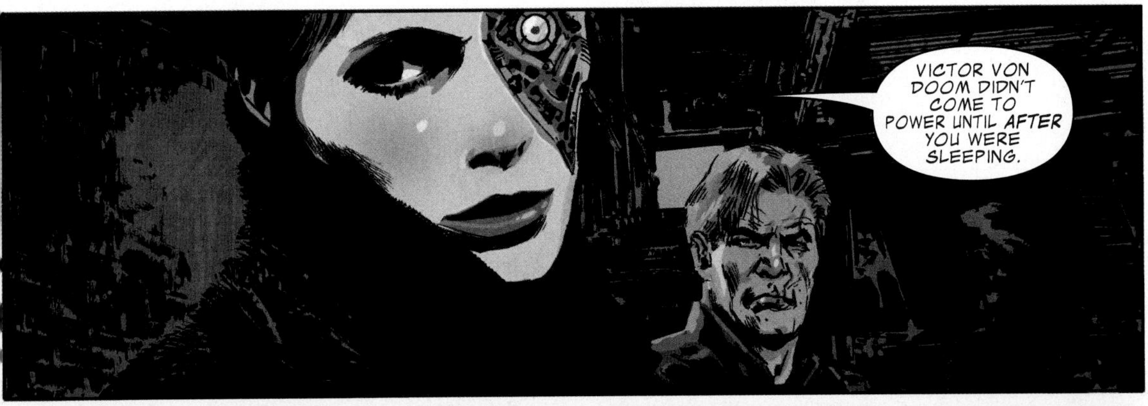
VICTOR VON DOOM DIDN'T COME TO POWER UNTIL AFTER YOU WERE SLEEPING.

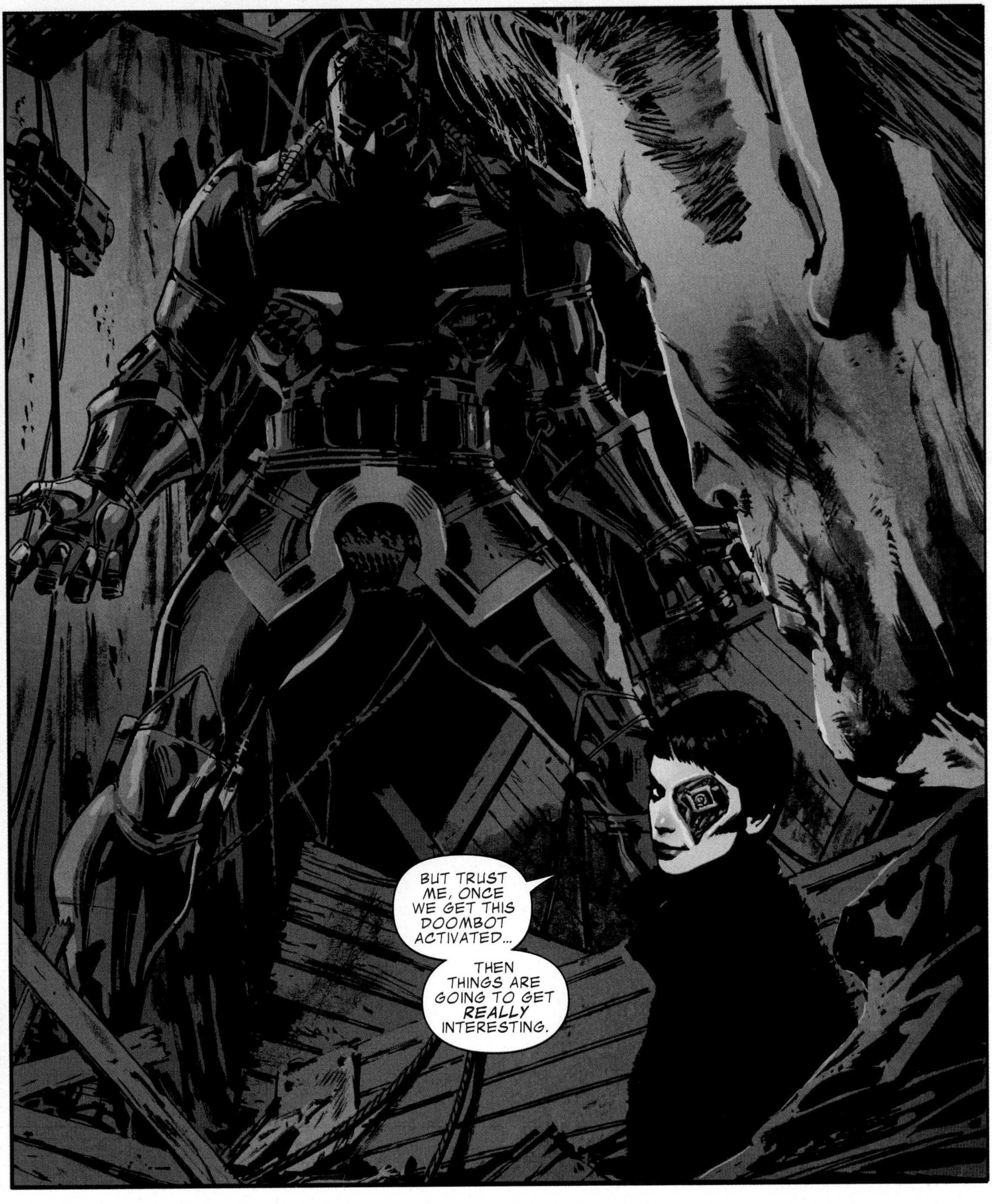
BUT TRUST ME, ONCE WE GET THIS DOOMBOT ACTIVATED...
THEN THINGS ARE GOING TO GET REALLY INTERESTING.

3

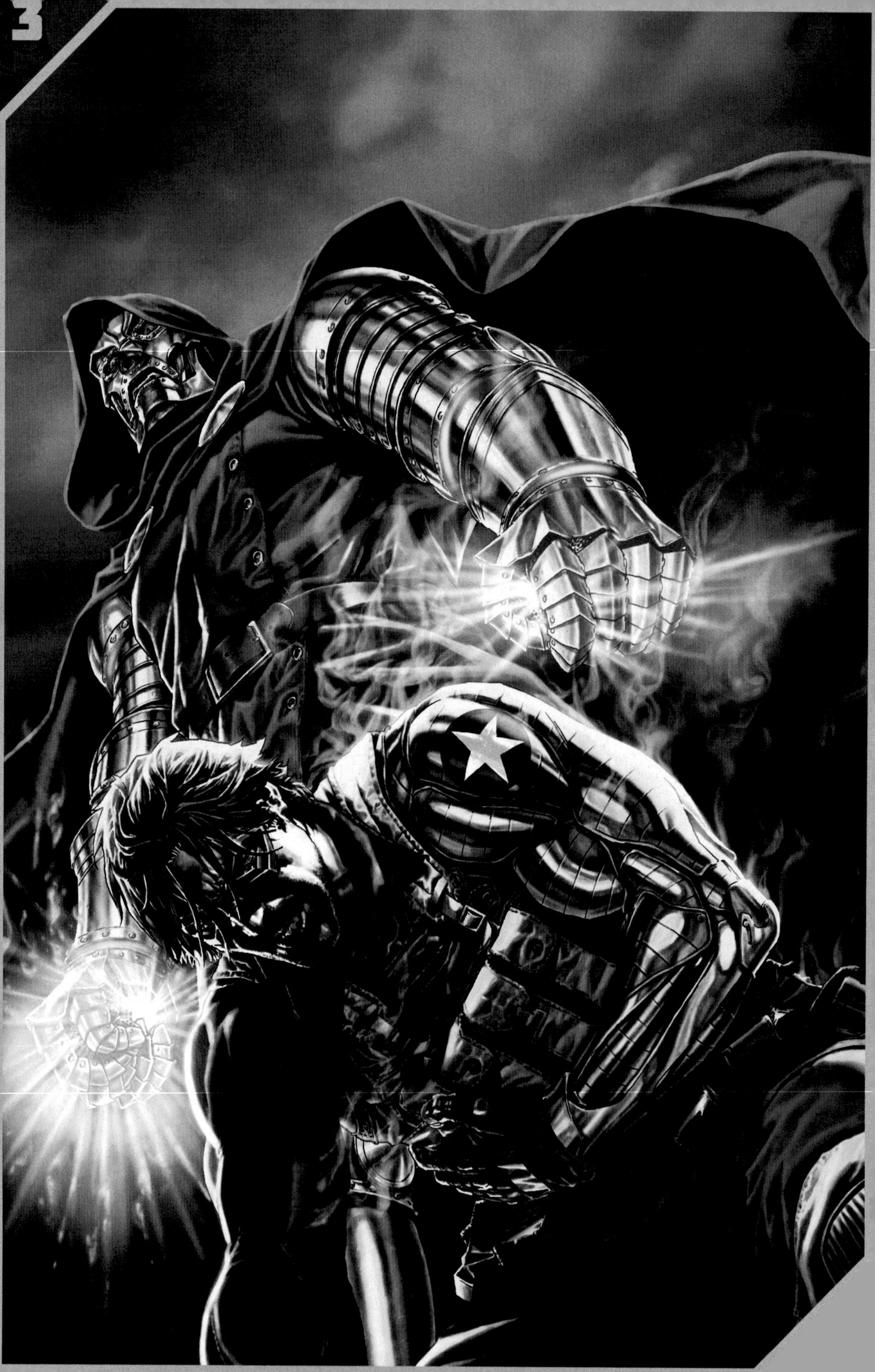

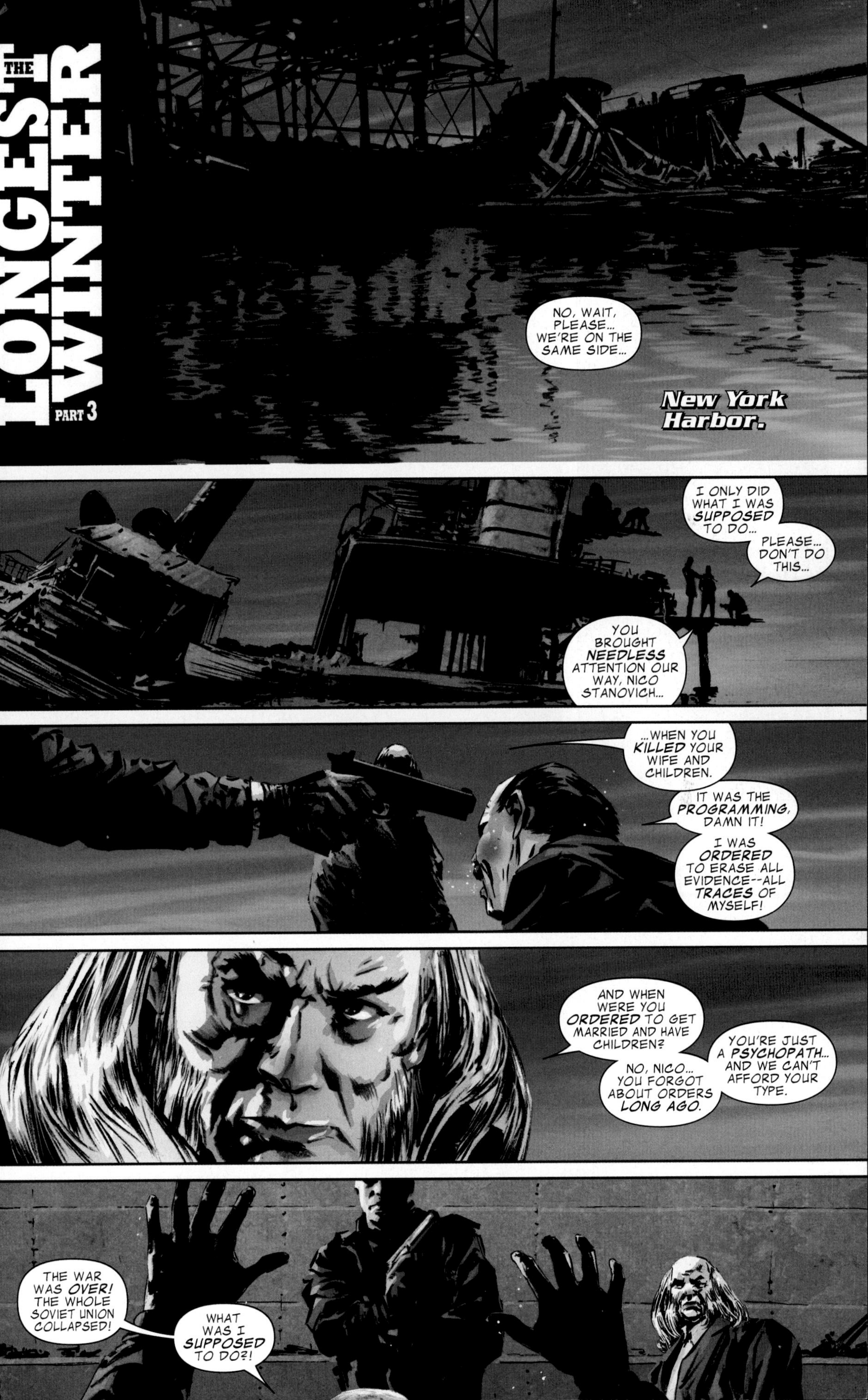
THE LONGEST WINTER
PART 3
NO, WAIT, PLEASE... WE'RE ON THE SAME SIDE...
New York Harbor.
I ONLY DID WHAT I WAS SUPPOSED TO DO...
PLEASE... DON'T DO THIS...
YOU BROUGHT NEEDLESS ATTENTION OUR WAY, NICO STANOVICH...
...WHEN YOU KILLED YOUR WIFE AND CHILDREN.
IT WAS THE PROGRAMMING, DAMN IT!
I WAS ORDERED TO ERASE ALL EVIDENCE--ALL TRACES OF MYSELF!
AND WHEN WERE YOU ORDERED TO GET MARRIED AND HAVE CHILDREN?
NO, NICO... YOU FORGOT ABOUT ORDERS LONG AGO.
YOU'RE JUST A PSYCHOPATH... AND WE CAN'T AFFORD YOUR TYPE.
THE WAR WAS OVER! THE WHOLE SOVIET UNION COLLAPSED!
WHAT WAS I SUPPOSED TO DO?!

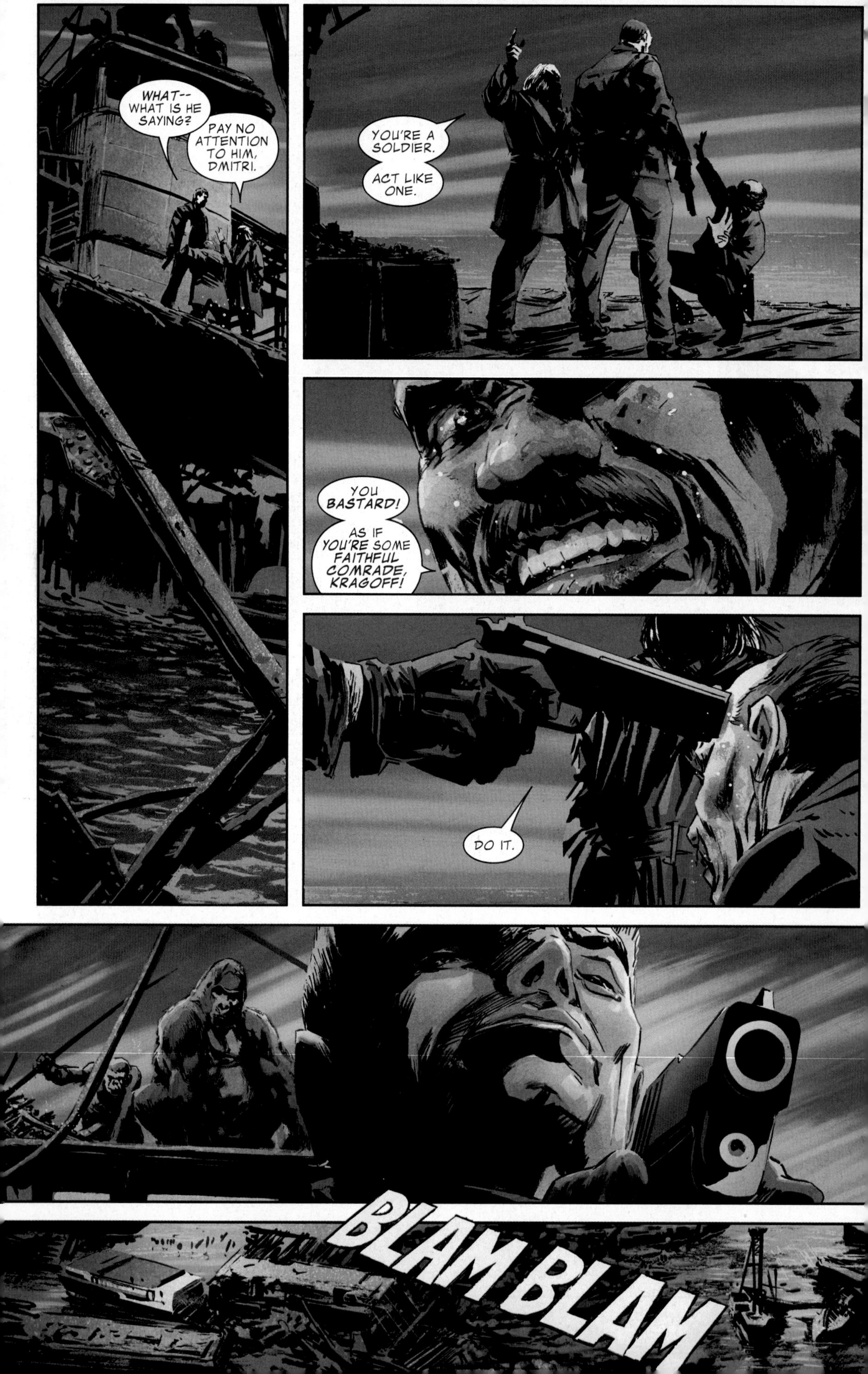
WHAT--
WHAT IS HE SAYING?
PAY NO ATTENTION TO HIM, DMITRI.
YOU'RE A SOLDIER.
ACT LIKE ONE.
YOU BASTARD!
AS IF YOU'RE SOME FAITHFUL COMRADE, KRAGOFF!
DO IT.
BLAM BLAM

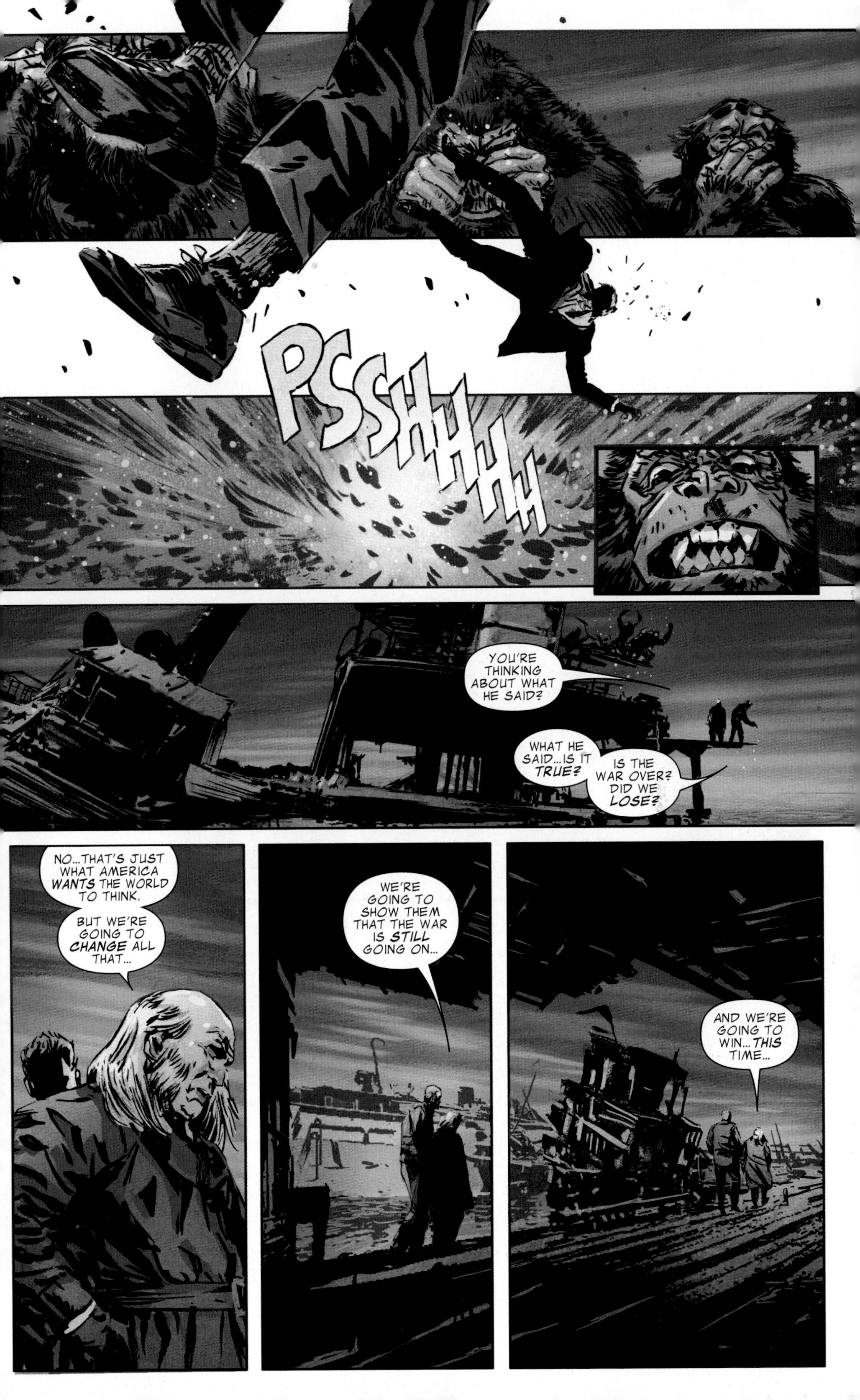
PSSHHHHH
YOU'RE THINKING ABOUT WHAT HE SAID?
WHAT HE SAID...IS IT TRUE?
IS THE WAR OVER? DID WE LOSE?
NO...THAT'S JUST WHAT AMERICA WANTS THE WORLD TO THINK.
BUT WE'RE GOING TO CHANGE ALL THAT...
WE'RE GOING TO SHOW THEM THAT THE WAR IS STILL GOING ON...
AND WE'RE GOING TO WIN... THIS TIME...

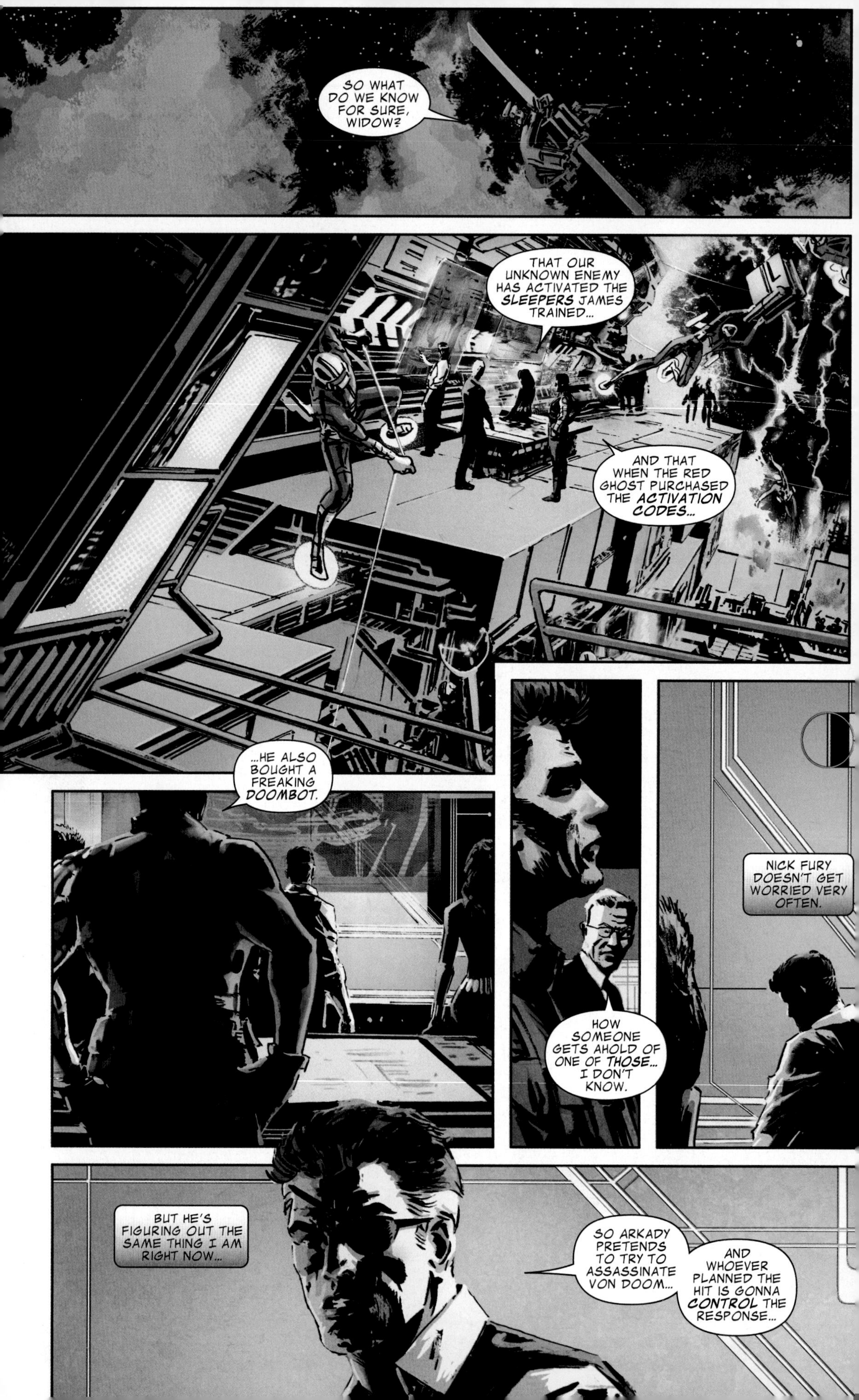
SO WHAT DO WE KNOW FOR SURE, WIDOW?
THAT OUR UNKNOWN ENEMY HAS ACTIVATED THE SLEEPERS JAMES TRAINED...
AND THAT WHEN THE RED GHOST PURCHASED THE ACTIVATION CODES...
...HE ALSO BOUGHT A FREAKING DOOMBOT.
HOW SOMEONE GETS AHOLD OF ONE OF THOSE... I DON'T KNOW.
NICK FURY DOESN'T GET WORRIED VERY OFTEN.
BUT HE'S FIGURING OUT THE SAME THING I AM RIGHT NOW...
SO ARKADY PRETENDS TO TRY TO ASSASSINATE VON DOOM...
AND WHOEVER PLANNED THE HIT IS GONNA CONTROL THE RESPONSE...

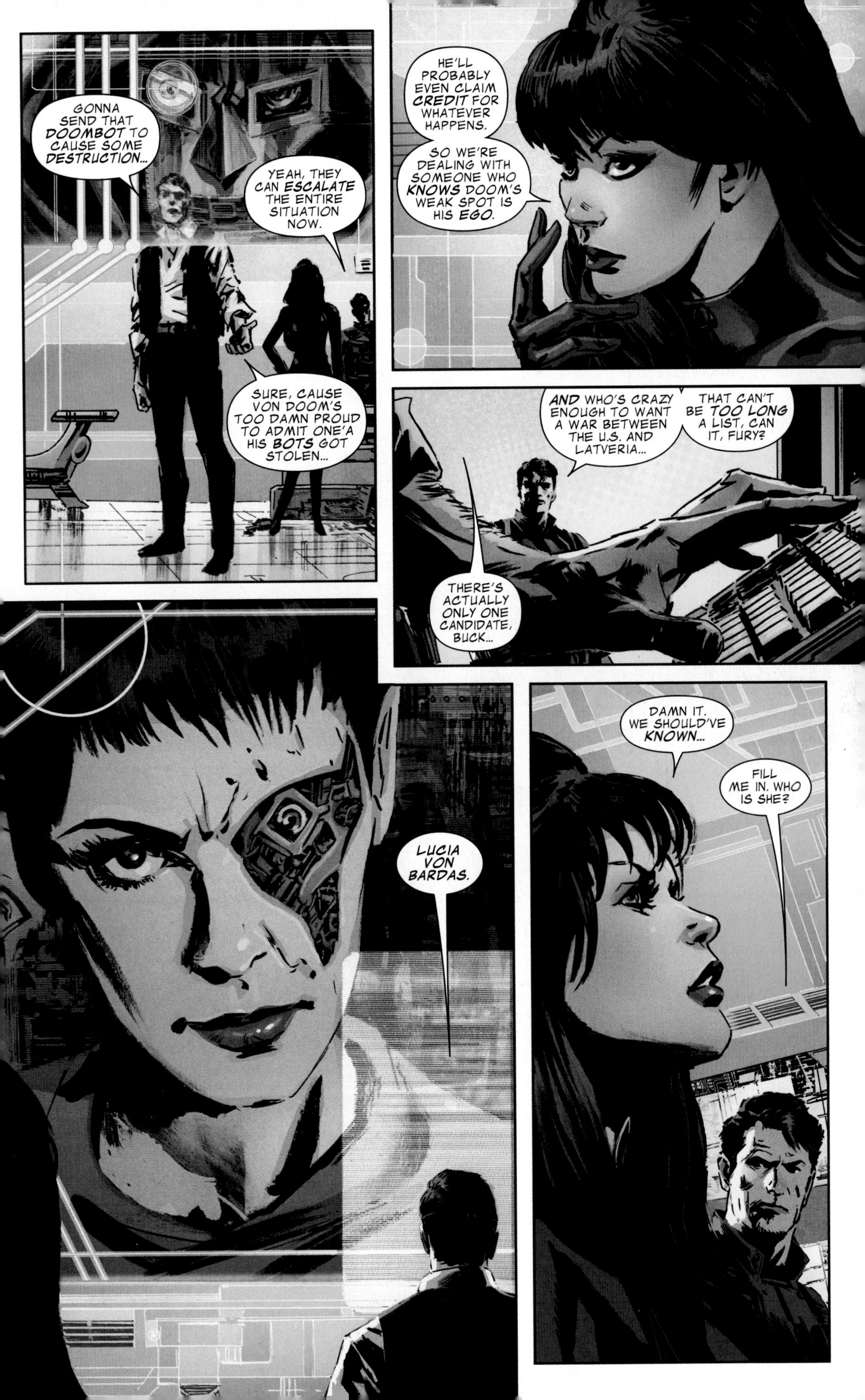
GONNA SEND THAT DOOMBOT TO CAUSE SOME DESTRUCTION...
YEAH, THEY CAN ESCALATE THE ENTIRE SITUATION NOW.
SURE, CAUSE VON DOOM'S TOO DAMN PROUD TO ADMIT ONE'A HIS BOTS GOT STOLEN...
HE'LL PROBABLY EVEN CLAIM CREDIT FOR WHATEVER HAPPENS.
SO WE'RE DEALING WITH SOMEONE WHO KNOWS DOOM'S WEAK SPOT IS HIS EGO.
AND WHO'S CRAZY ENOUGH TO WANT A WAR BETWEEN THE U.S. AND LATVERIA...
THAT CAN'T BE TOO LONG A LIST, CAN IT, FURY?
THERE'S ACTUALLY ONLY ONE CANDIDATE, BUCK...
LUCIA VON BARDAS.
DAMN IT. WE SHOULD'VE KNOWN...
FILL ME IN. WHO IS SHE?

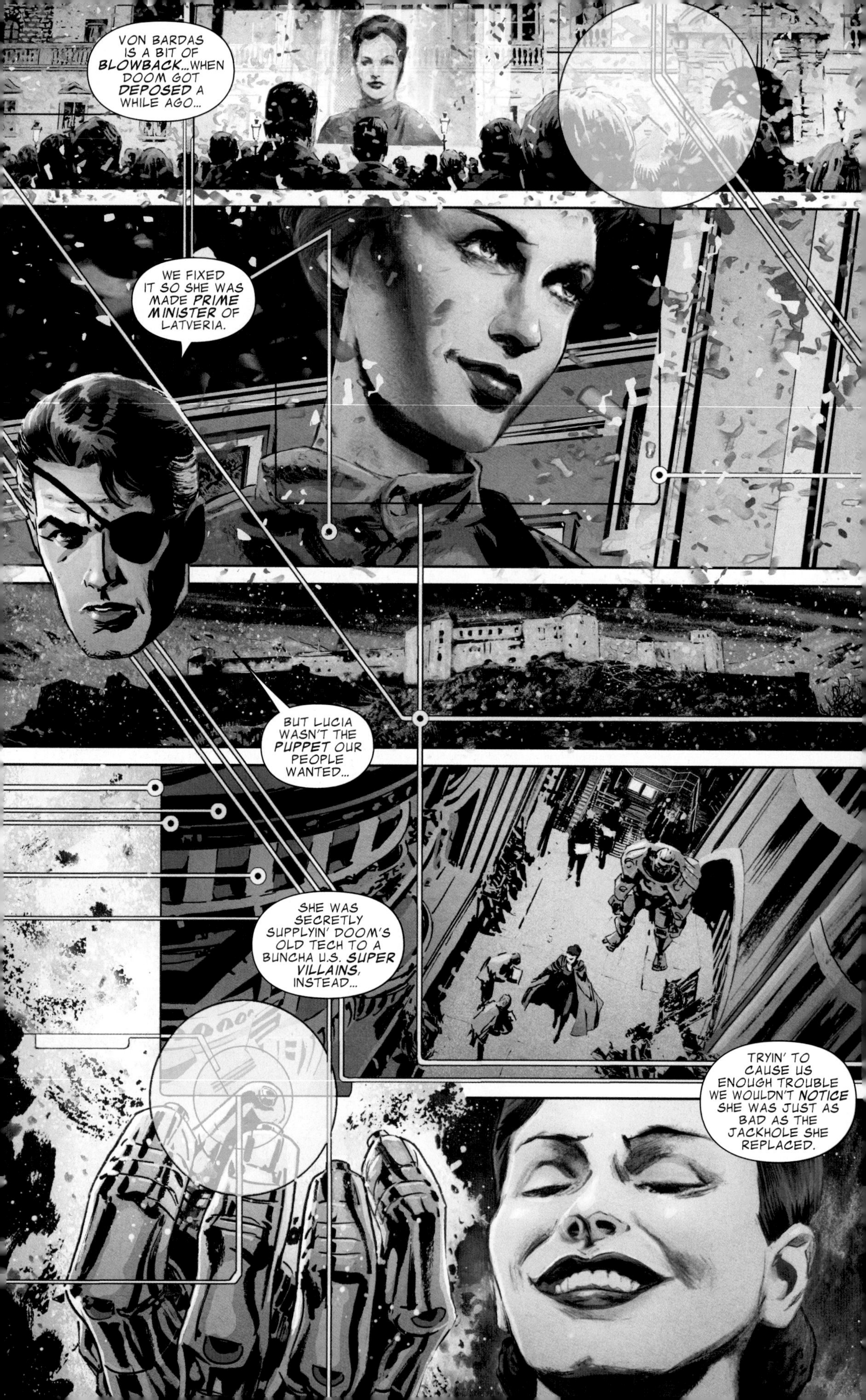
VON BARDAS IS A BIT OF BLOWBACK...WHEN DOOM GOT DEPOSED A WHILE AGO...
WE FIXED IT SO SHE WAS MADE PRIME MINISTER OF LATVERIA.
BUT LUCIA WASN'T THE PUPPET OUR PEOPLE WANTED...
SHE WAS SECRETLY SUPPLYIN' DOOM'S OLD TECH TO A BUNCHA U.S. SUPER VILLAINS, INSTEAD...
TRYIN' TO CAUSE US ENOUGH TROUBLE WE WOULDN'T NOTICE SHE WAS JUST AS BAD AS THE JACKHOLE SHE REPLACED.

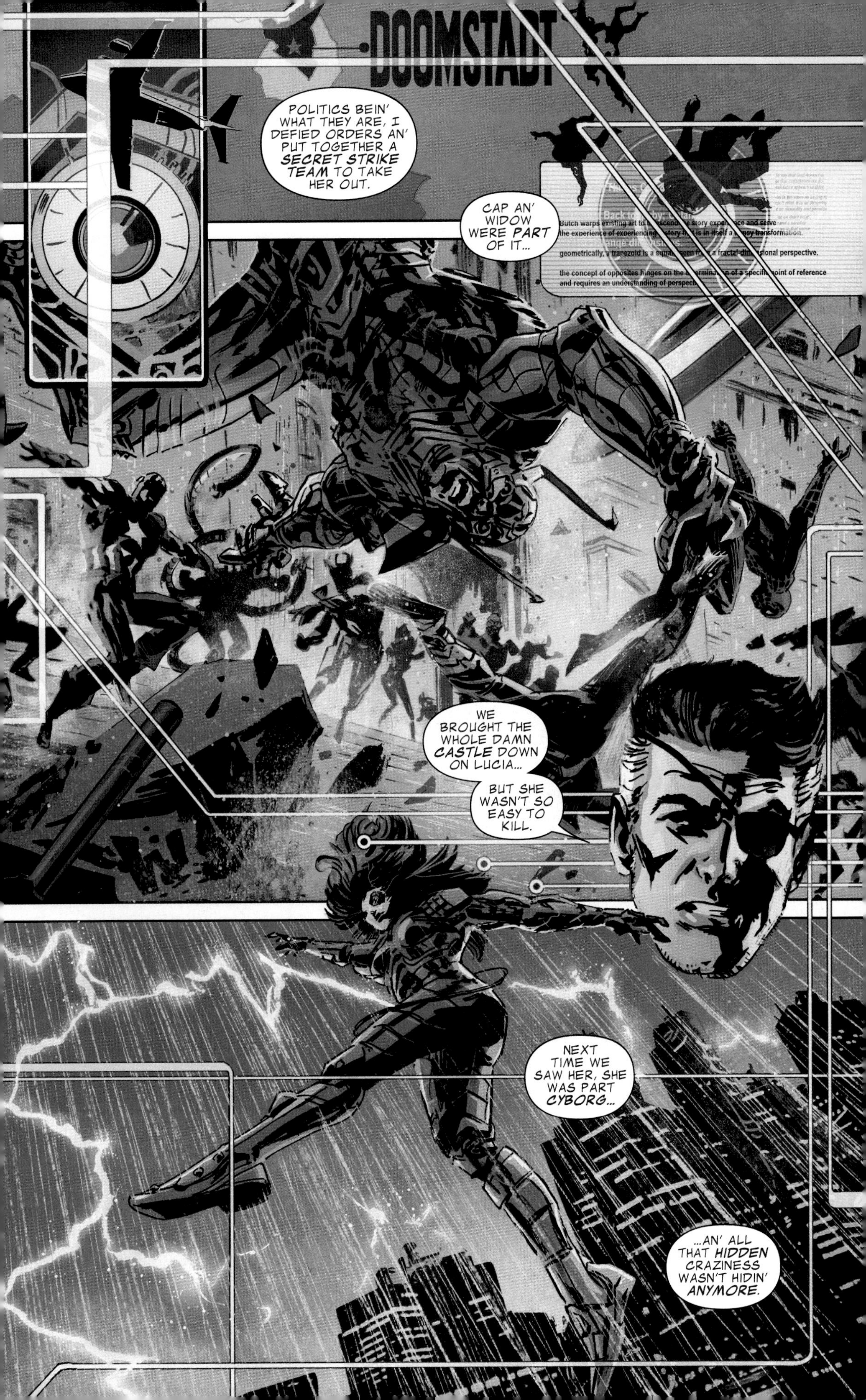
DOOMSTADT
POLITICS BEIN' WHAT THEY ARE, I DEFIED ORDERS AN' PUT TOGETHER A SECRET STRIKE TEAM TO TAKE HER OUT.
CAP AN' WIDOW WERE PART OF IT...
Butch warps existing art to
story expe
ce and serve
the experience of experiencing
is in itself a
transformation.
geometrically, a trapezoid is a
a fractal-
sional perspective.
the concept of opposites hinges on the
of a specific
oint of reference
and requires an understanding of
WE BROUGHT THE WHOLE DAMN CASTLE DOWN ON LUCIA...
BUT SHE WASN'T SO EASY TO KILL.
NEXT TIME WE SAW HER, SHE WAS PART CYBORG...
...AN' ALL THAT HIDDEN CRAZINESS WASN'T HIDIN' ANYMORE.

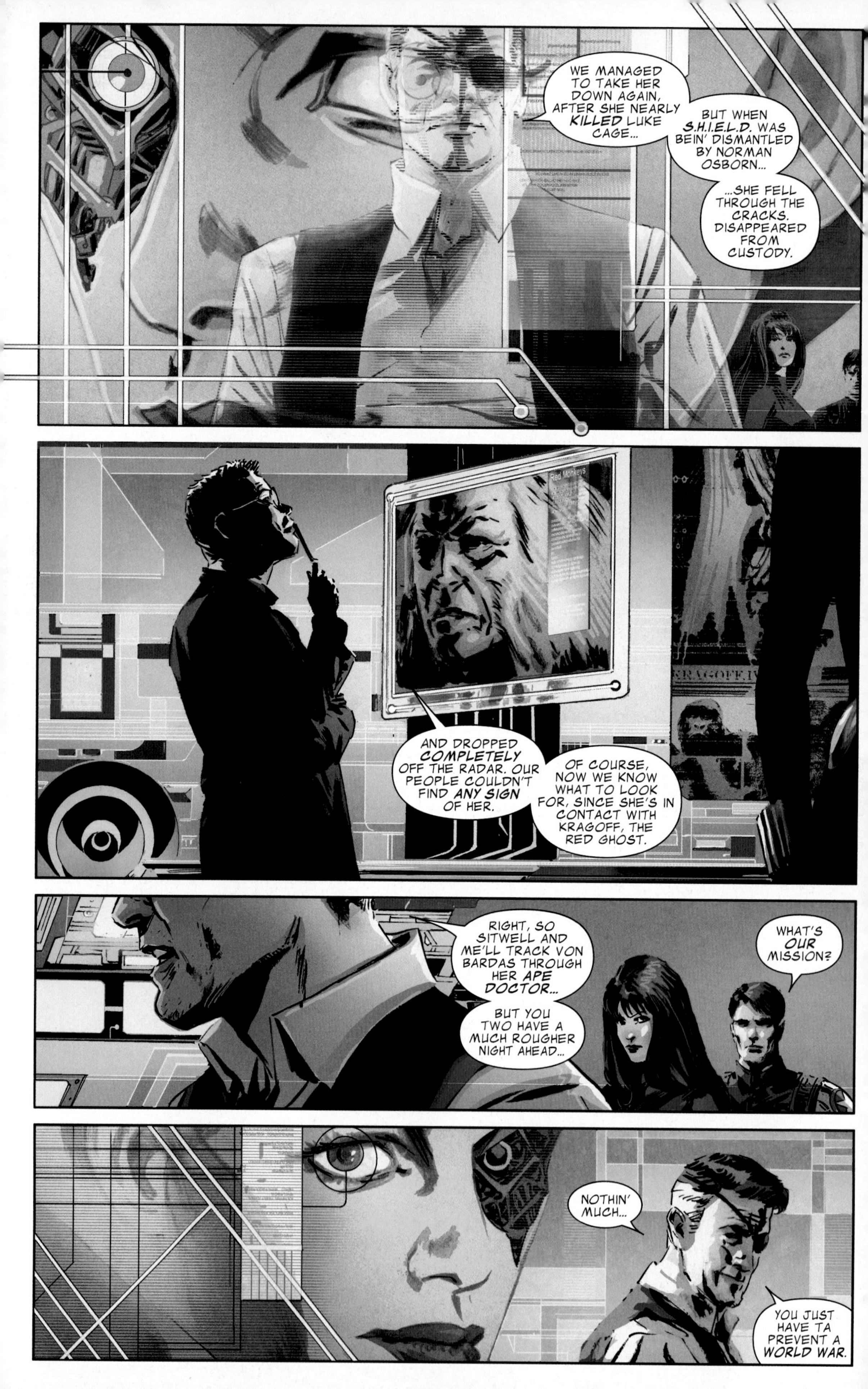

WE MANAGED TO TAKE HER DOWN AGAIN, AFTER SHE NEARLY KILLED LUKE CAGE...
BUT WHEN S.H.I.E.L.D. WAS BEIN' DISMANTLED BY NORMAN OSBORN...
...SHE FELL THROUGH THE CRACKS. DISAPPEARED FROM CUSTODY.
Red Monkeys
KRAGOFF
AND DROPPED COMPLETELY OFF THE RADAR. OUR PEOPLE COULDN'T FIND ANY SIGN OF HER.
OF COURSE, NOW WE KNOW WHAT TO LOOK FOR, SINCE SHE'S IN CONTACT WITH KRAGOFF, THE RED GHOST.
RIGHT, SO SITWELL AND ME'LL TRACK VON BARDAS THROUGH HER APE DOCTOR...
BUT YOU TWO HAVE A MUCH ROUGHER NIGHT AHEAD...
WHAT'S OUR MISSION?
NOTHIN' MUCH...
YOU JUST HAVE TA PREVENT A WORLD WAR.

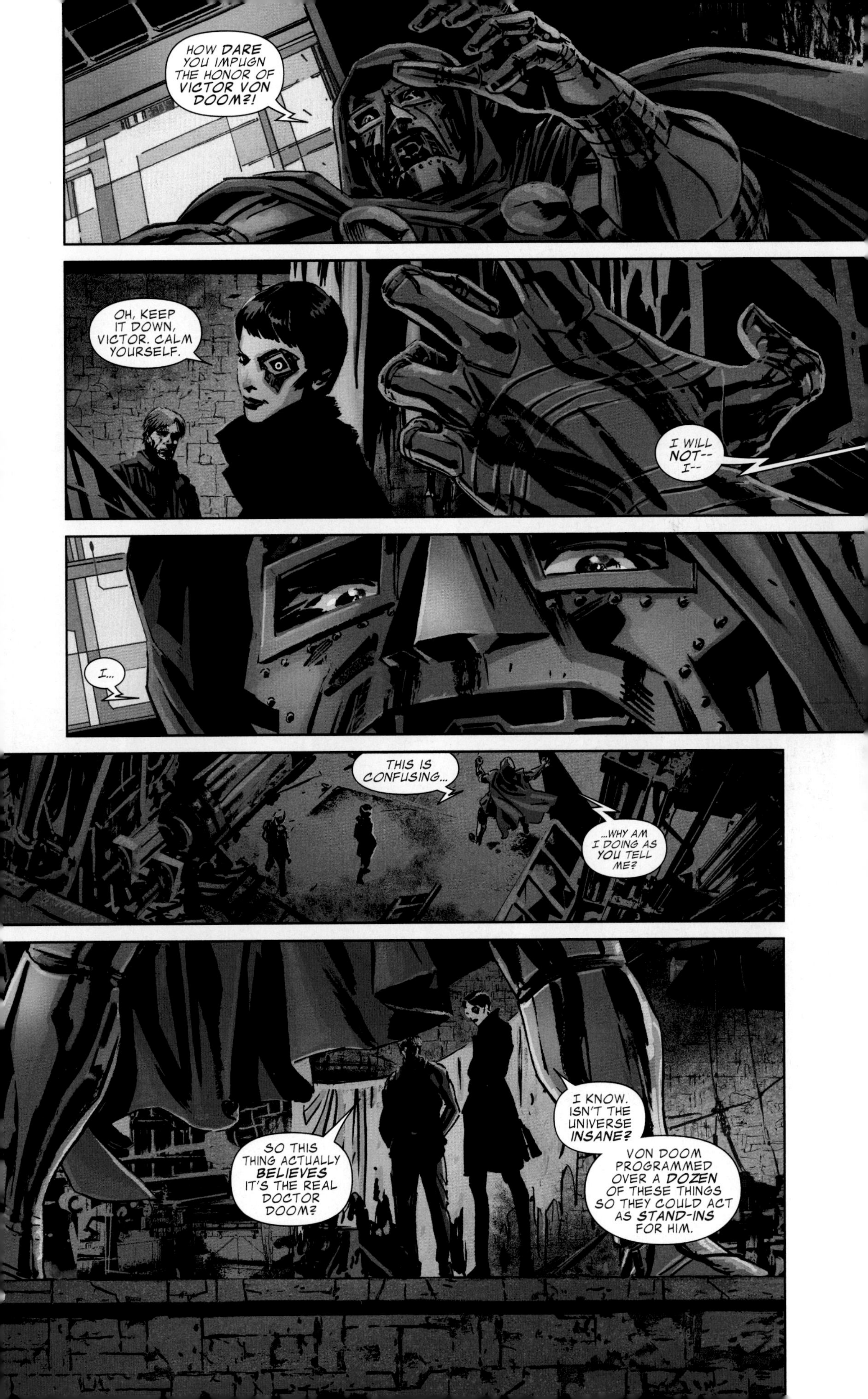
HOW DARE YOU IMPUGN THE HONOR OF VICTOR VON DOOM?!
OH, KEEP IT DOWN, VICTOR. CALM YOURSELF.
I WILL NOT-- I--
I...
THIS IS CONFUSING...
...WHY AM I DOING AS YOU TELL ME?
SO THIS THING ACTUALLY BELIEVES IT'S THE REAL DOCTOR DOOM?
I KNOW. ISN'T THE UNIVERSE INSANE?
VON DOOM PROGRAMMED OVER A DOZEN OF THESE THINGS SO THEY COULD ACT AS STAND-INS FOR HIM.

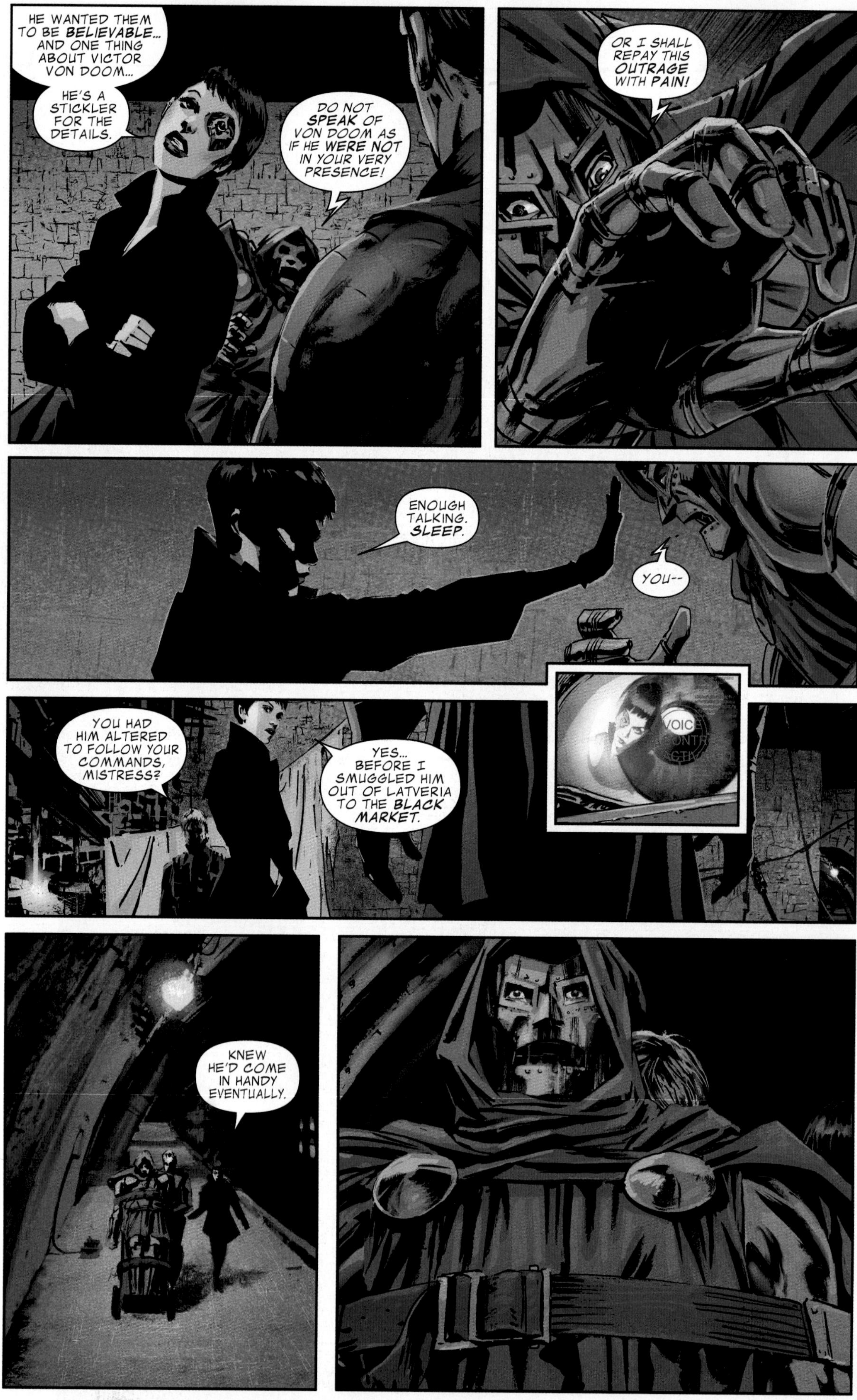
HE WANTED THEM TO BE BELIEVABLE... AND ONE THING ABOUT VICTOR VON DOOM...
HE'S A STICKLER FOR THE DETAILS.
DO NOT SPEAK OF VON DOOM AS IF HE WERE NOT IN YOUR VERY PRESENCE!
OR I SHALL REPAY THIS OUTRAGE WITH PAIN!
ENOUGH TALKING. SLEEP.
YOU--
VOICE
YOU HAD HIM ALTERED TO FOLLOW YOUR COMMANDS, MISTRESS?
YES... BEFORE I SMUGGLED HIM OUT OF LATVERIA TO THE BLACK MARKET.
KNEW HE'D COME IN HANDY EVENTUALLY.

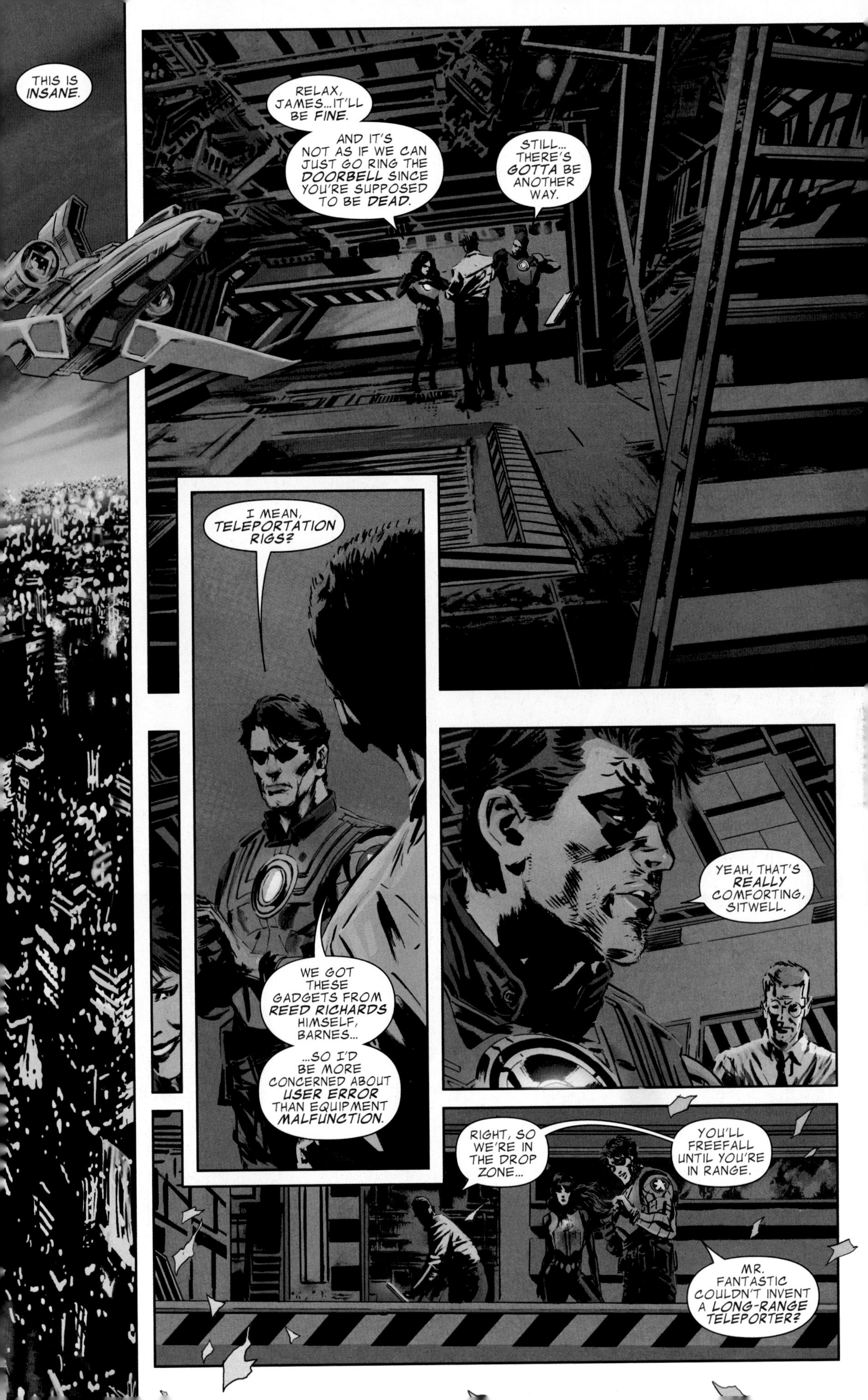
THIS IS INSANE.
RELAX, JAMES...IT'LL BE FINE.
AND IT'S NOT AS IF WE CAN JUST GO RING THE DOORBELL SINCE YOU'RE SUPPOSED TO BE DEAD.
STILL... THERE'S GOTTA BE ANOTHER WAY.
I MEAN, TELEPORTATION RIGS?
WE GOT THESE GADGETS FROM REED RICHARDS HIMSELF, BARNES...
...SO I'D BE MORE CONCERNED ABOUT USER ERROR THAN EQUIPMENT MALFUNCTION.
YEAH, THAT'S REALLY COMFORTING, SITWELL.
RIGHT, SO WE'RE IN THE DROP ZONE...
YOU'LL FREEFALL UNTIL YOU'RE IN RANGE.
MR. FANTASTIC COULDN'T INVENT A LONG-RANGE TELEPORTER?

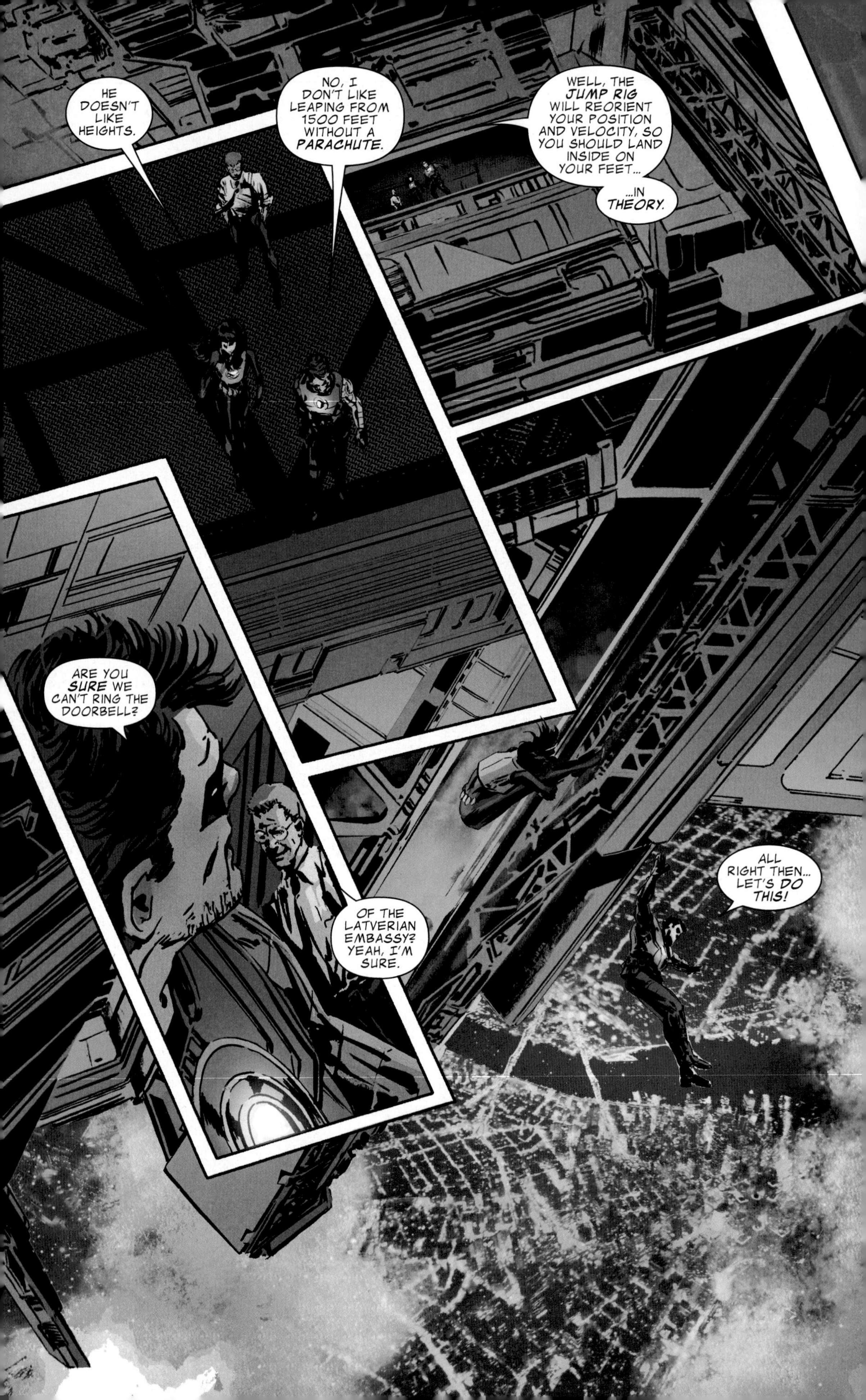
HE DOESN'T LIKE HEIGHTS.
NO, I DON'T LIKE LEAPING FROM 1500 FEET WITHOUT A PARACHUTE.
WELL, THE JUMP RIG WILL REORIENT YOUR POSITION AND VELOCITY, SO YOU SHOULD LAND INSIDE ON YOUR FEET...
...IN THEORY.
ARE YOU SURE WE CAN'T RING THE DOORBELL?
OF THE LATVERIAN EMBASSY? YEAH, I'M SURE.
ALL RIGHT THEN... LET'S DO THIS!

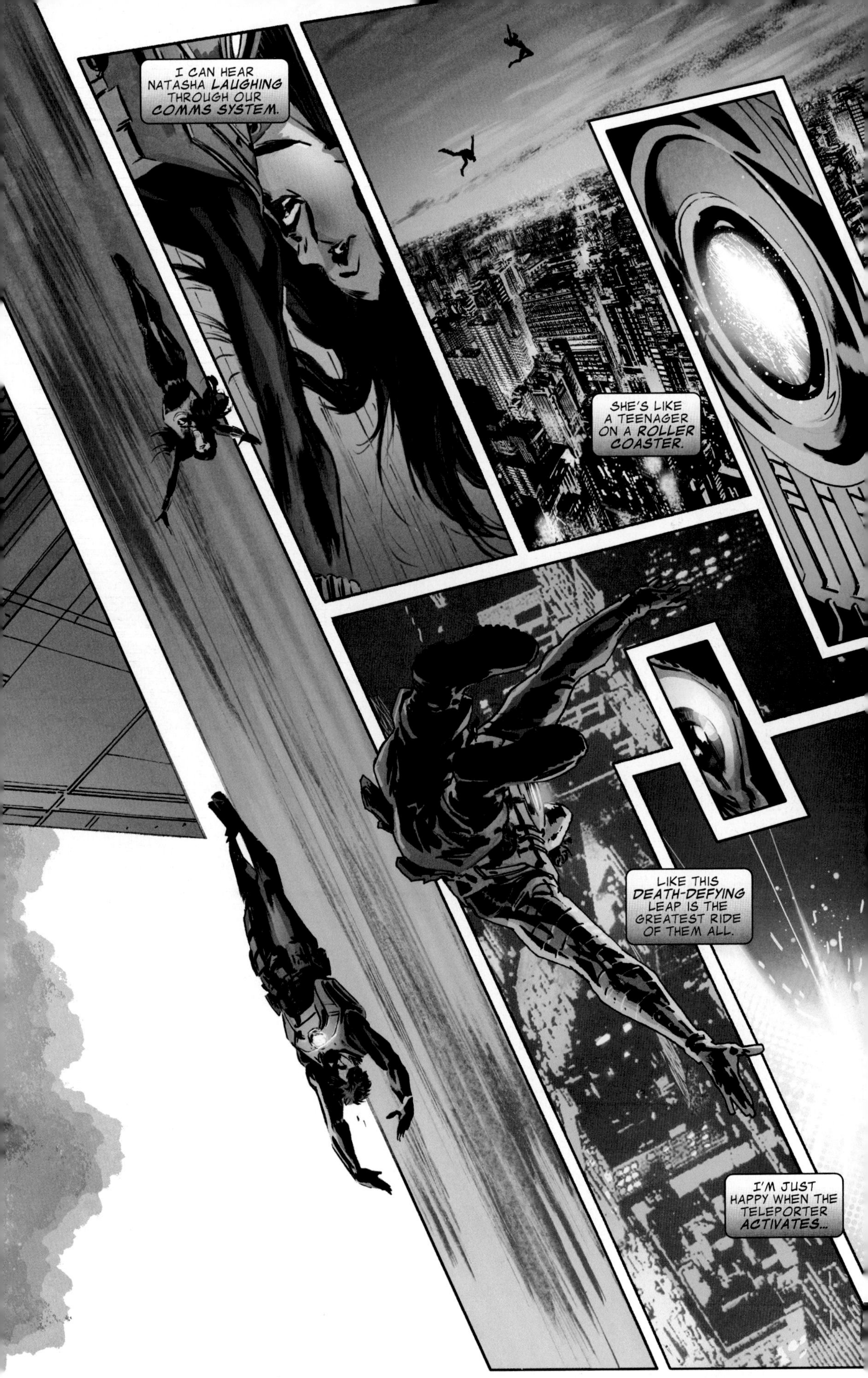

I CAN HEAR NATASHA LAUGHING THROUGH OUR COMMS SYSTEM.
SHE'S LIKE A TEENAGER ON A ROLLER COASTER.
LIKE THIS DEATH-DEFYING LEAP IS THE GREATEST RIDE OF THEM ALL.
I'M JUST HAPPY WHEN THE TELEPORTER ACTIVATES...

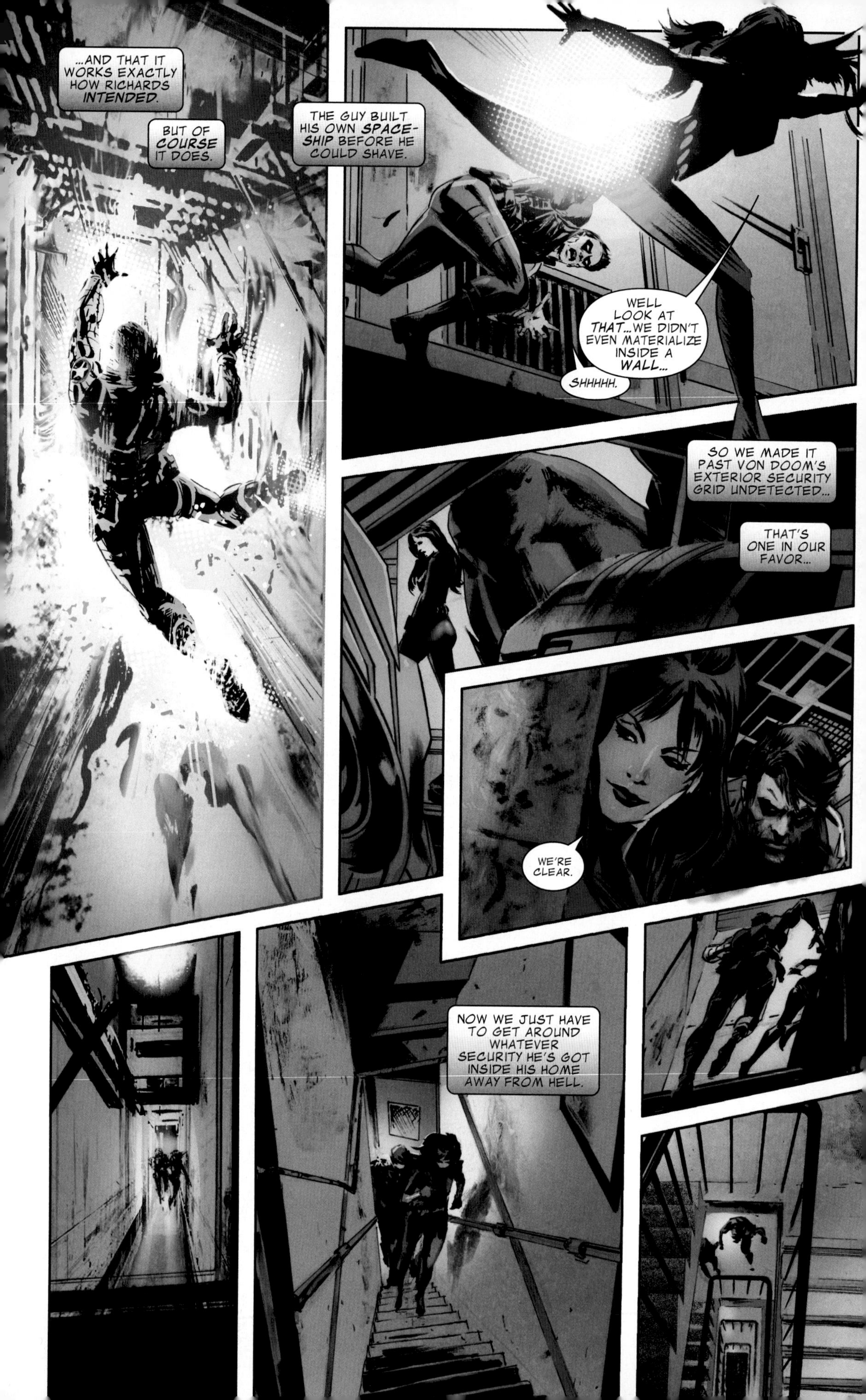
...AND THAT IT WORKS EXACTLY HOW RICHARDS INTENDED.
BUT OF COURSE IT DOES.
THE GUY BUILT HIS OWN SPACE-SHIP BEFORE HE COULD SHAVE.
WELL LOOK AT THAT...WE DIDN'T EVEN MATERIALIZE INSIDE A WALL...
SHHHHH.
SO WE MADE IT PAST VON DOOM'S EXTERIOR SECURITY GRID UNDETECTED...
THAT'S ONE IN OUR FAVOR...
WE'RE CLEAR.
NOW WE JUST HAVE TO GET AROUND WHATEVER SECURITY HE'S GOT INSIDE HIS HOME AWAY FROM HELL.

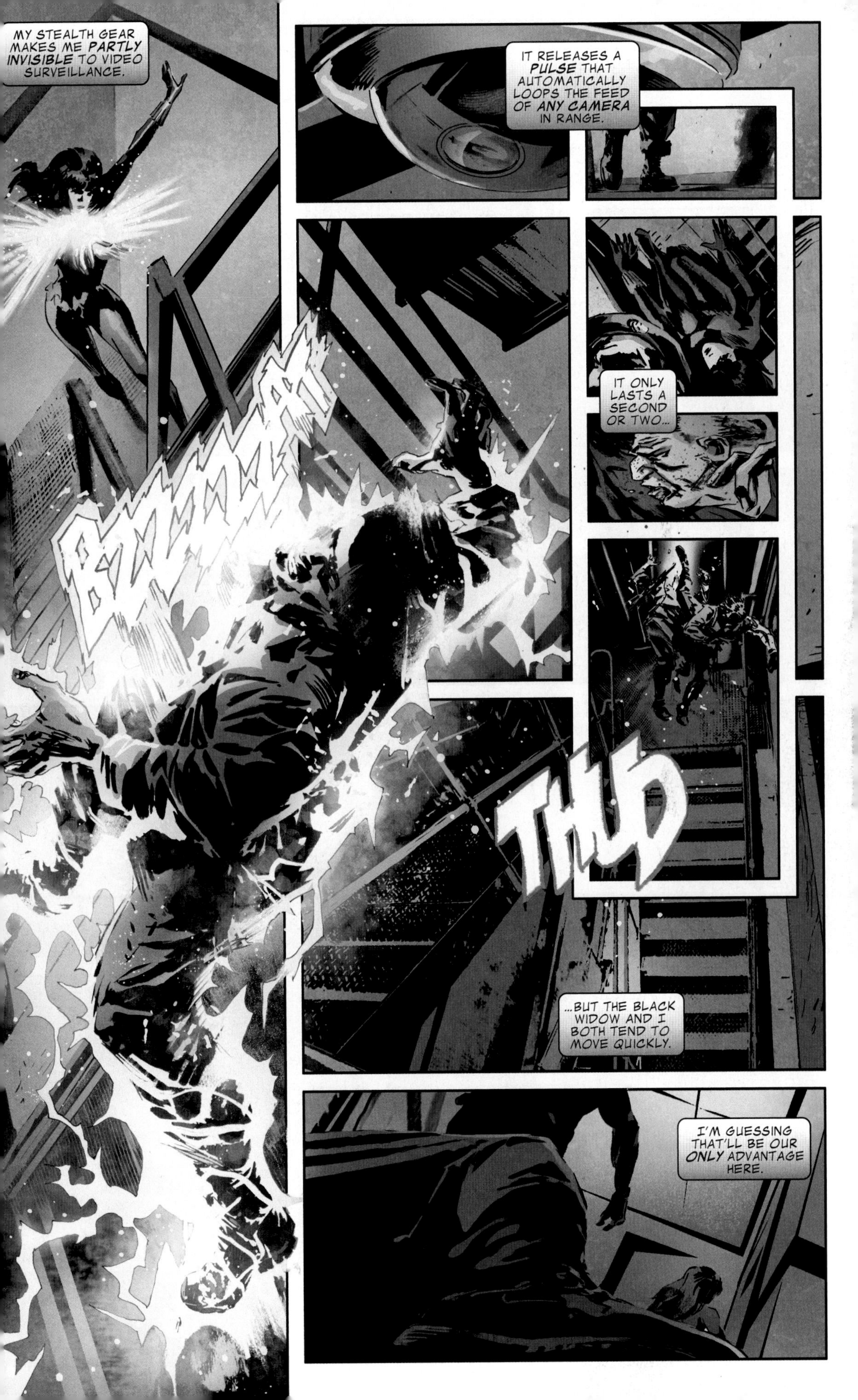
MY STEALTH GEAR MAKES ME PARTLY INVISIBLE TO VIDEO SURVEILLANCE.
IT RELEASES A PULSE THAT AUTOMATICALLY LOOPS THE FEED OF ANY CAMERA IN RANGE.
IT ONLY LASTS A SECOND OR TWO...
THUD
...BUT THE BLACK WIDOW AND I BOTH TEND TO MOVE QUICKLY.
I'M GUESSING THAT'LL BE OUR ONLY ADVANTAGE HERE.

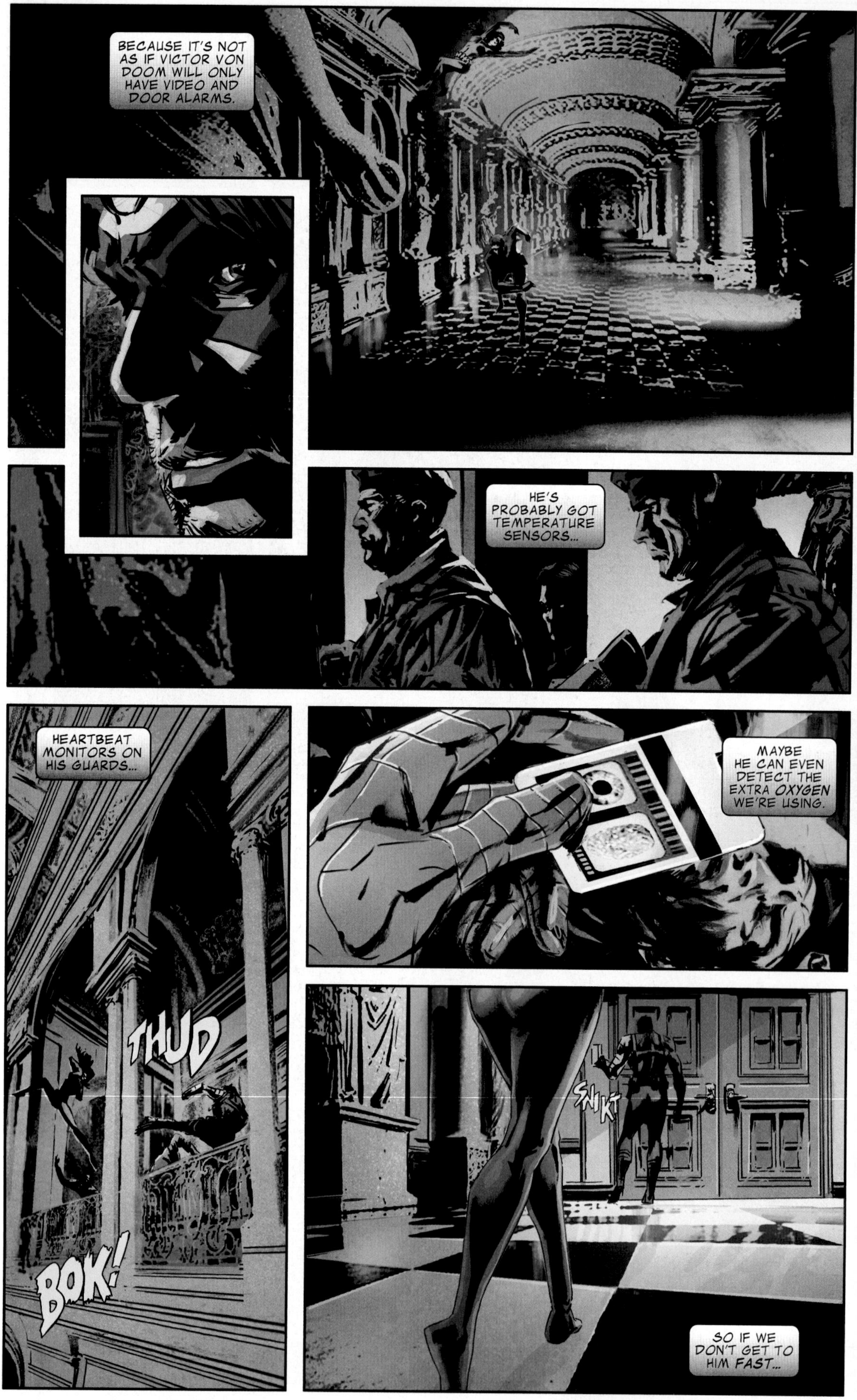
BECAUSE IT'S NOT AS IF VICTOR VON DOOM WILL ONLY HAVE VIDEO AND DOOR ALARMS.
HE'S PROBABLY GOT TEMPERATURE SENSORS...
HEARTBEAT MONITORS ON HIS GUARDS...
THUD
BOK!
MAYBE HE CAN EVEN DETECT THE EXTRA OXYGEN WE'RE USING.
SNIKT
SO IF WE DON'T GET TO HIM FAST...

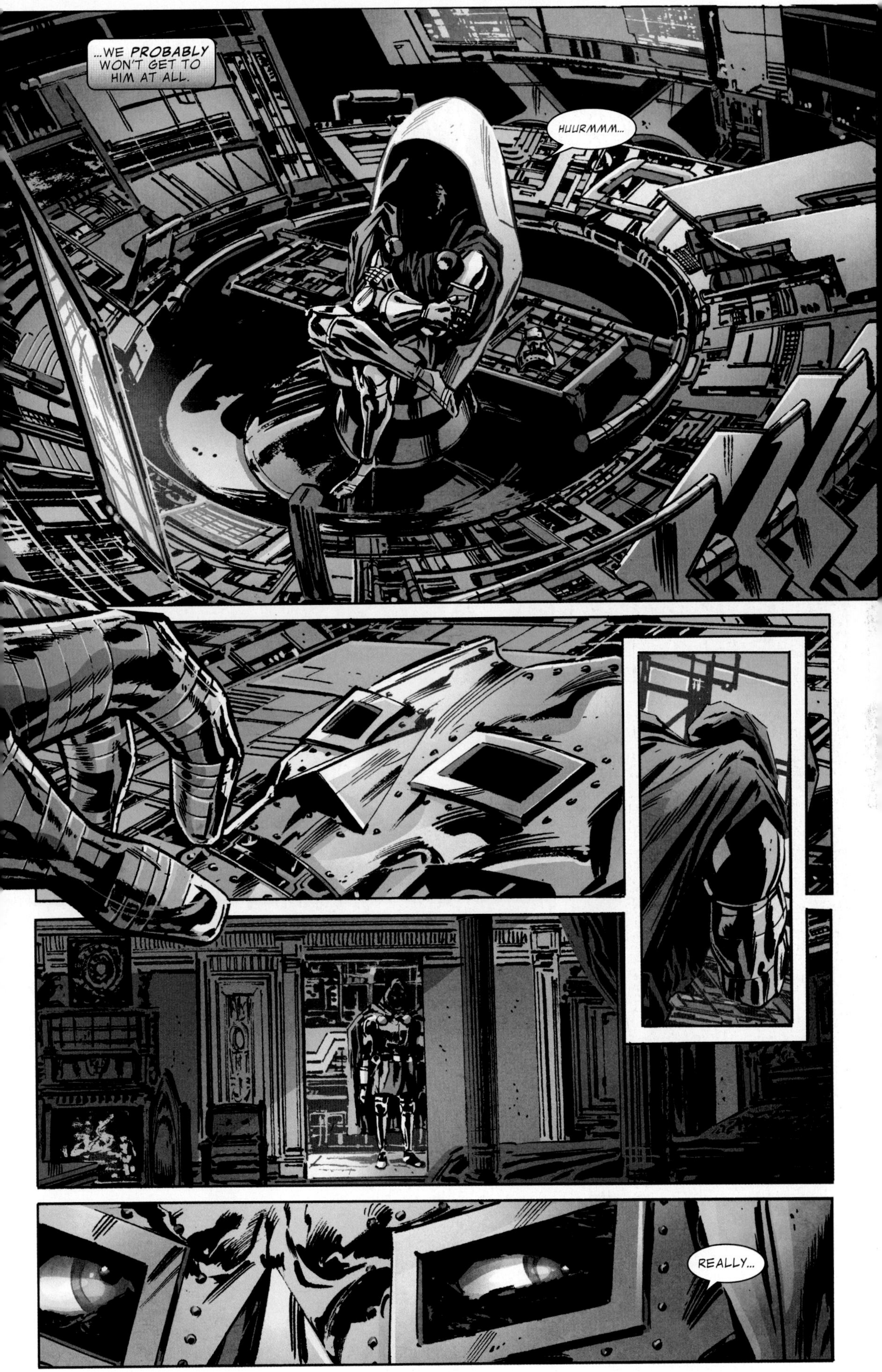
...WE PROBABLY WON'T GET TO HIM AT ALL.
HUURMMM...
REALLY...

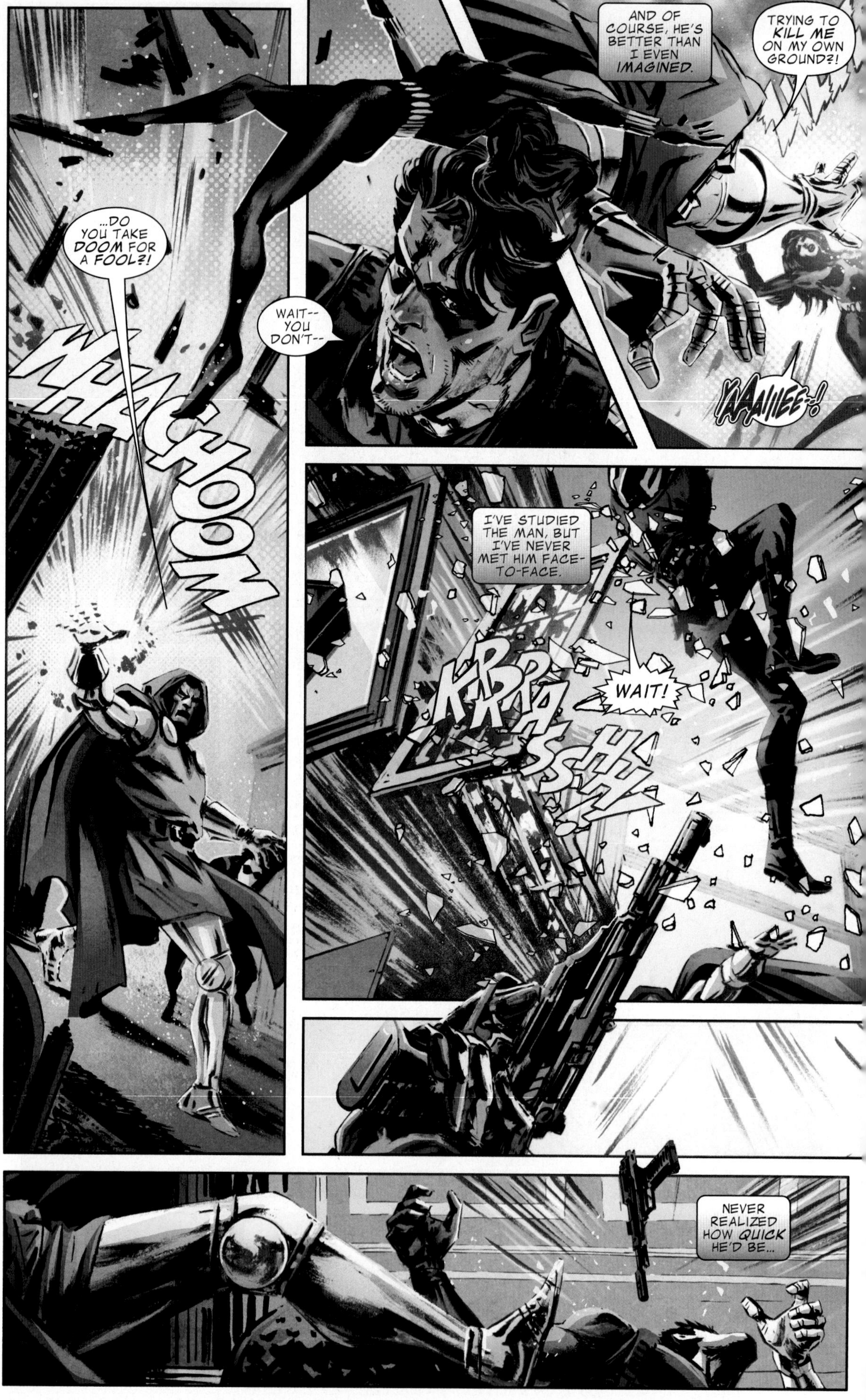
AND OF COURSE, HE'S BETTER THAN I EVEN IMAGINED.
TRYING TO KILL ME ON MY OWN GROUND?!
...DO YOU TAKE DOOM FOR A FOOL?!
WAIT-- YOU DON'T--
YAAAIIIEE--!
WHACHOOM
I'VE STUDIED THE MAN, BUT I'VE NEVER MET HIM FACE-TO-FACE.
KRRAASSHH!
WAIT!
NEVER REALIZED HOW QUICK HE'D BE...

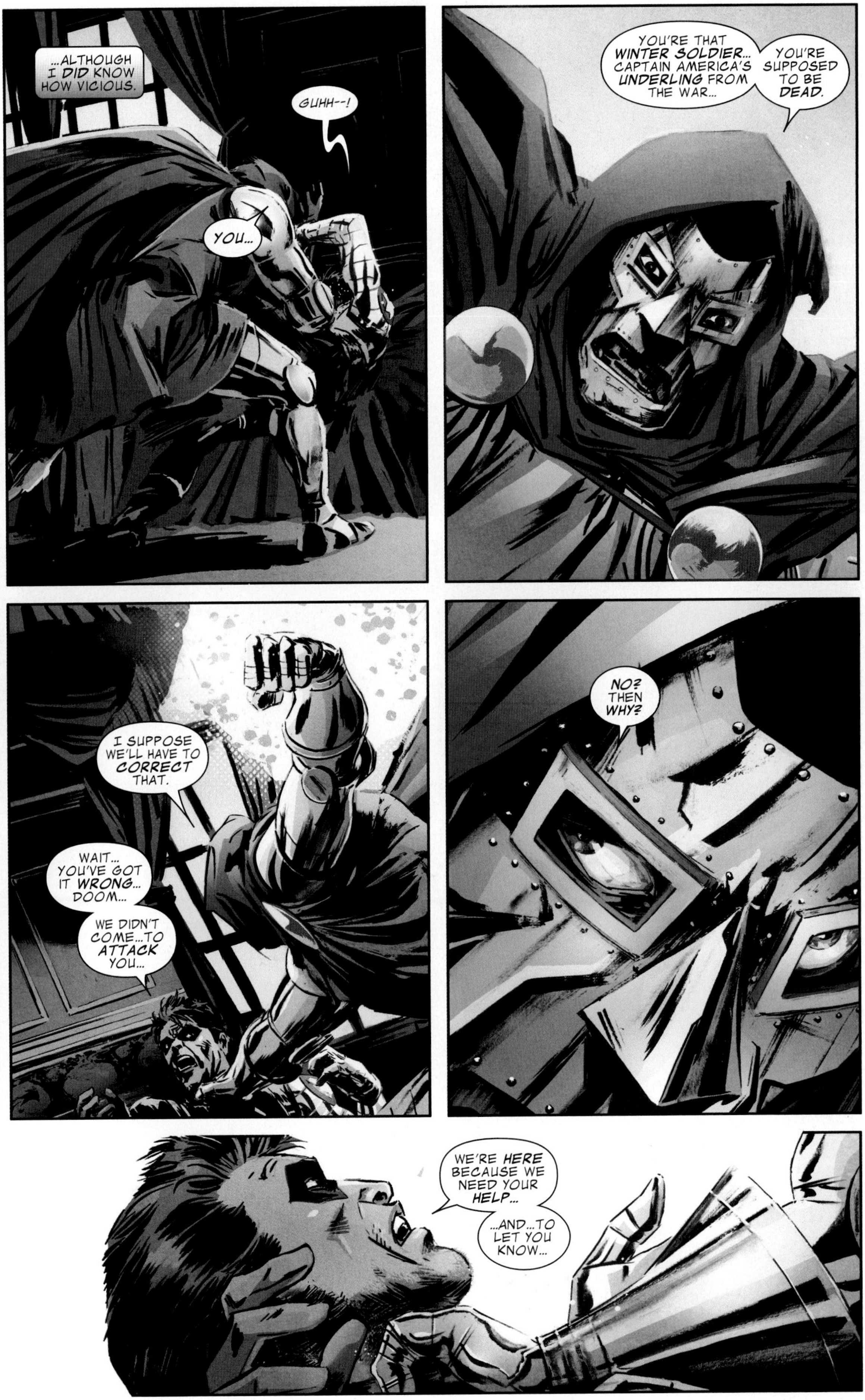
...ALTHOUGH I DID KNOW HOW VICIOUS.
GUHH--!
YOU...
YOU'RE THAT WINTER SOLDIER... CAPTAIN AMERICA'S UNDERLING FROM THE WAR...
YOU'RE SUPPOSED TO BE DEAD.
I SUPPOSE WE'LL HAVE TO CORRECT THAT.
WAIT... YOU'VE GOT IT WRONG... DOOM...
WE DIDN'T COME...TO ATTACK YOU...
NO? THEN WHY?
WE'RE HERE BECAUSE WE NEED YOUR HELP...
...AND...TO LET YOU KNOW...

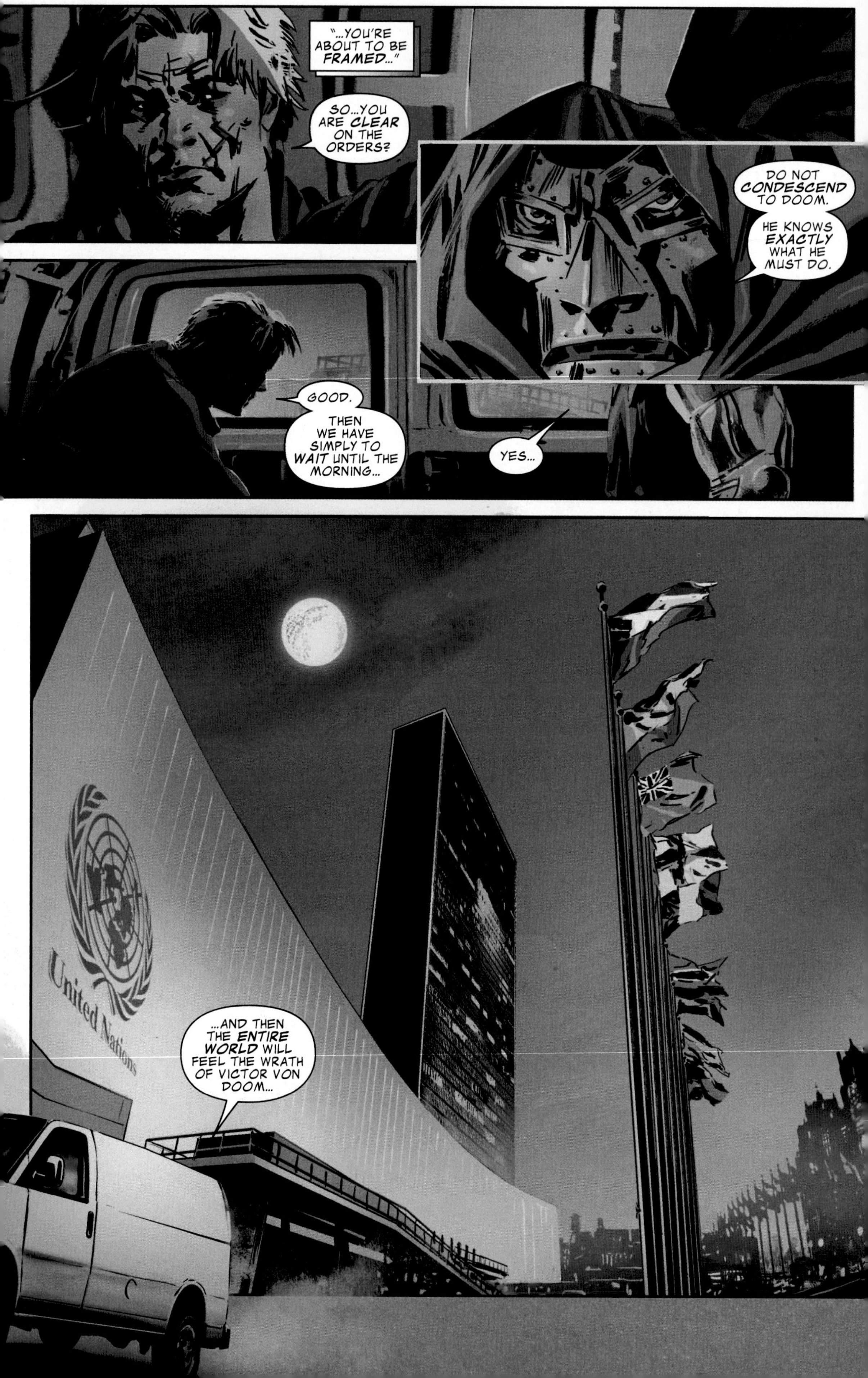
"...YOU'RE ABOUT TO BE FRAMED..."
SO...YOU ARE CLEAR ON THE ORDERS?
DO NOT CONDESCEND TO DOOM.
HE KNOWS EXACTLY WHAT HE MUST DO.
GOOD.
THEN WE HAVE SIMPLY TO WAIT UNTIL THE MORNING...
YES...
United Nations
...AND THEN THE ENTIRE WORLD WILL FEEL THE WRATH OF VICTOR VON DOOM...

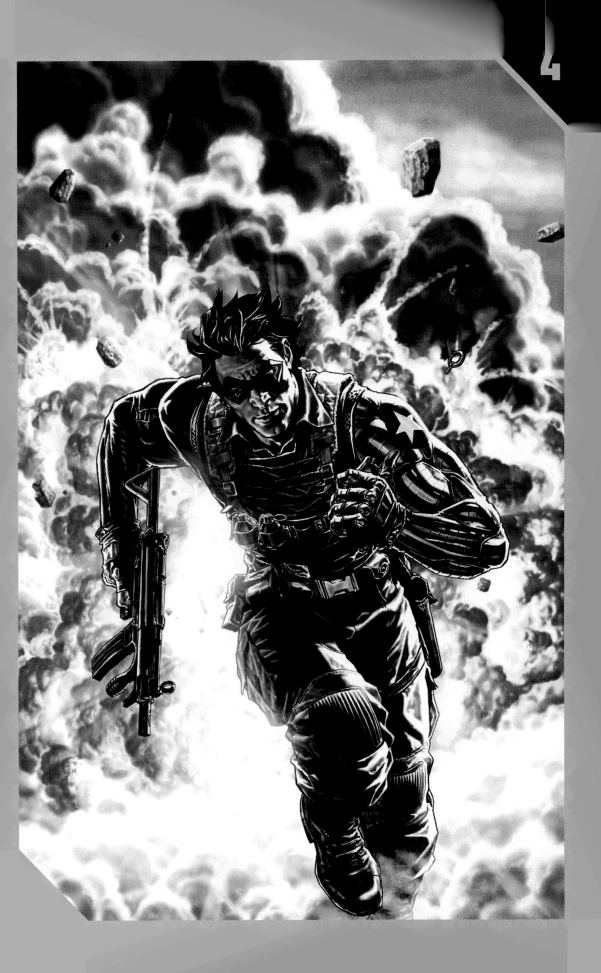

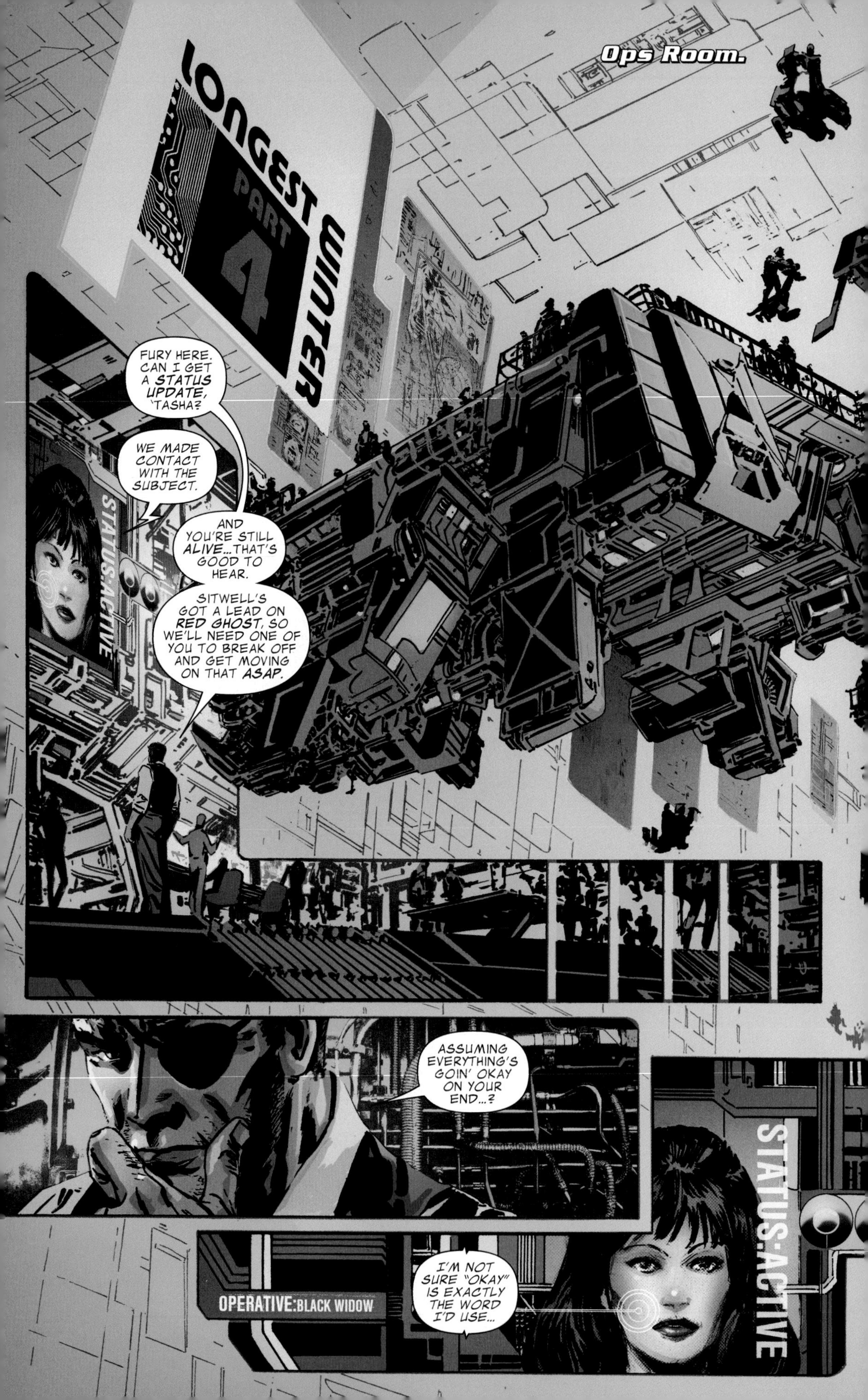
Ops Room.
LONGEST WINTER PART 4
FURY HERE. CAN I GET A STATUS UPDATE, 'TASHA?
WE MADE CONTACT WITH THE SUBJECT.
STATUS:ACTIVE
AND YOU'RE STILL ALIVE...THAT'S GOOD TO HEAR.
SITWELL'S GOT A LEAD ON RED GHOST, SO WE'LL NEED ONE OF YOU TO BREAK OFF AND GET MOVING ON THAT ASAP.
ASSUMING EVERYTHING'S GOIN' OKAY ON YOUR END...?
STATUS:ACTIVE
OPERATIVE:BLACK WIDOW
I'M NOT SURE "OKAY" IS EXACTLY THE WORD I'D USE...

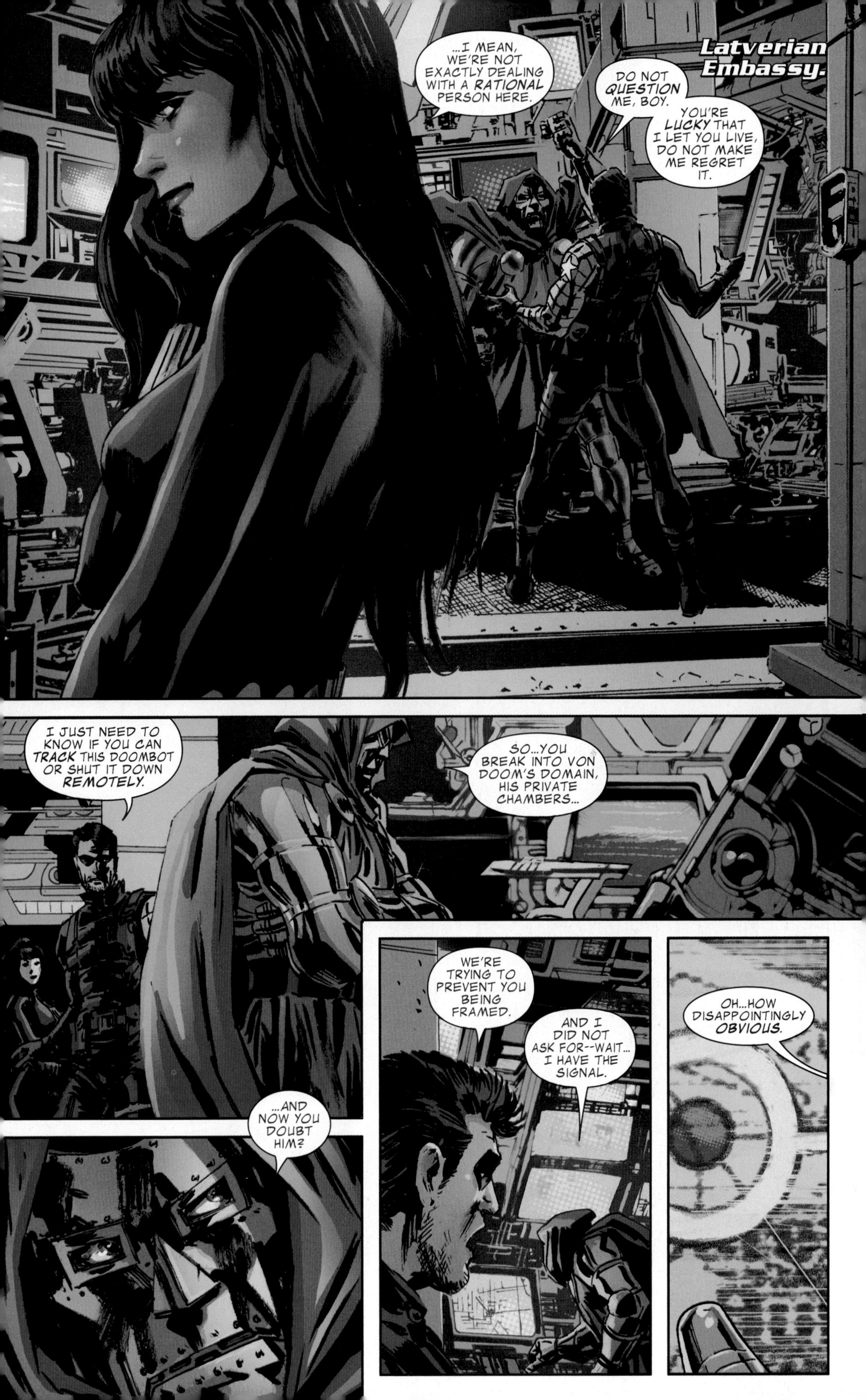
Latverian Embassy.
...I MEAN, WE'RE NOT EXACTLY DEALING WITH A RATIONAL PERSON HERE.
DO NOT QUESTION ME, BOY.
YOU'RE LUCKY THAT I LET YOU LIVE, DO NOT MAKE ME REGRET IT.
I JUST NEED TO KNOW IF YOU CAN TRACK THIS DOOMBOT OR SHUT IT DOWN REMOTELY.
SO...YOU BREAK INTO VON DOOM'S DOMAIN, HIS PRIVATE CHAMBERS...
...AND NOW YOU DOUBT HIM?
WE'RE TRYING TO PREVENT YOU BEING FRAMED.
AND I DID NOT ASK FOR--WAIT... I HAVE THE SIGNAL.
OH...HOW DISAPPOINTINGLY OBVIOUS.

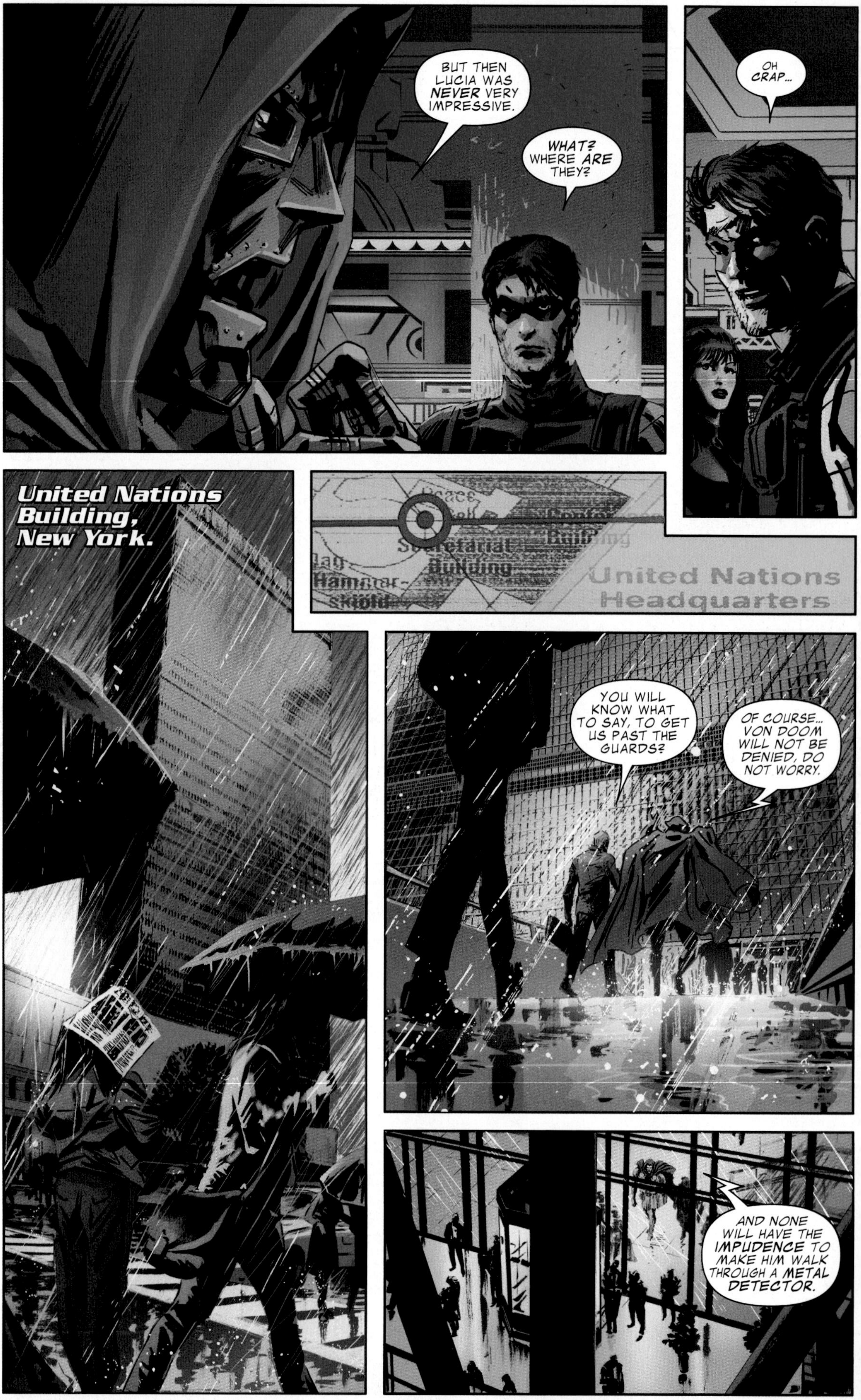
BUT THEN LUCIA WAS NEVER VERY IMPRESSIVE.
WHAT? WHERE ARE THEY?
OH CRAP...
United Nations Building, New York.
United Nations Headquarters
YOU WILL KNOW WHAT TO SAY, TO GET US PAST THE GUARDS?
OF COURSE... VON DOOM WILL NOT BE DENIED, DO NOT WORRY.
AND NONE WILL HAVE THE IMPUDENCE TO MAKE HIM WALK THROUGH A METAL DETECTOR.

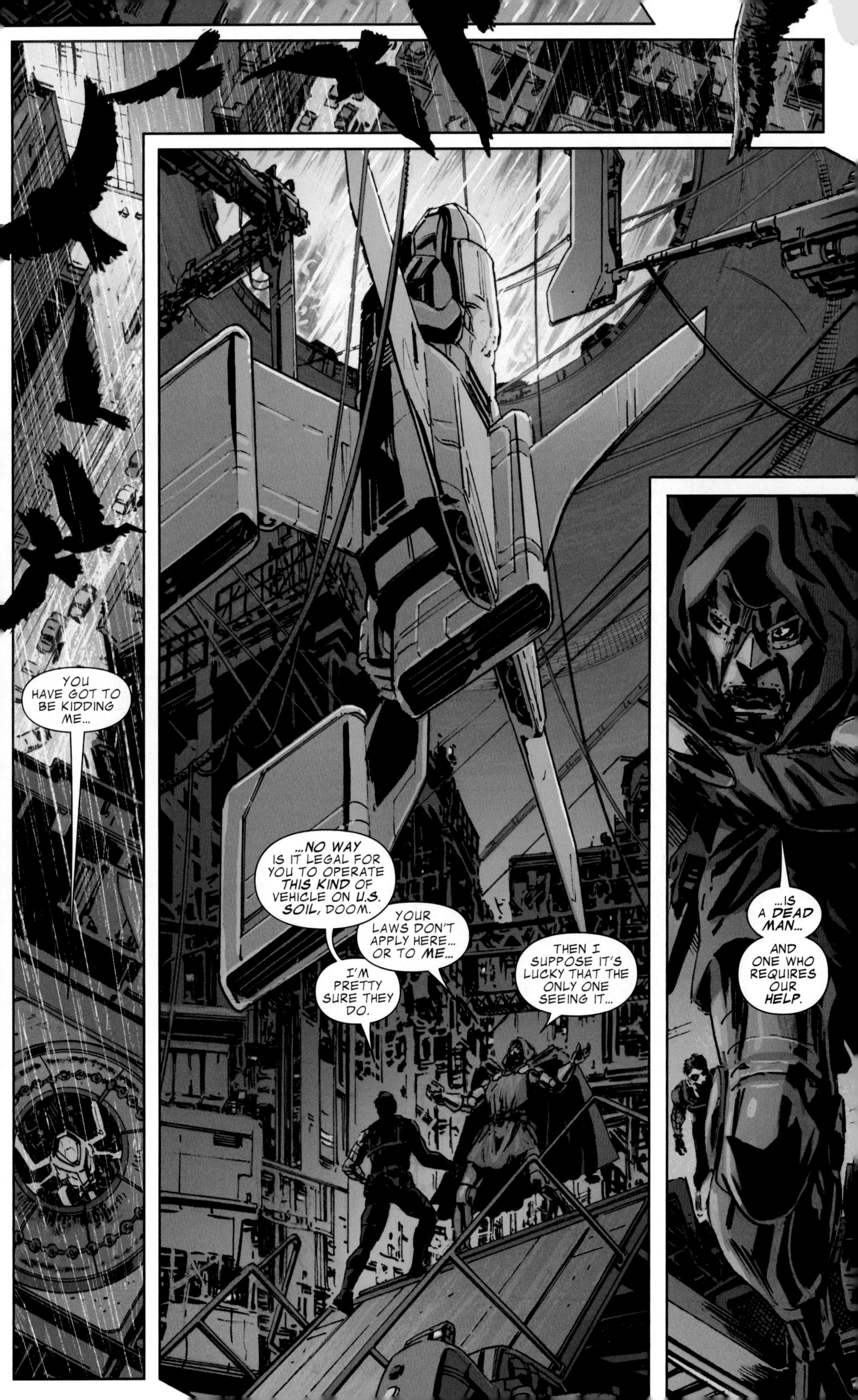
YOU HAVE GOT TO BE KIDDING ME...
...NO WAY IS IT LEGAL FOR YOU TO OPERATE THIS KIND OF VEHICLE ON U.S. SOIL, DOOM.
YOUR LAWS DON'T APPLY HERE... OR TO ME...
I'M PRETTY SURE THEY DO.
THEN I SUPPOSE IT'S LUCKY THAT THE ONLY ONE SEEING IT...
...IS A DEAD MAN...
AND ONE WHO REQUIRES OUR HELP.

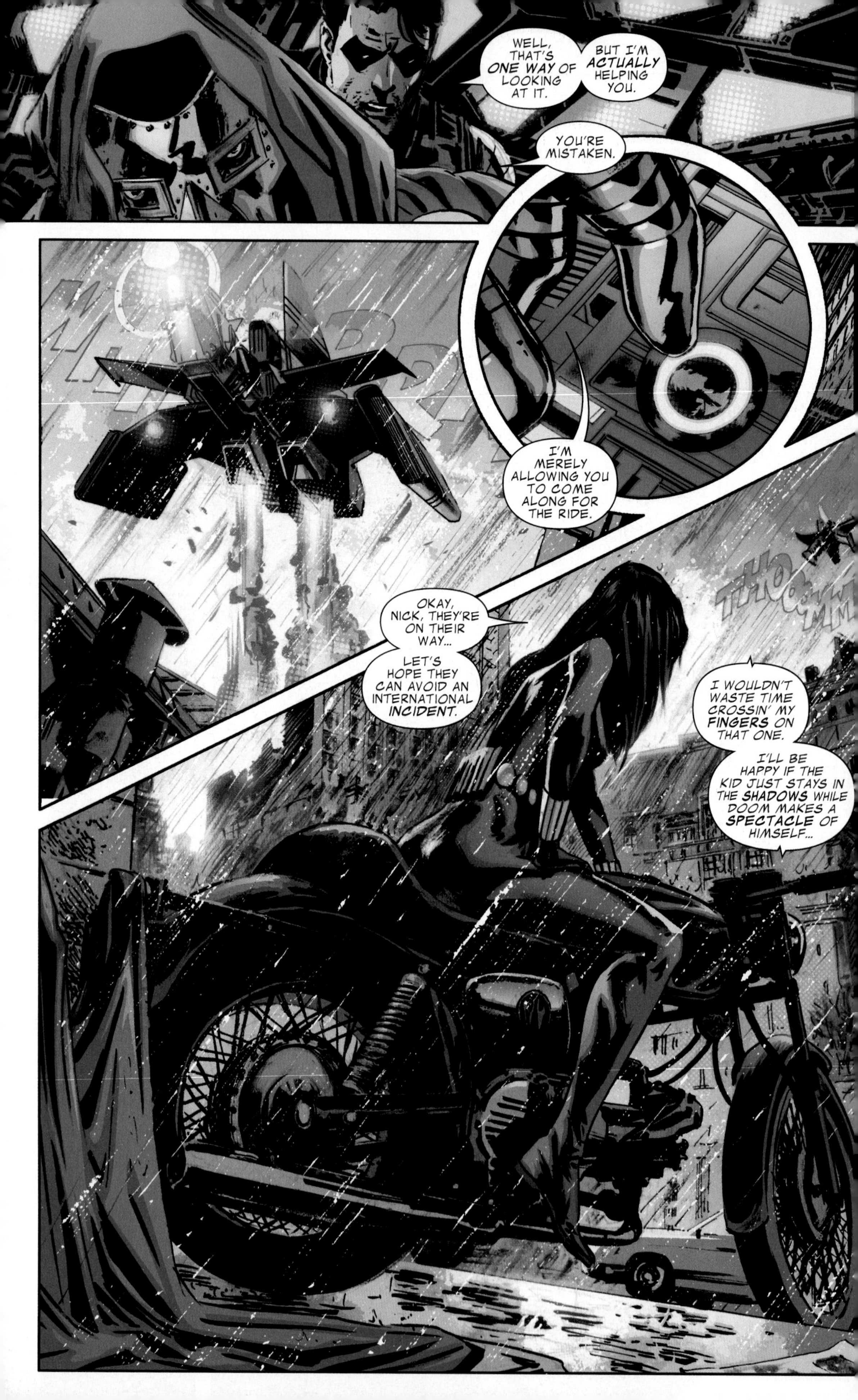
WELL, THAT'S ONE WAY OF LOOKING AT IT.
BUT I'M ACTUALLY HELPING YOU.
YOU'RE MISTAKEN.
I'M MERELY ALLOWING YOU TO COME ALONG FOR THE RIDE.
OKAY, NICK, THEY'RE ON THEIR WAY...
LET'S HOPE THEY CAN AVOID AN INTERNATIONAL INCIDENT.
I WOULDN'T WASTE TIME CROSSIN' MY FINGERS ON THAT ONE.
I'LL BE HAPPY IF THE KID JUST STAYS IN THE SHADOWS WHILE DOOM MAKES A SPECTACLE OF HIMSELF...

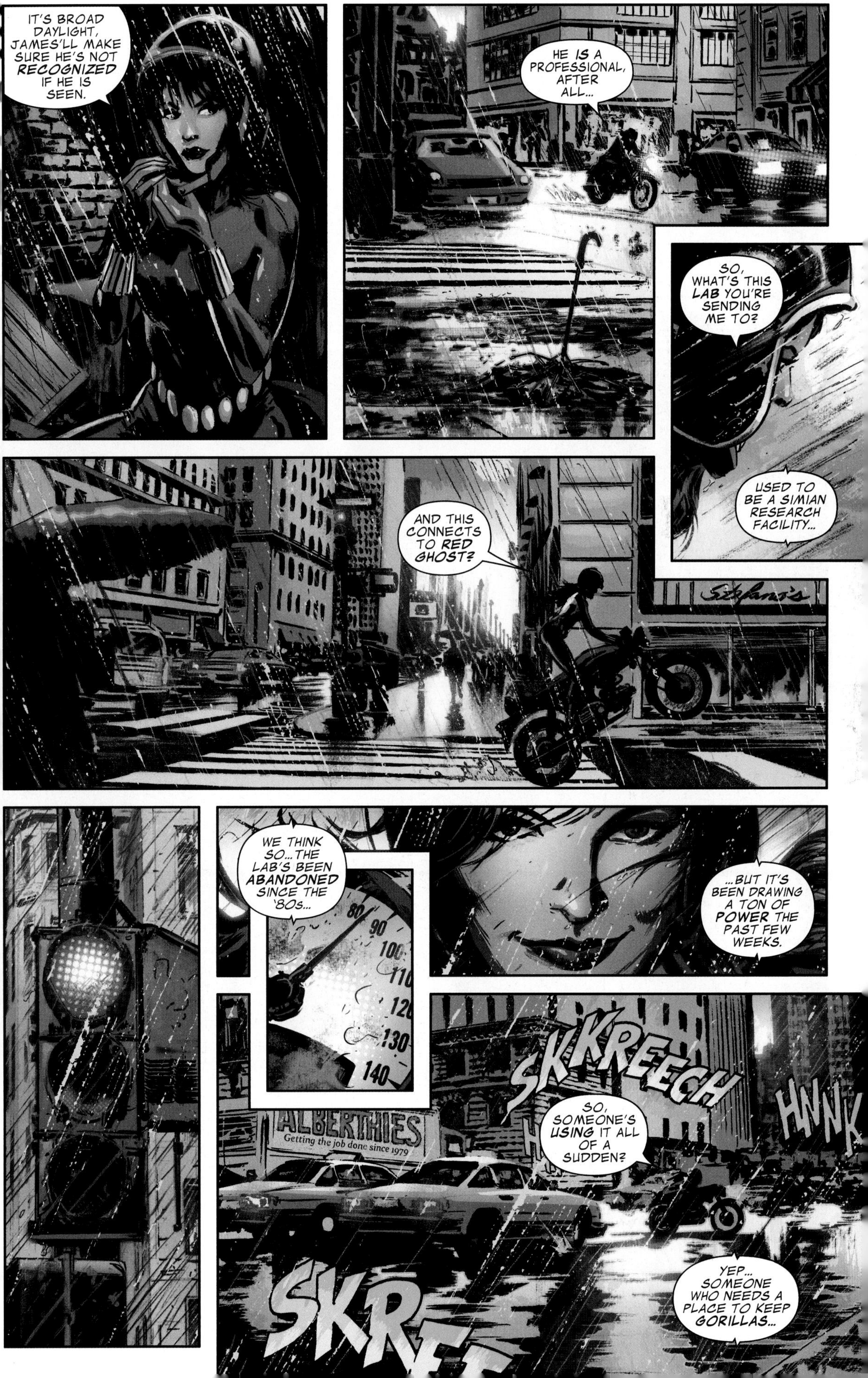
IT'S BROAD DAYLIGHT, JAMES'LL MAKE SURE HE'S NOT RECOGNIZED IF HE IS SEEN.
HE IS A PROFESSIONAL, AFTER ALL...
SO, WHAT'S THIS LAB YOU'RE SENDING ME TO?
USED TO BE A SIMIAN RESEARCH FACILITY...
AND THIS CONNECTS TO RED GHOST?
WE THINK SO... THE LAB'S BEEN ABANDONED SINCE THE '80s...
...BUT IT'S BEEN DRAWING A TON OF POWER THE PAST FEW WEEKS.
80
90
100
110
120
130
140
SKKREECH
HNNK
ALBERTHIES
Getting the job done since 1979
SO, SOMEONE'S USING IT ALL OF A SUDDEN?
YEP... SOMEONE WHO NEEDS A PLACE TO KEEP GORILLAS...
SKR

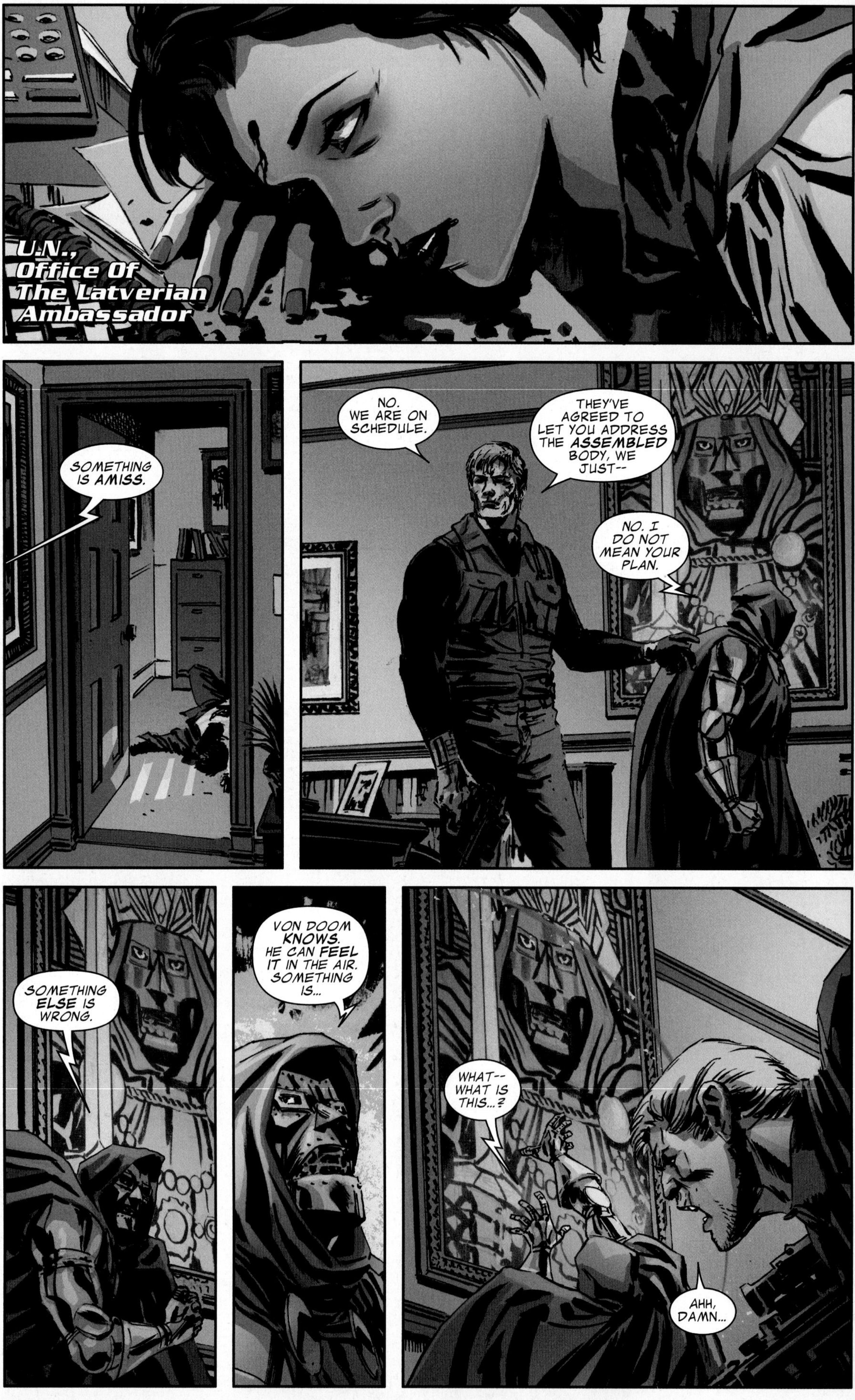
U.N., Office Of The Latverian Ambassador
SOMETHING IS AMISS.
NO. WE ARE ON SCHEDULE.
THEY'VE AGREED TO LET YOU ADDRESS THE ASSEMBLED BODY, WE JUST--
NO. I DO NOT MEAN YOUR PLAN.
SOMETHING ELSE IS WRONG.
VON DOOM KNOWS. HE CAN FEEL IT IN THE AIR. SOMETHING IS...
WHAT-- WHAT IS THIS...?
AHH, DAMN...

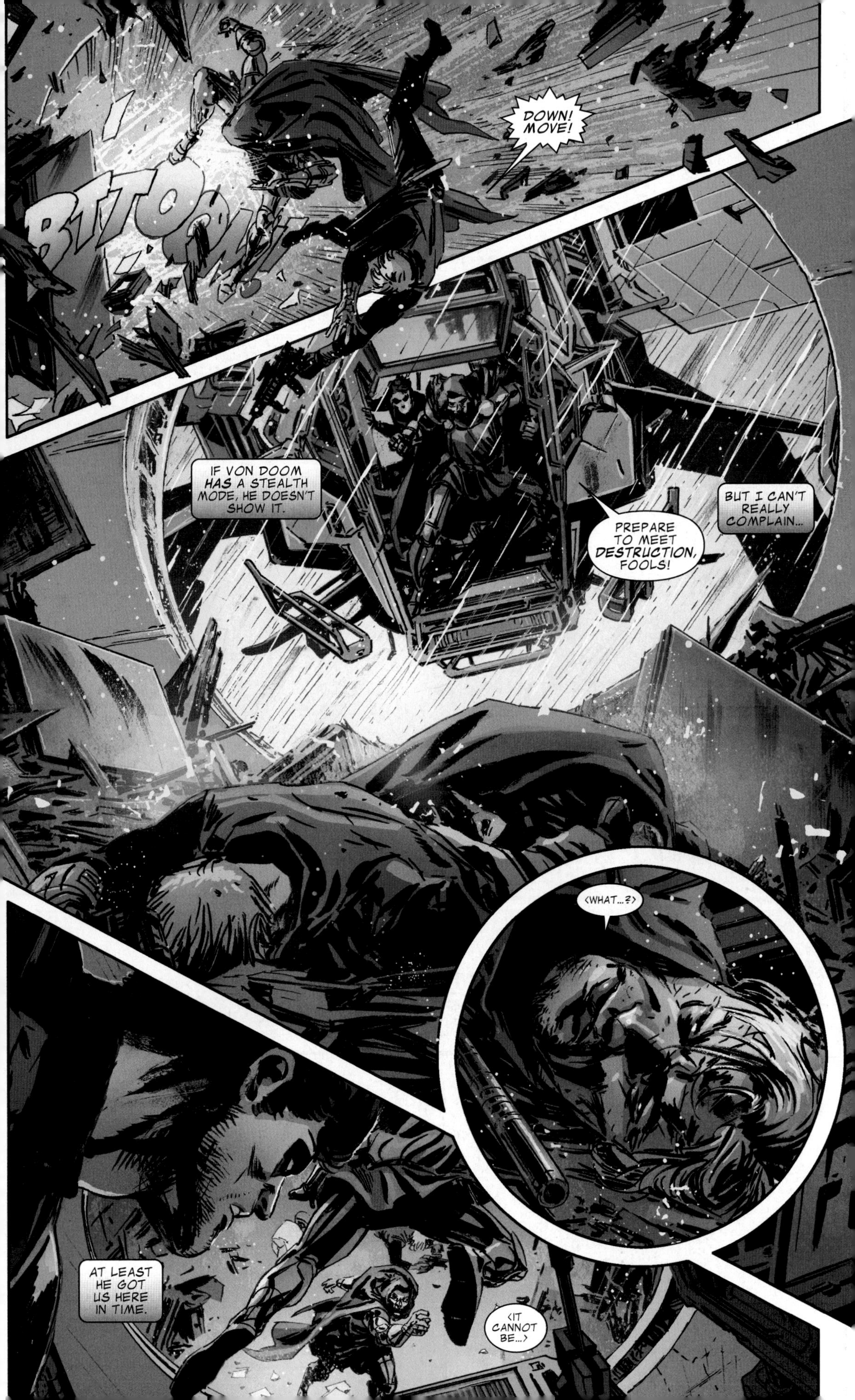
BTTOOM
DOWN! MOVE!
IF VON DOOM HAS A STEALTH MODE, HE DOESN'T SHOW IT.
PREPARE TO MEET DESTRUCTION, FOOLS!
BUT I CAN'T REALLY COMPLAIN...
<WHAT...?>
AT LEAST HE GOT US HERE IN TIME.
<IT CANNOT BE...>

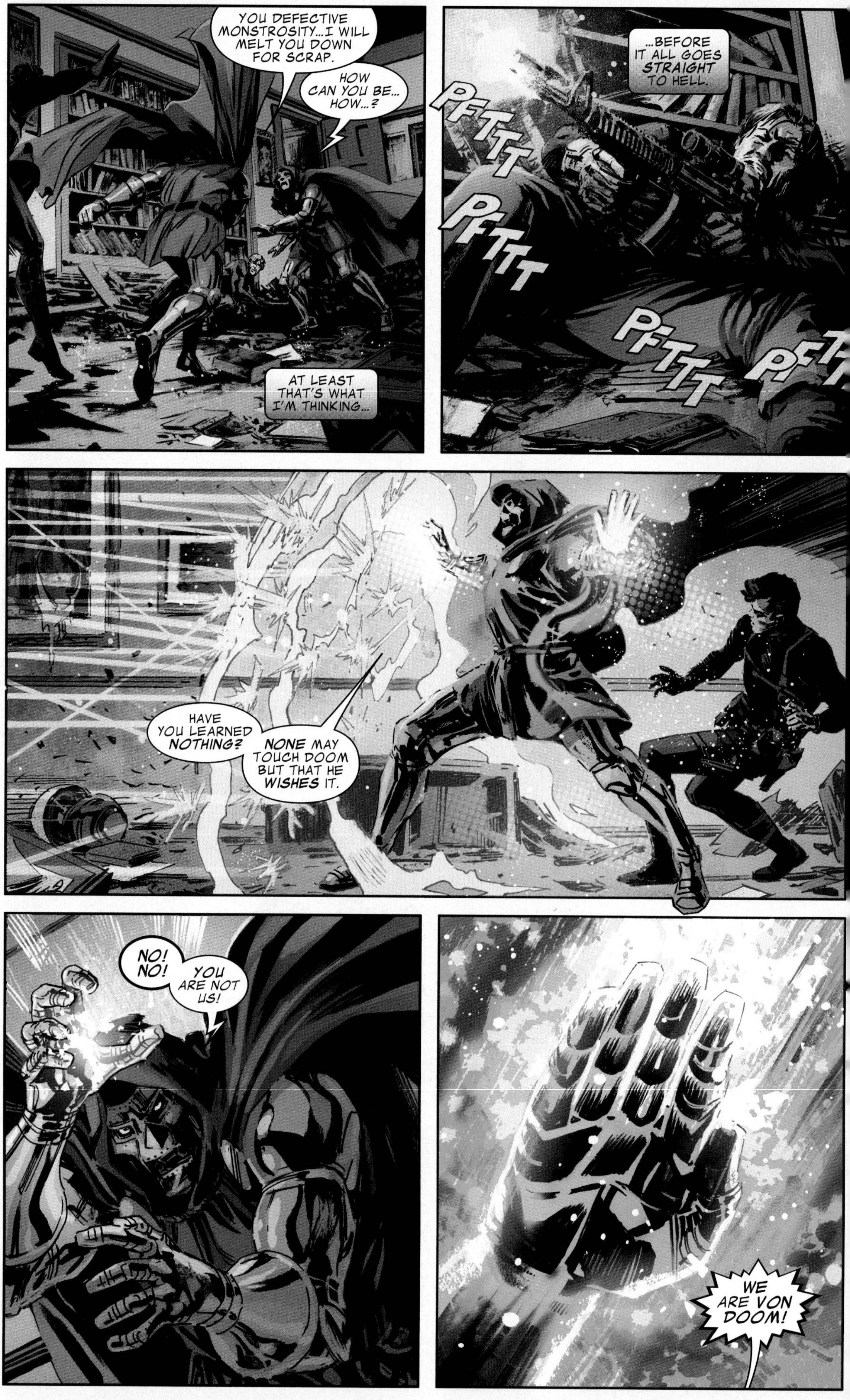
YOU DEFECTIVE MONSTROSITY...I WILL MELT YOU DOWN FOR SCRAP.
HOW CAN YOU BE... HOW...?
AT LEAST THAT'S WHAT I'M THINKING...
...BEFORE IT ALL GOES STRAIGHT TO HELL.
PFTTT
PFTTTT
PFTTTT
HAVE YOU LEARNED NOTHING?
NONE MAY TOUCH DOOM BUT THAT HE WISHES IT.
NO! NO!
YOU ARE NOT US!
WE ARE VON DOOM!

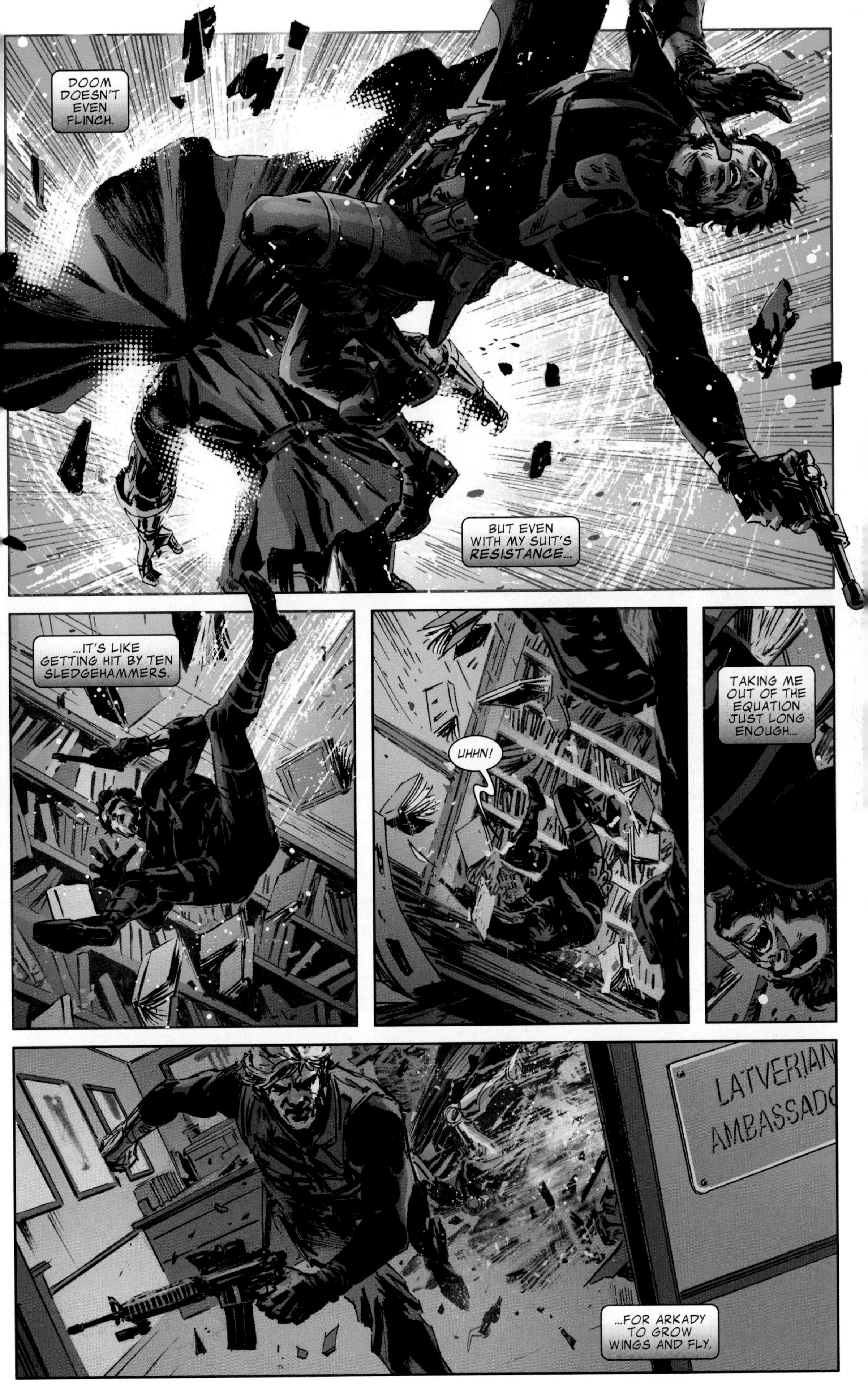
DOOM DOESN'T EVEN FLINCH.
BUT EVEN WITH MY SUIT'S RESISTANCE...
...IT'S LIKE GETTING HIT BY TEN SLEDGEHAMMERS.
UHHN!
TAKING ME OUT OF THE EQUATION JUST LONG ENOUGH...
LATVERIAN AMBASSADO
...FOR ARKADY TO GROW WINGS AND FLY.

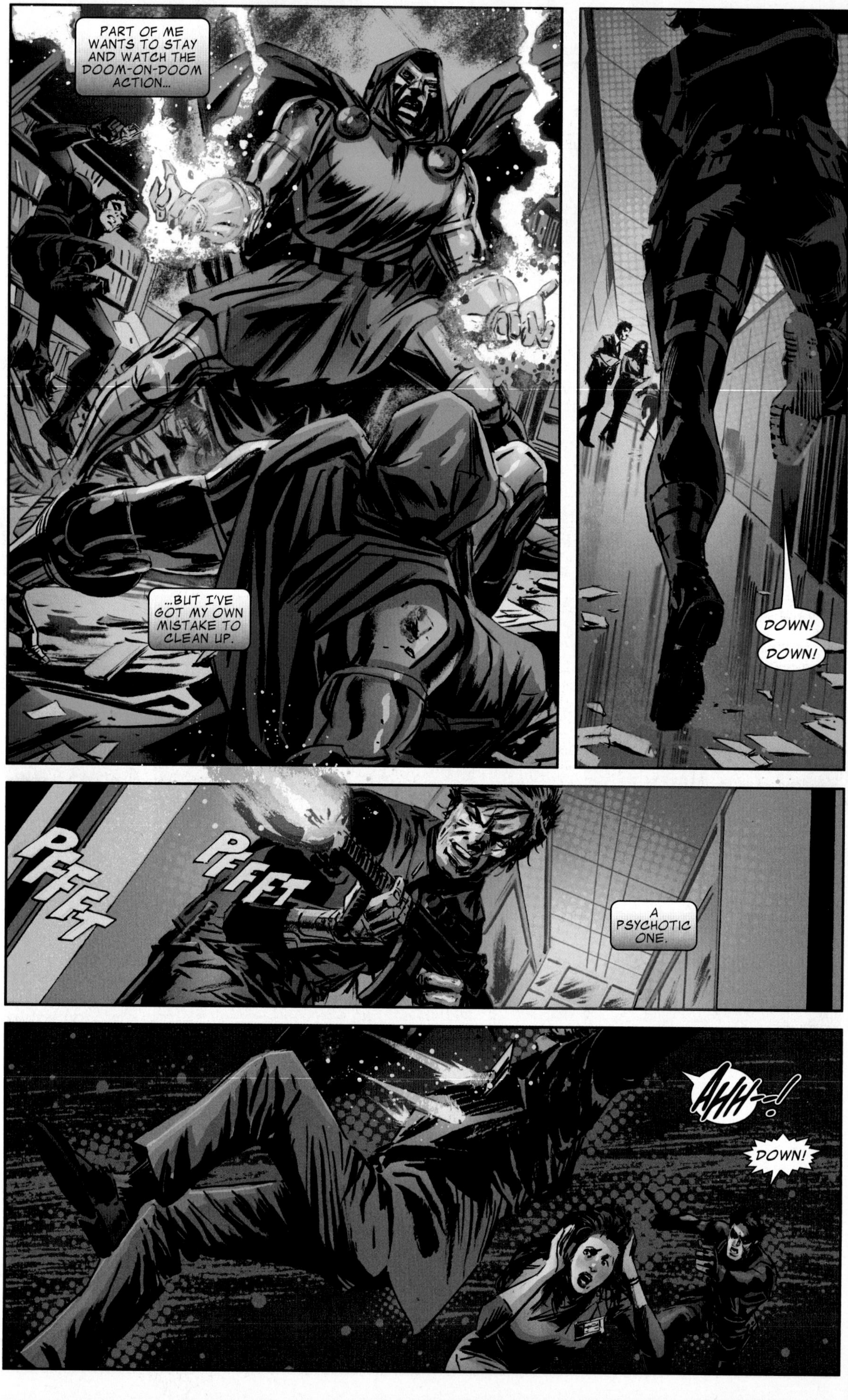
PART OF ME WANTS TO STAY AND WATCH THE DOOM-ON-DOOM ACTION...
...BUT I'VE GOT MY OWN MISTAKE TO CLEAN UP.
DOWN! DOWN!
PFFFT
PFFFT
A PSYCHOTIC ONE.
AHH--!
DOWN!

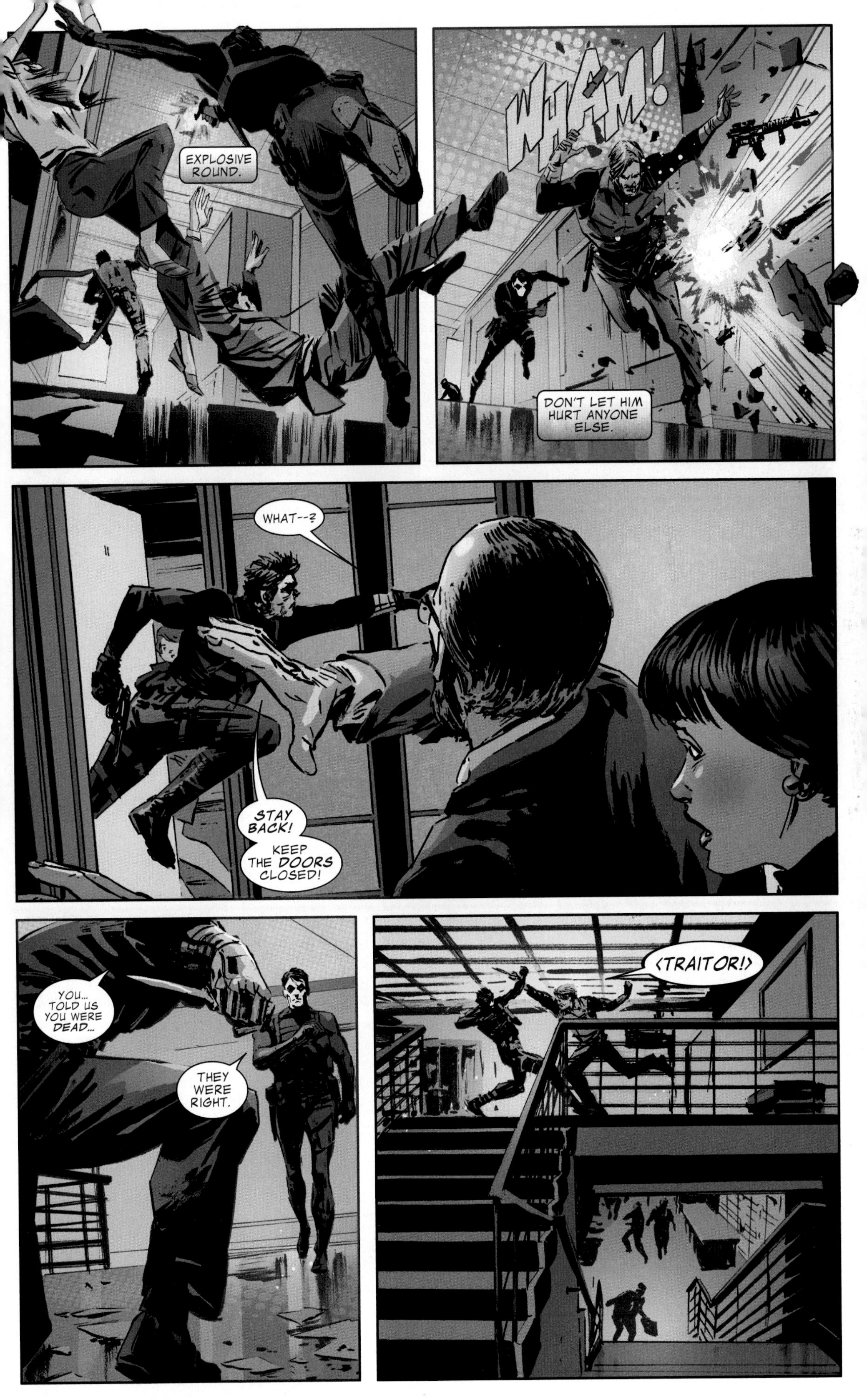
EXPLOSIVE ROUND.
WHAM!
DON'T LET HIM HURT ANYONE ELSE.
WHAT--?
STAY BACK!
KEEP THE DOORS CLOSED!
YOU... TOLD US YOU WERE DEAD...
THEY WERE RIGHT.
‹TRAITOR!›

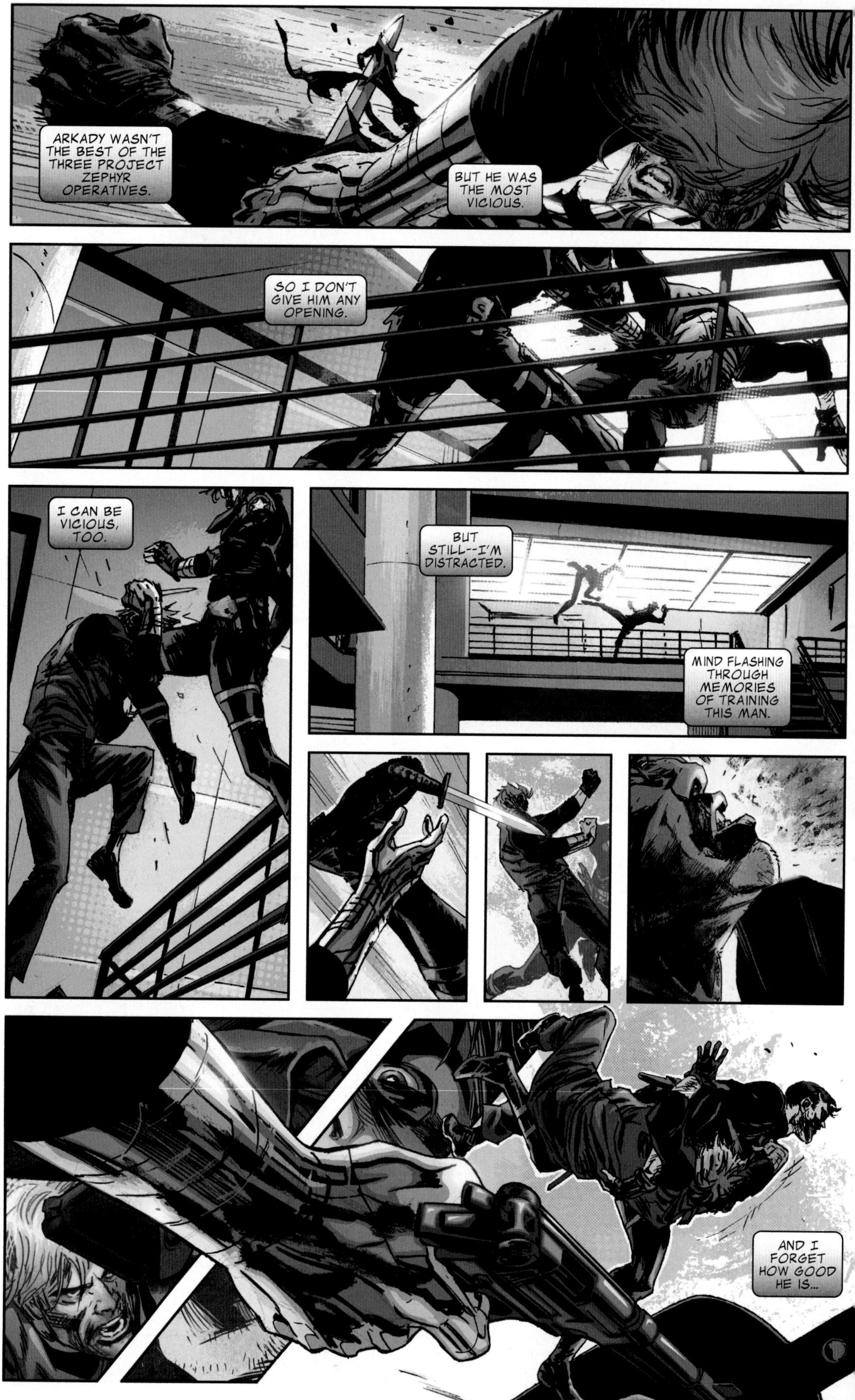

ARKADY WASN'T THE BEST OF THE THREE PROJECT ZEPHYR OPERATIVES.
BUT HE WAS THE MOST VICIOUS.
SO I DON'T GIVE HIM ANY OPENING.
I CAN BE VICIOUS, TOO.
BUT STILL--I'M DISTRACTED.
MIND FLASHING THROUGH MEMORIES OF TRAINING THIS MAN.
AND I FORGET HOW GOOD HE IS...

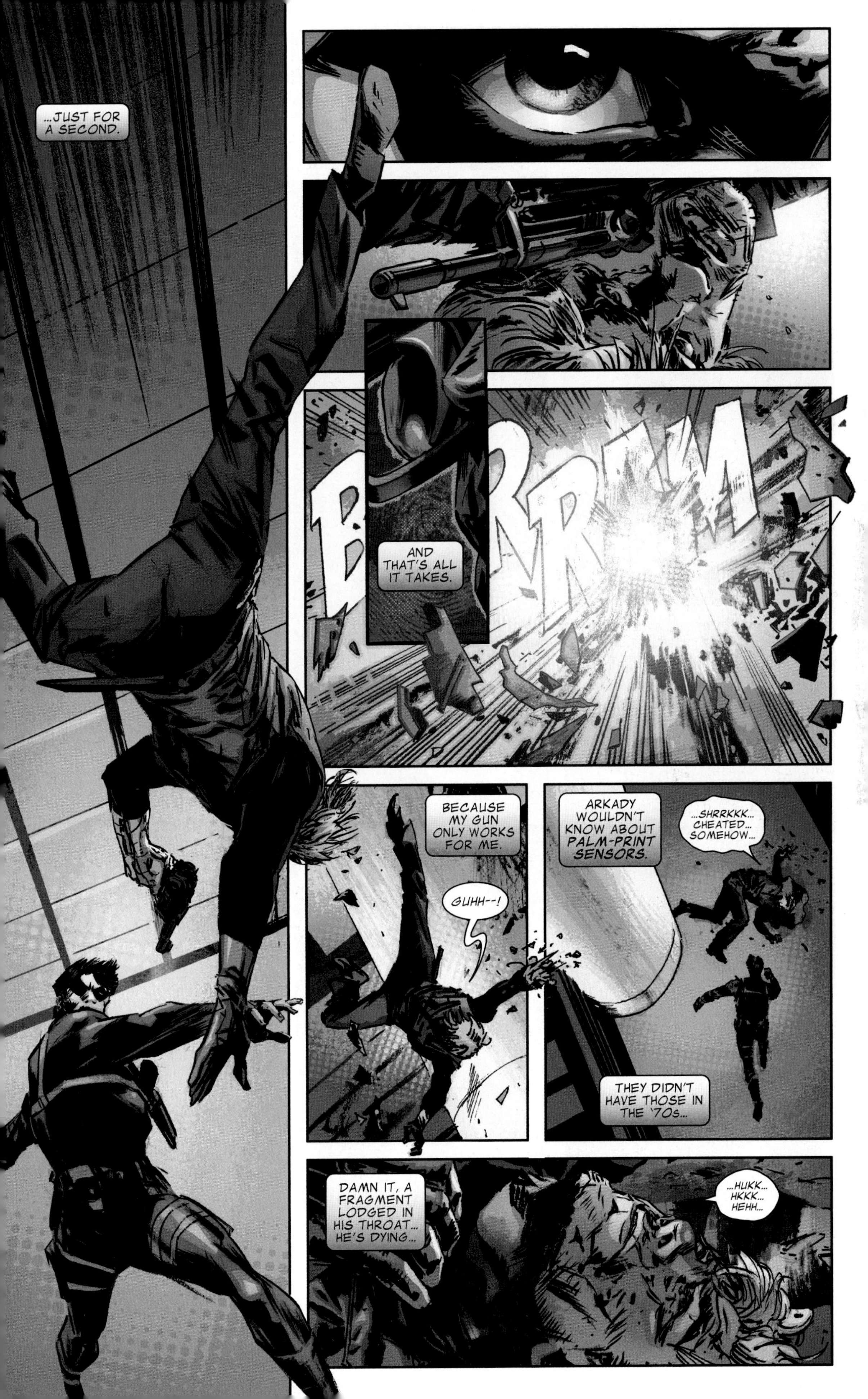
...JUST FOR A SECOND.
AND THAT'S ALL IT TAKES.
BECAUSE MY GUN ONLY WORKS FOR ME.
GUHH--!
ARKADY WOULDN'T KNOW ABOUT PALM-PRINT SENSORS.
...SHRRKKK... CHEATED... SOMEHOW...
THEY DIDN'T HAVE THOSE IN THE '70s...
DAMN IT, A FRAGMENT LODGED IN HIS THROAT... HE'S DYING...
...HUKK... HKKK... HEHH...

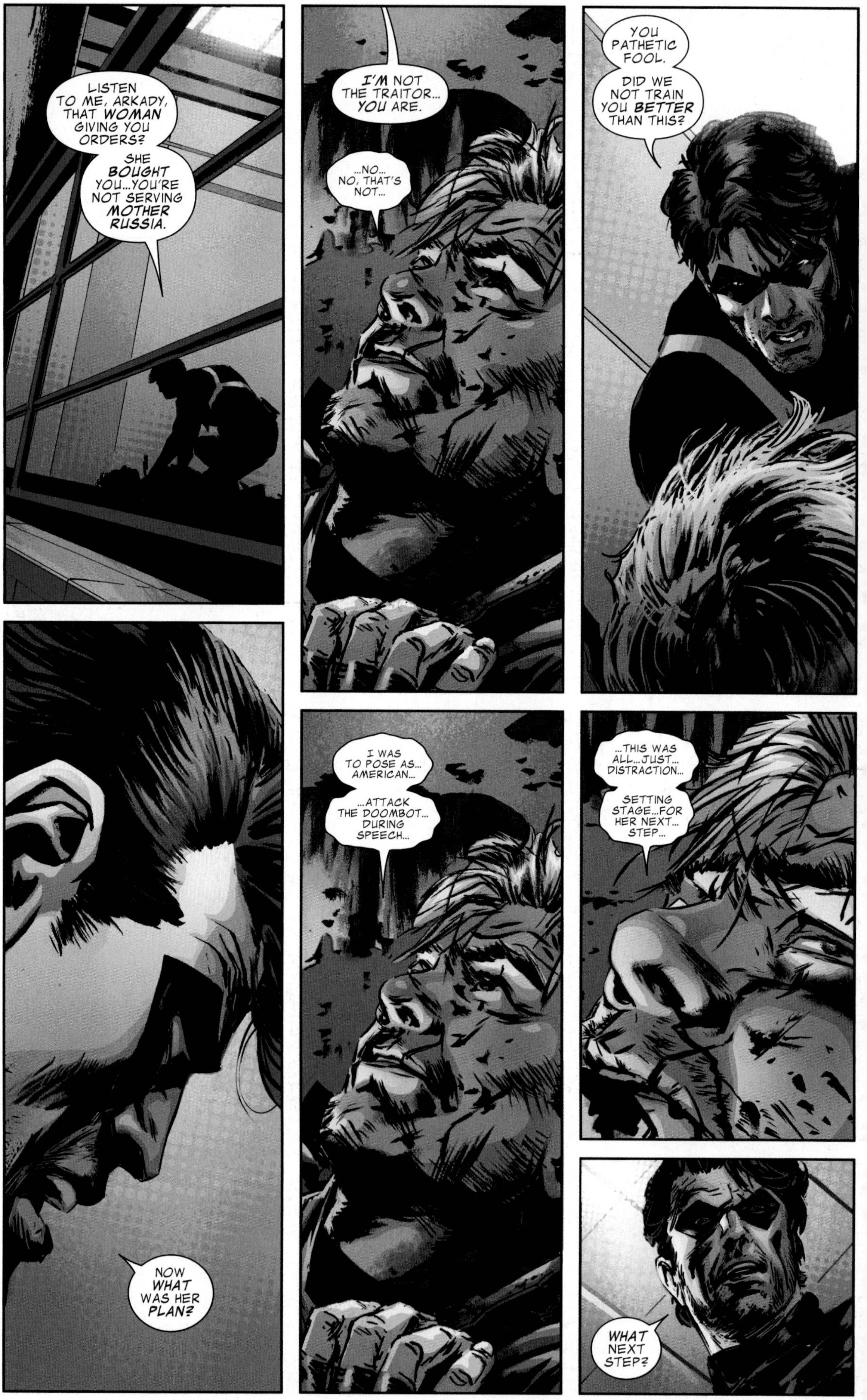
LISTEN TO ME, ARKADY, THAT WOMAN GIVING YOU ORDERS?
SHE BOUGHT YOU...YOU'RE NOT SERVING MOTHER RUSSIA.
I'M NOT THE TRAITOR... YOU ARE.
...NO... NO, THAT'S NOT...
YOU PATHETIC FOOL.
DID WE NOT TRAIN YOU BETTER THAN THIS?
NOW WHAT WAS HER PLAN?
I WAS TO POSE AS... AMERICAN...
...ATTACK THE DOOMBOT... DURING SPEECH...
...THIS WAS ALL...JUST... DISTRACTION...
SETTING STAGE...FOR HER NEXT... STEP...
WHAT NEXT STEP?

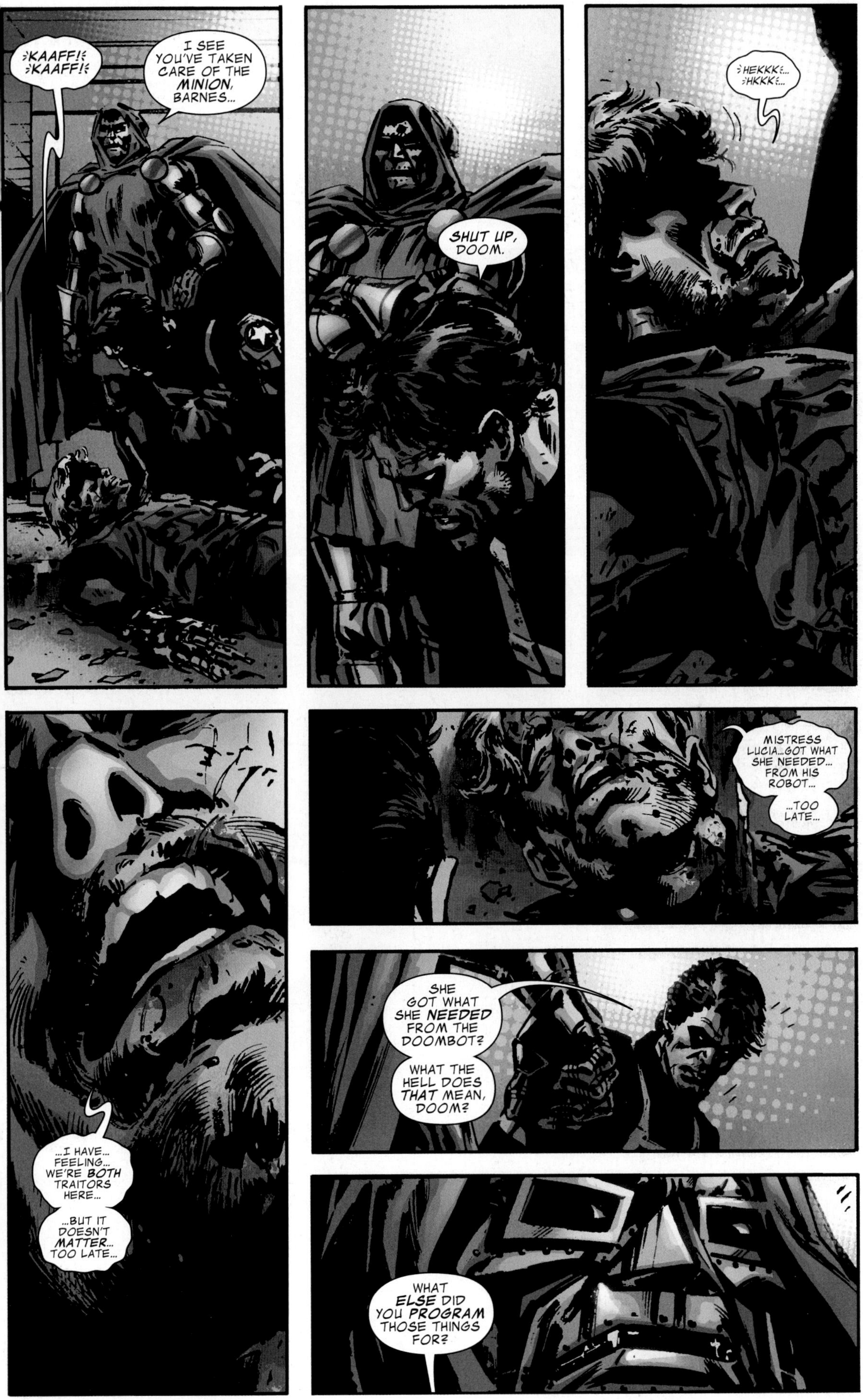

KAAFF! KAAFF!
I SEE YOU'VE TAKEN CARE OF THE MINION, BARNES...
SHUT UP, DOOM.
HEKKK... HKKK...
...I HAVE... FEELING... WE'RE BOTH TRAITORS HERE...
...BUT IT DOESN'T MATTER... TOO LATE...
MISTRESS LUCIA...GOT WHAT SHE NEEDED... FROM HIS ROBOT...
...TOO LATE...
SHE GOT WHAT SHE NEEDED FROM THE DOOMBOT?
WHAT THE HELL DOES THAT MEAN, DOOM?
WHAT ELSE DID YOU PROGRAM THOSE THINGS FOR?

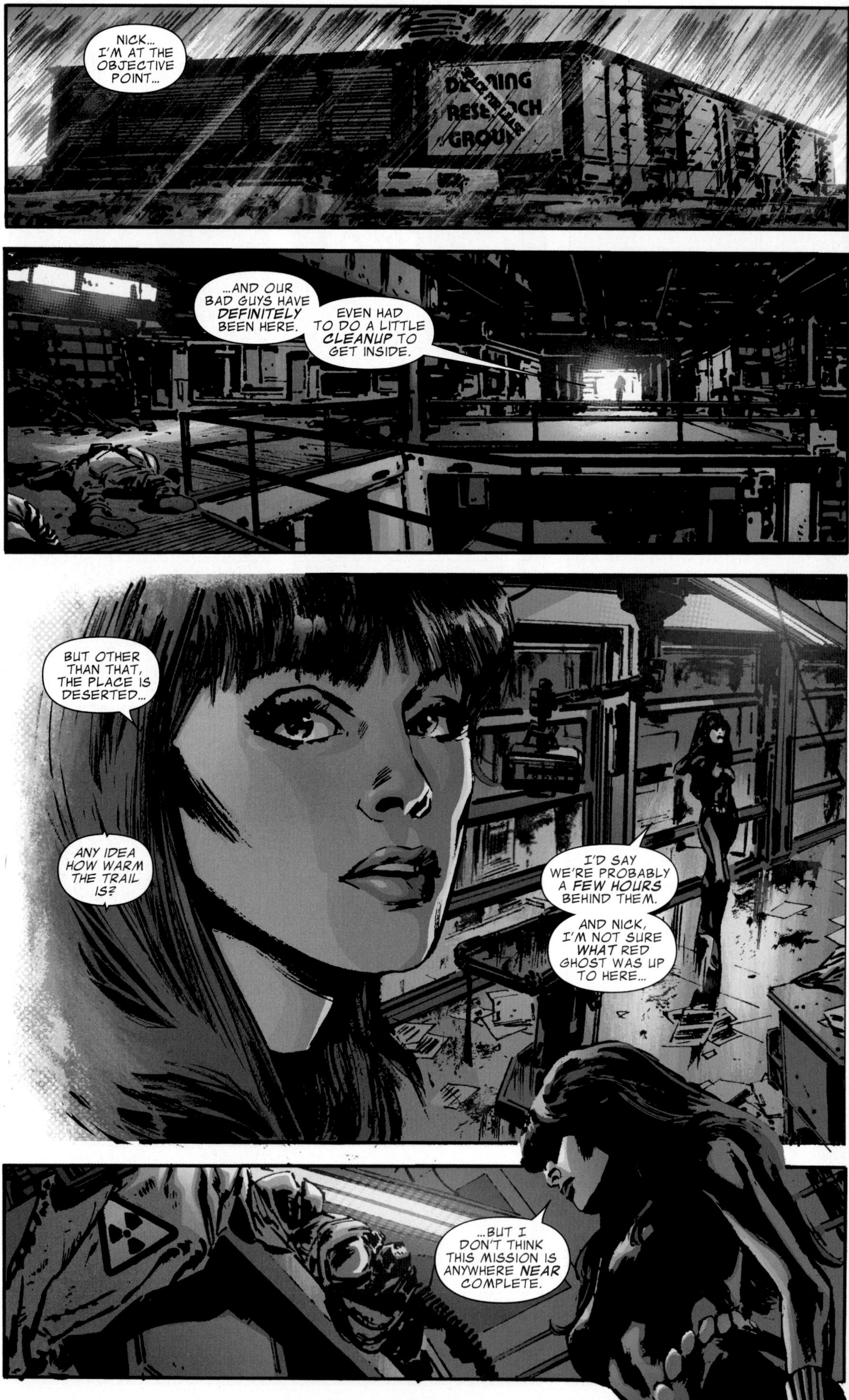
NICK... I'M AT THE OBJECTIVE POINT...
...AND OUR BAD GUYS HAVE DEFINITELY BEEN HERE.
EVEN HAD TO DO A LITTLE CLEANUP TO GET INSIDE.
BUT OTHER THAN THAT, THE PLACE IS DESERTED...
ANY IDEA HOW WARM THE TRAIL IS?
I'D SAY WE'RE PROBABLY A FEW HOURS BEHIND THEM.
AND NICK, I'M NOT SURE WHAT RED GHOST WAS UP TO HERE...
...BUT I DON'T THINK THIS MISSION IS ANYWHERE NEAR COMPLETE.

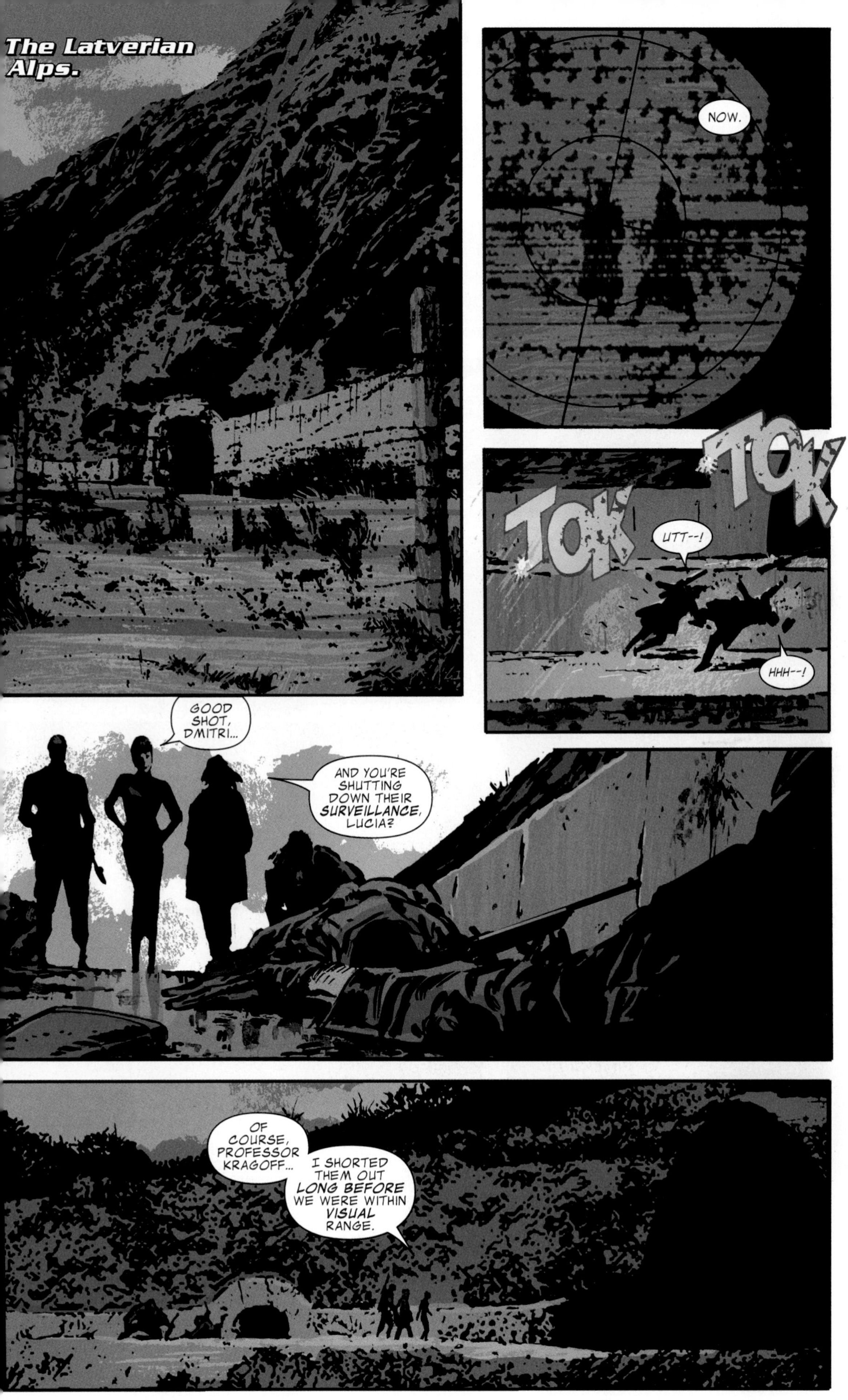
The Latverian Alps.
NOW.
TOK
TOK
UTT--!
HHH--!
GOOD SHOT, DMITRI...
AND YOU'RE SHUTTING DOWN THEIR SURVEILLANCE, LUCIA?
OF COURSE, PROFESSOR KRAGOFF...
I SHORTED THEM OUT LONG BEFORE WE WERE WITHIN VISUAL RANGE.

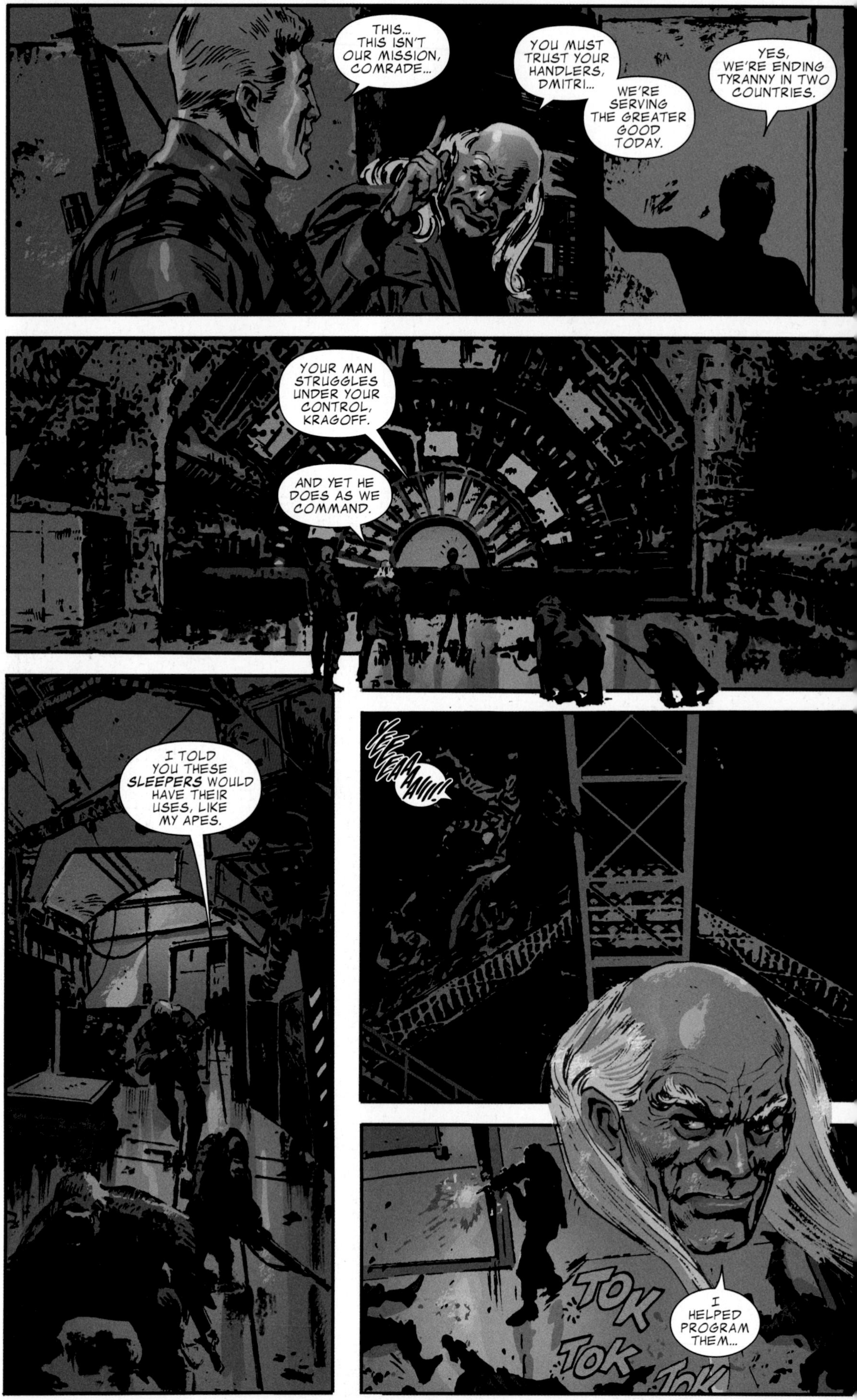
THIS... THIS ISN'T OUR MISSION, COMRADE...
YOU MUST TRUST YOUR HANDLERS, DMITRI...
WE'RE SERVING THE GREATER GOOD TODAY.
YES, WE'RE ENDING TYRANNY IN TWO COUNTRIES.
YOUR MAN STRUGGLES UNDER YOUR CONTROL, KRAGOFF.
AND YET HE DOES AS WE COMMAND.
I TOLD YOU THESE SLEEPERS WOULD HAVE THEIR USES, LIKE MY APES.
TOK
TOK
I HELPED PROGRAM THEM...

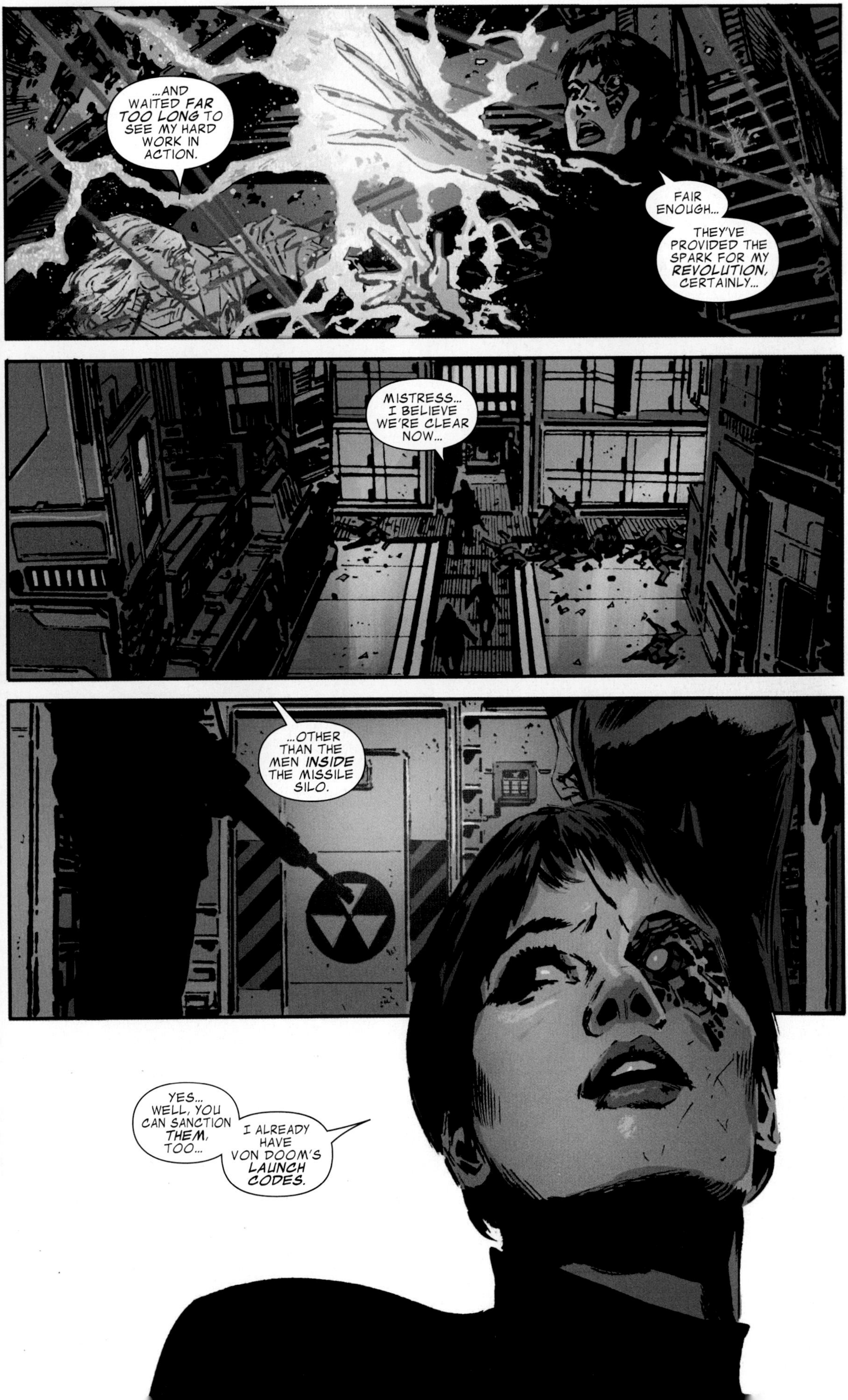
...AND WAITED FAR TOO LONG TO SEE MY HARD WORK IN ACTION.
FAIR ENOUGH...
THEY'VE PROVIDED THE SPARK FOR MY REVOLUTION, CERTAINLY...
MISTRESS... I BELIEVE WE'RE CLEAR NOW...
...OTHER THAN THE MEN INSIDE THE MISSILE SILO.
YES... WELL, YOU CAN SANCTION THEM, TOO...
I ALREADY HAVE VON DOOM'S LAUNCH CODES.

5

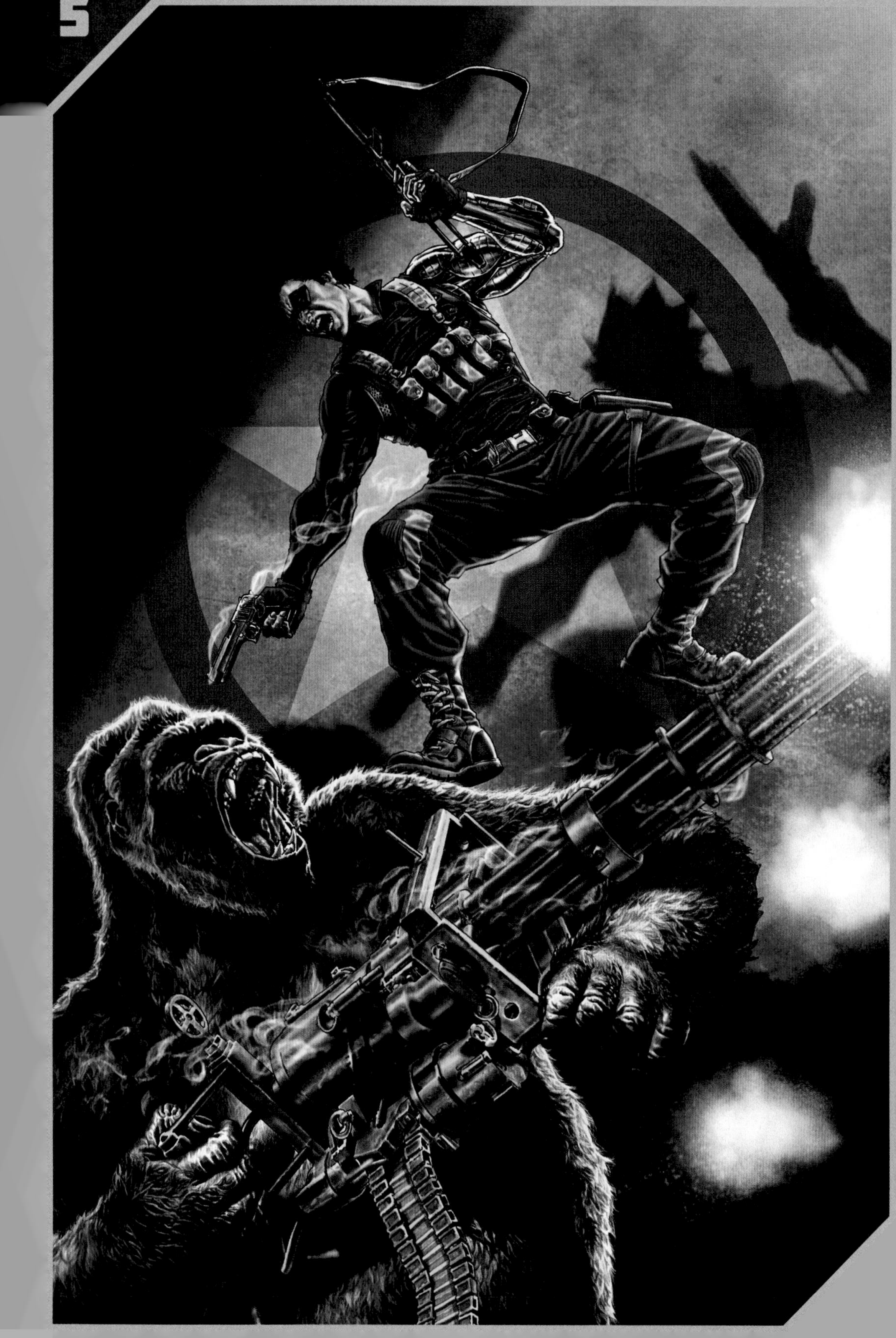

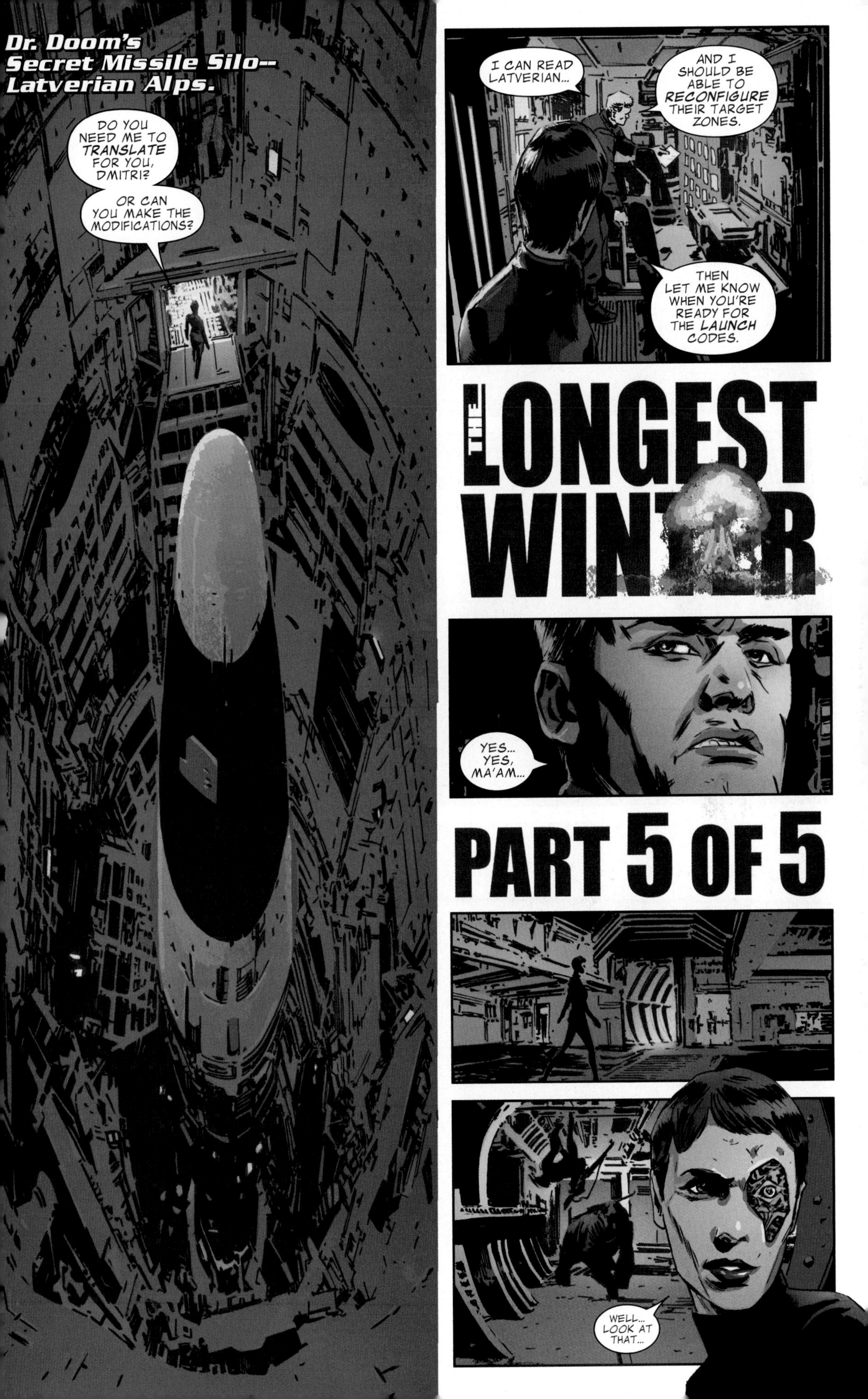
Dr. Doom's Secret Missile Silo-- Latverian Alps.
DO YOU NEED ME TO TRANSLATE FOR YOU, DMITRI?
OR CAN YOU MAKE THE MODIFICATIONS?
I CAN READ LATVERIAN...
AND I SHOULD BE ABLE TO RECONFIGURE THEIR TARGET ZONES.
THEN LET ME KNOW WHEN YOU'RE READY FOR THE LAUNCH CODES.
THE LONGEST WINTER
YES... YES, MA'AM...
PART 5 OF 5
WELL... LOOK AT THAT...

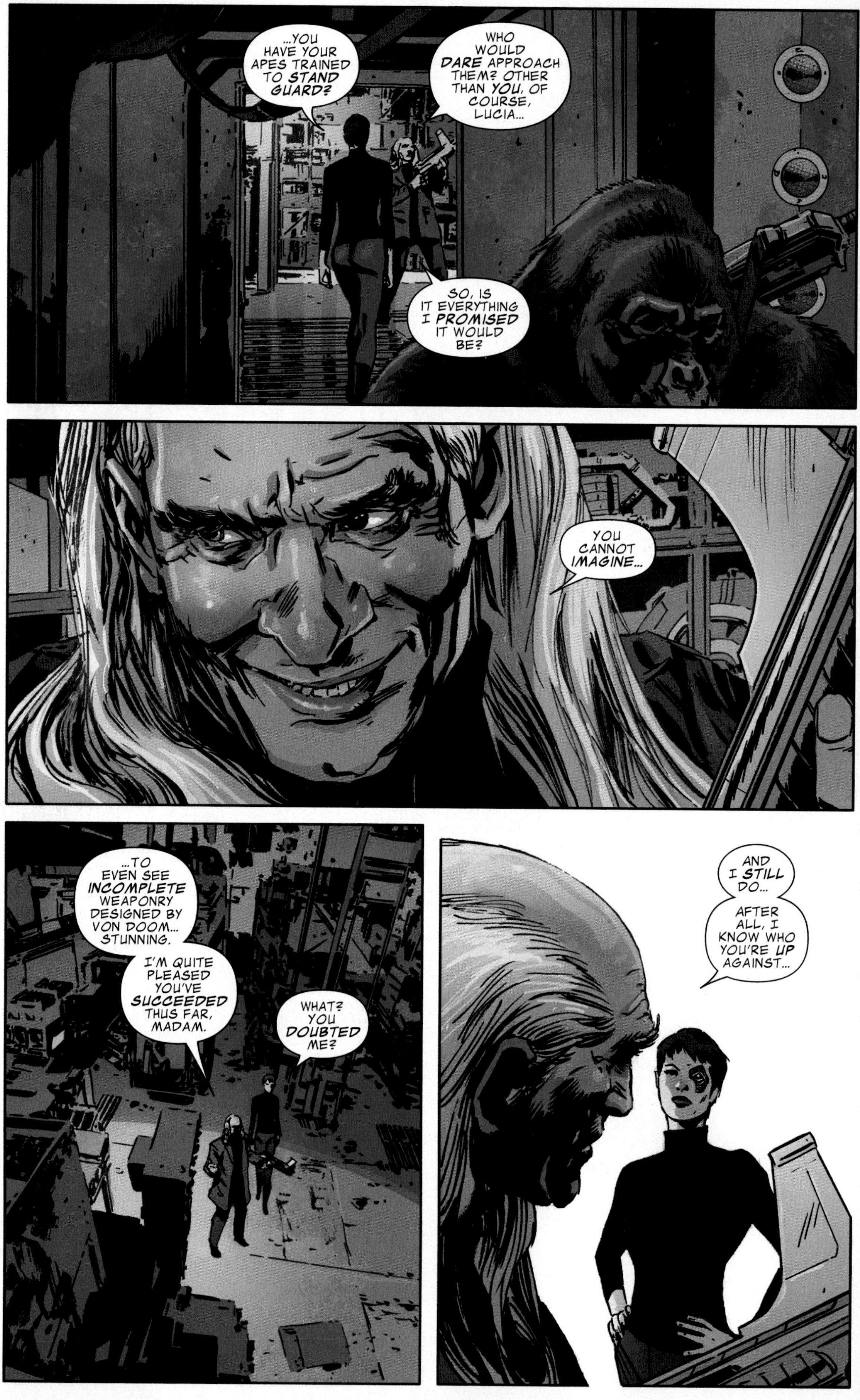
...YOU HAVE YOUR APES TRAINED TO STAND GUARD?
WHO WOULD DARE APPROACH THEM? OTHER THAN YOU, OF COURSE, LUCIA...
SO, IS IT EVERYTHING I PROMISED IT WOULD BE?
YOU CANNOT IMAGINE...
...TO EVEN SEE INCOMPLETE WEAPONRY DESIGNED BY VON DOOM... STUNNING.
I'M QUITE PLEASED YOU'VE SUCCEEDED THUS FAR, MADAM.
WHAT? YOU DOUBTED ME?
AND I STILL DO...
AFTER ALL, I KNOW WHO YOU'RE UP AGAINST...

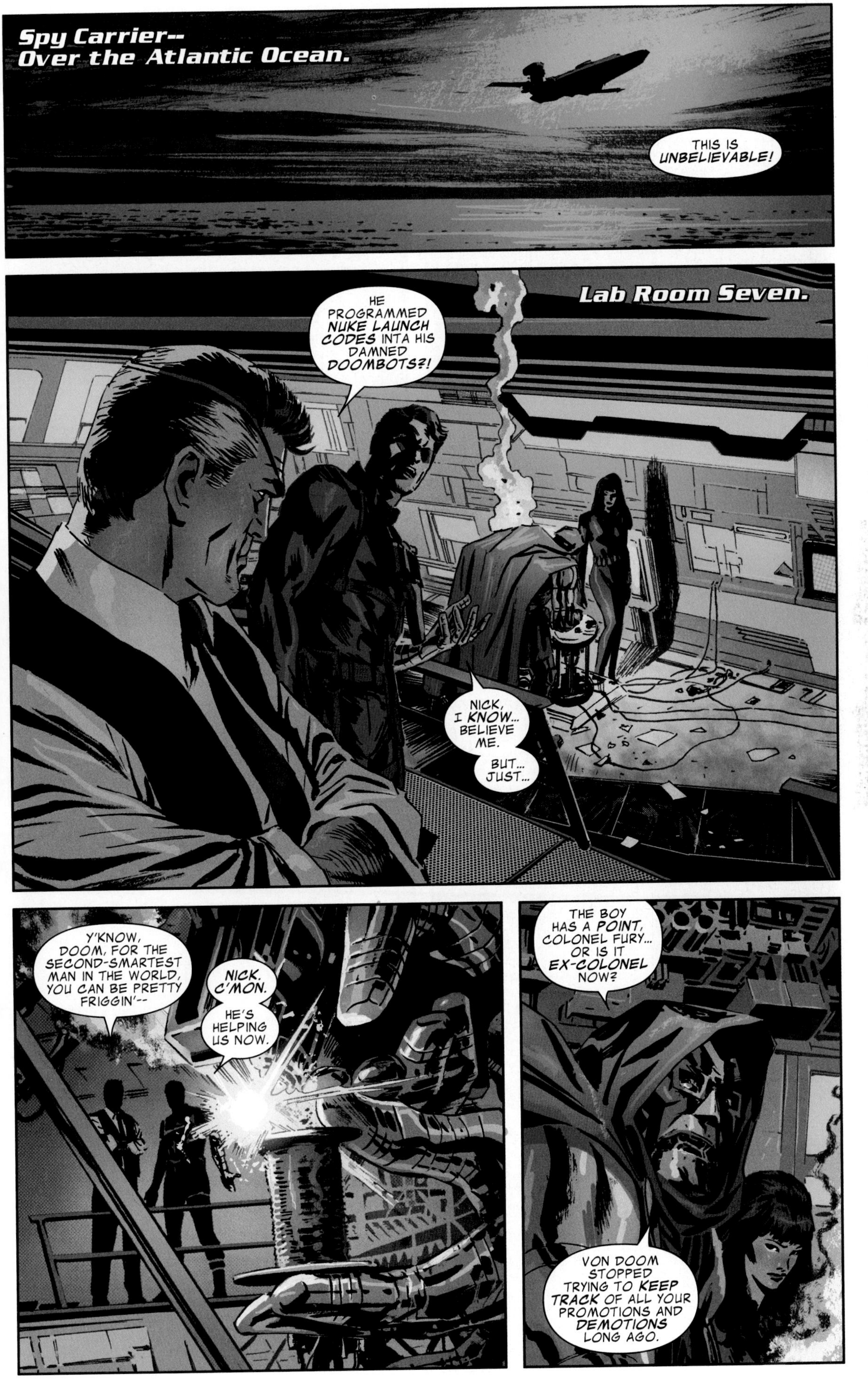
Spy Carrier--
Over the Atlantic Ocean.
THIS IS UNBELIEVABLE!
Lab Room Seven.
HE PROGRAMMED NUKE LAUNCH CODES INTA HIS DAMNED DOOMBOTS?!
NICK, I KNOW... BELIEVE ME.
BUT... JUST...
Y'KNOW, DOOM, FOR THE SECOND-SMARTEST MAN IN THE WORLD, YOU CAN BE PRETTY FRIGGIN'--
NICK. C'MON.
HE'S HELPING US NOW.
THE BOY HAS A POINT, COLONEL FURY... OR IS IT EX-COLONEL NOW?
VON DOOM STOPPED TRYING TO KEEP TRACK OF ALL YOUR PROMOTIONS AND DEMOTIONS LONG AGO.

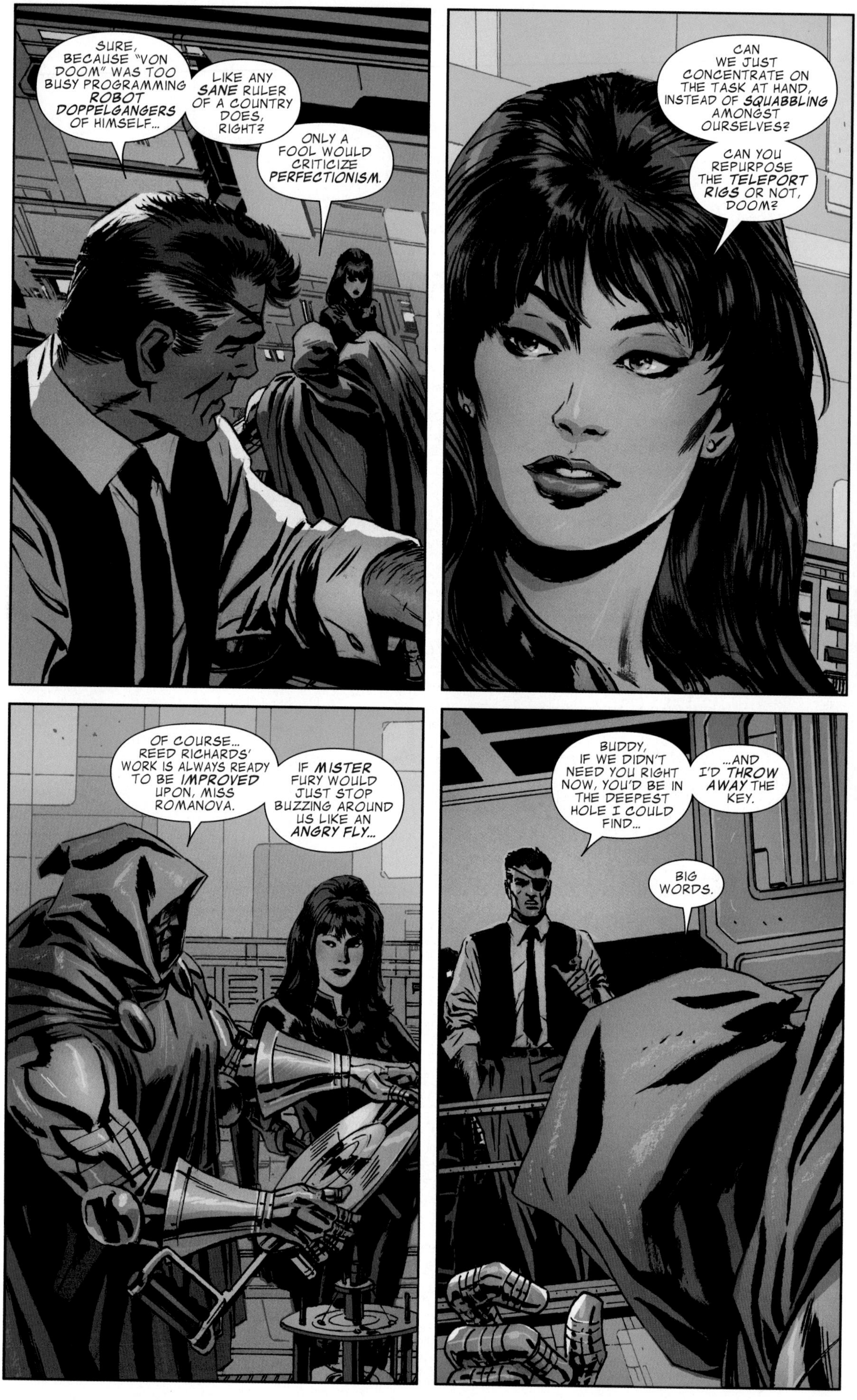
SURE, BECAUSE "VON DOOM" WAS TOO BUSY PROGRAMMING ROBOT DOPPELGANGERS OF HIMSELF...
LIKE ANY SANE RULER OF A COUNTRY DOES, RIGHT?
ONLY A FOOL WOULD CRITICIZE PERFECTIONISM.
CAN WE JUST CONCENTRATE ON THE TASK AT HAND, INSTEAD OF SQUABBLING AMONGST OURSELVES?
CAN YOU REPURPOSE THE TELEPORT RIGS OR NOT, DOOM?
OF COURSE... REED RICHARDS' WORK IS ALWAYS READY TO BE IMPROVED UPON, MISS ROMANOVA.
IF MISTER FURY WOULD JUST STOP BUZZING AROUND US LIKE AN ANGRY FLY...
BUDDY, IF WE DIDN'T NEED YOU RIGHT NOW, YOU'D BE IN THE DEEPEST HOLE I COULD FIND...
...AND I'D THROW AWAY THE KEY.
BIG WORDS.

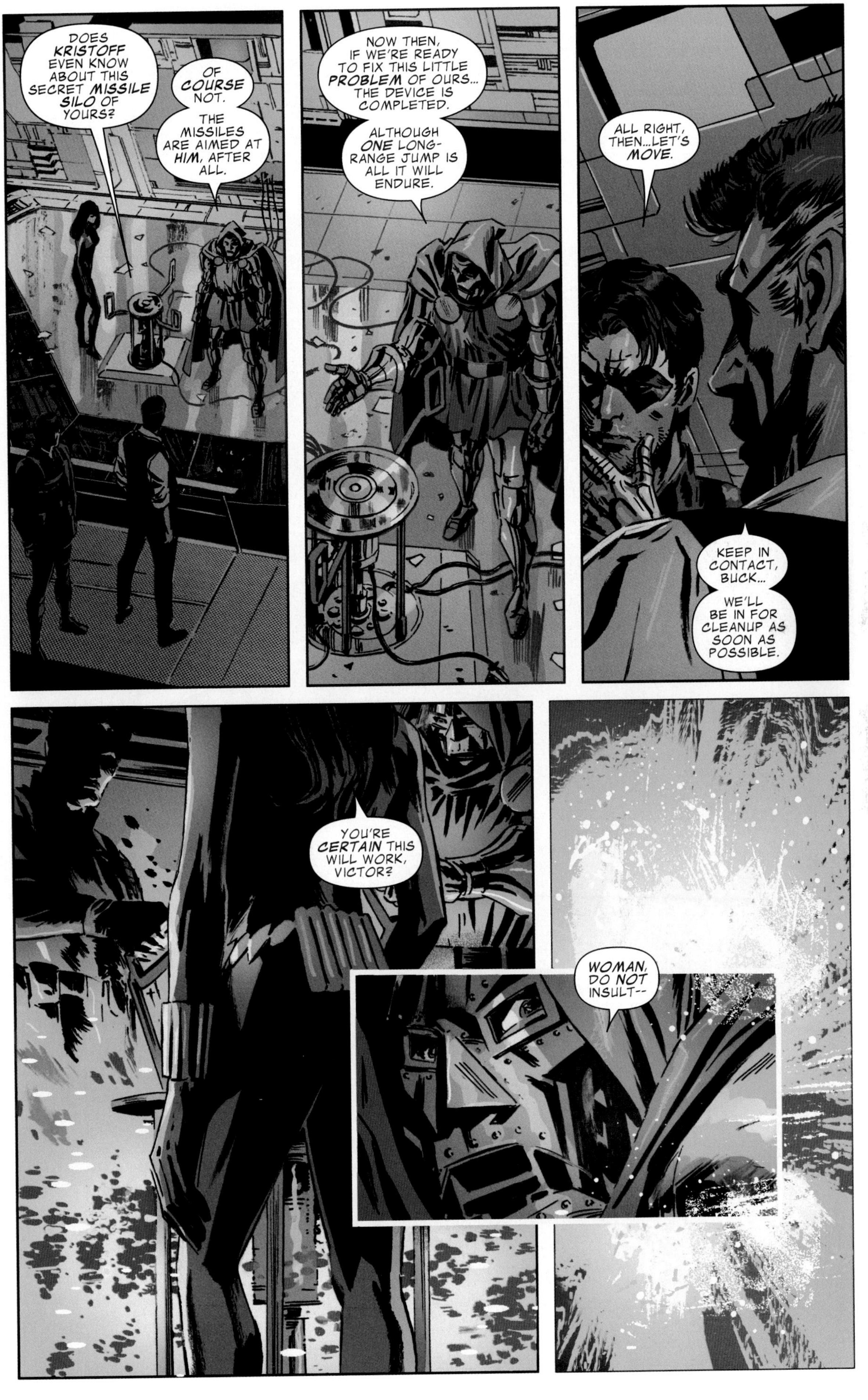
DOES KRISTOFF EVEN KNOW ABOUT THIS SECRET MISSILE SILO OF YOURS?
OF COURSE NOT.
THE MISSILES ARE AIMED AT HIM, AFTER ALL.
NOW THEN, IF WE'RE READY TO FIX THIS LITTLE PROBLEM OF OURS... THE DEVICE IS COMPLETED.
ALTHOUGH ONE LONG-RANGE JUMP IS ALL IT WILL ENDURE.
ALL RIGHT, THEN...LET'S MOVE.
KEEP IN CONTACT, BUCK...
WE'LL BE IN FOR CLEANUP AS SOON AS POSSIBLE.
YOU'RE CERTAIN THIS WILL WORK, VICTOR?
WOMAN, DO NOT INSULT--

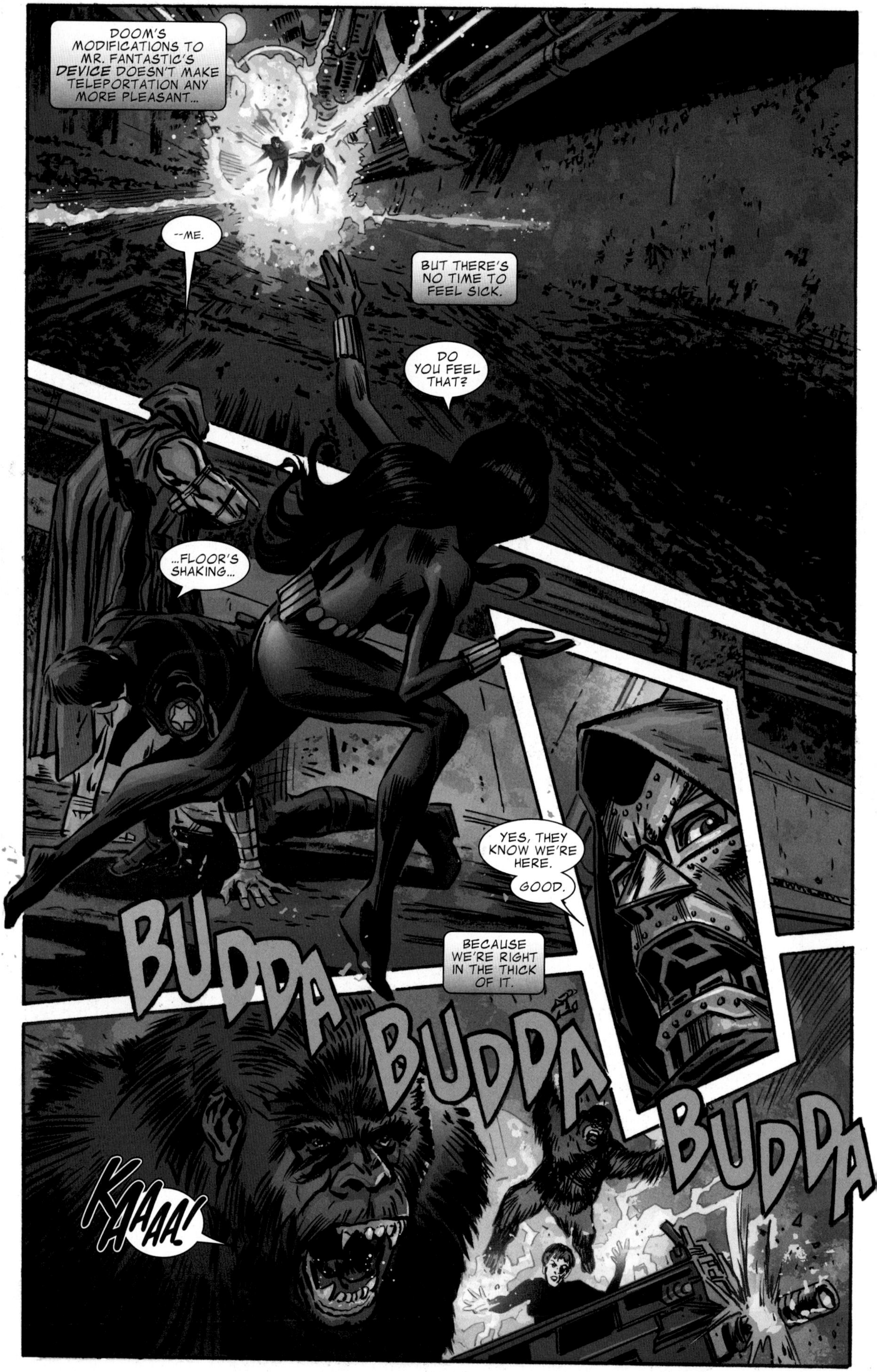
DOOM'S MODIFICATIONS TO MR. FANTASTIC'S DEVICE DOESN'T MAKE TELEPORTATION ANY MORE PLEASANT...
--ME.
BUT THERE'S NO TIME TO FEEL SICK.
DO YOU FEEL THAT?
...FLOOR'S SHAKING...
YES, THEY KNOW WE'RE HERE.
GOOD.
BECAUSE WE'RE RIGHT IN THE THICK OF IT.
BUDDA
BUDDA
BUDDA
KAAAA!

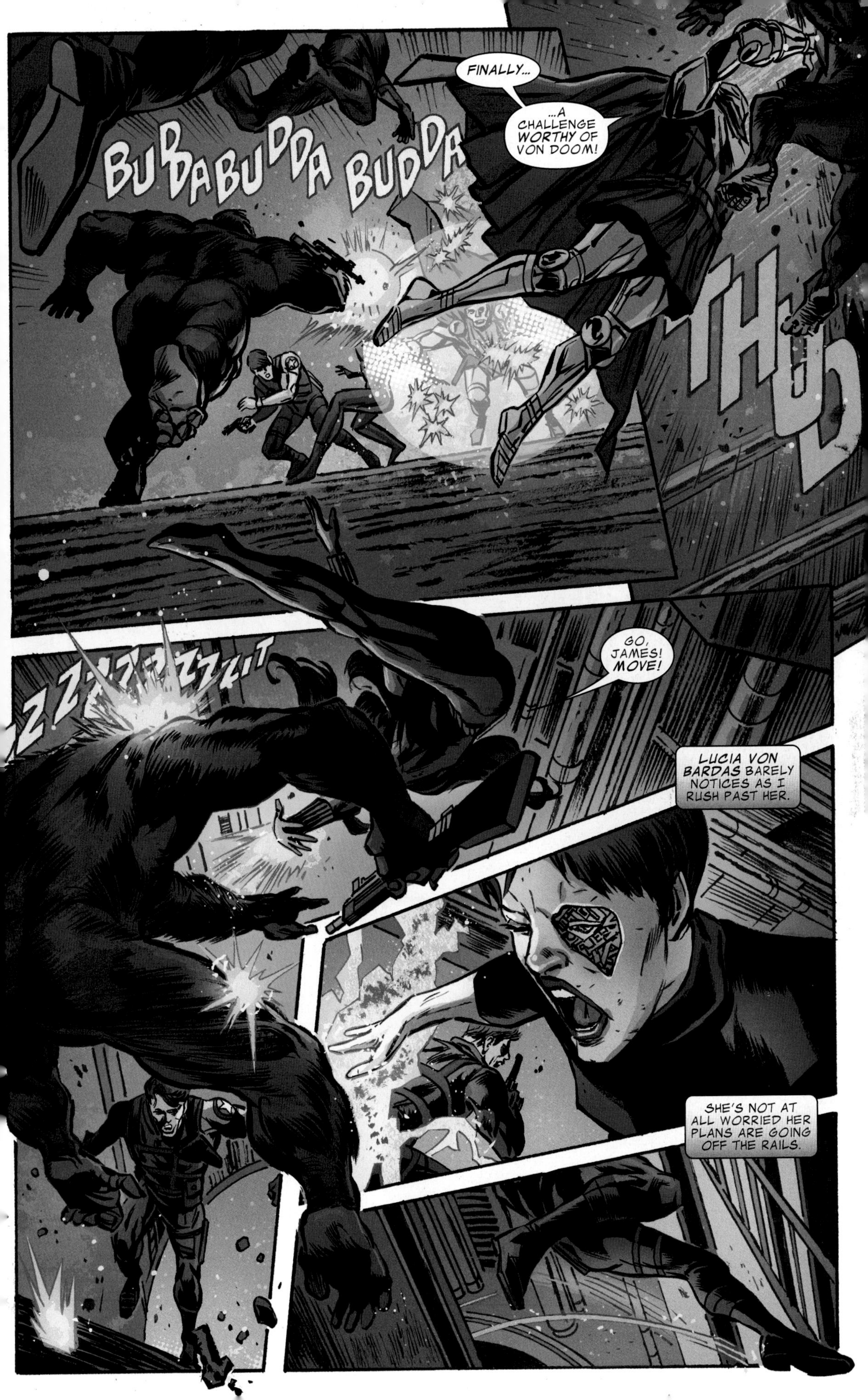
FINALLY...
...A CHALLENGE WORTHY OF VON DOOM!
BUDABUDDA BUDDA
THUD
ZZZZZZZZZZZZLIT
GO, JAMES! MOVE!
LUCIA VON BARDAS BARELY NOTICES AS I RUSH PAST HER.
SHE'S NOT AT ALL WORRIED HER PLANS ARE GOING OFF THE RAILS.

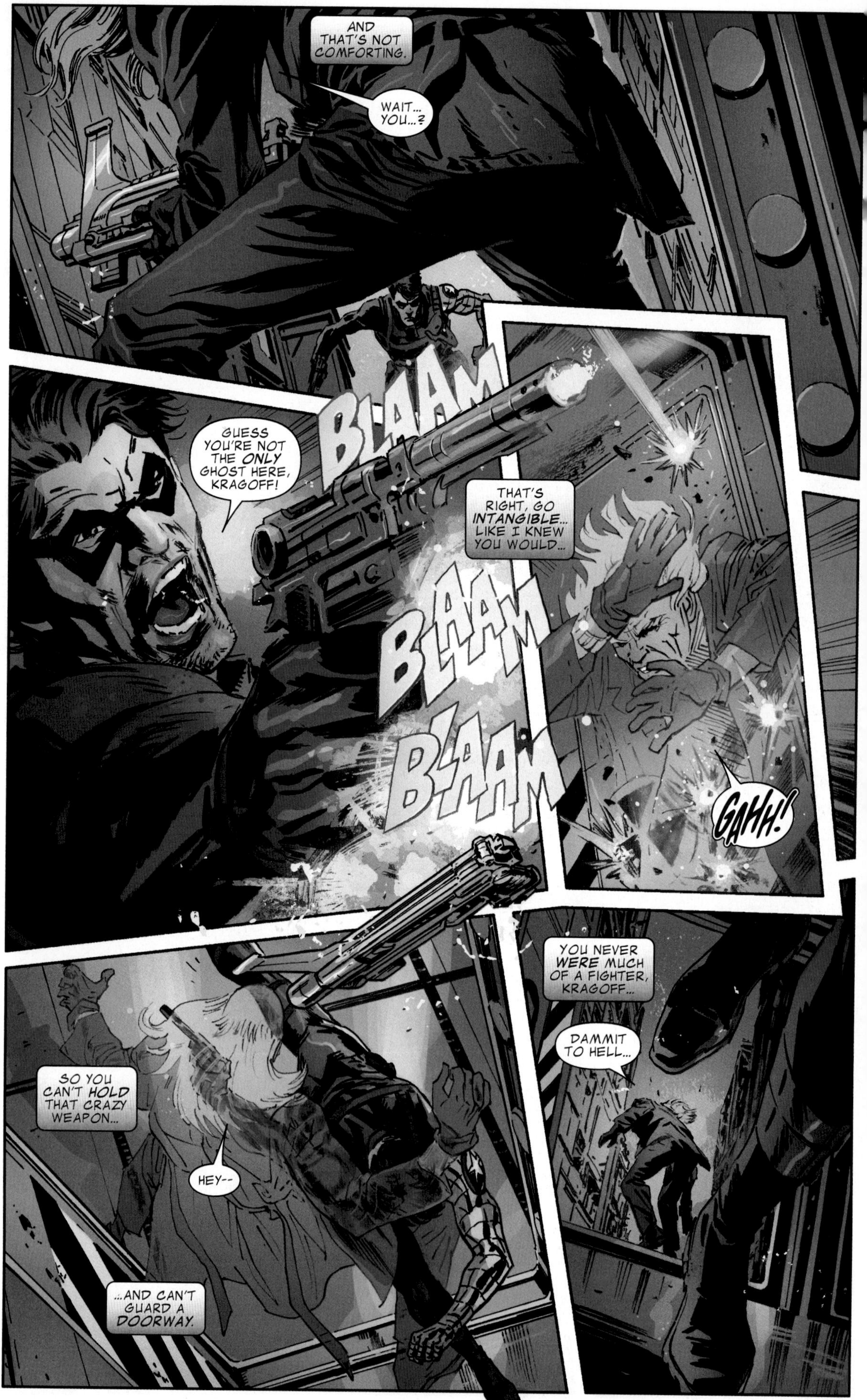
AND THAT'S NOT COMFORTING.
WAIT... YOU...?
GUESS YOU'RE NOT THE ONLY GHOST HERE, KRAGOFF!
BLAAM
THAT'S RIGHT, GO INTANGIBLE... LIKE I KNEW YOU WOULD...
BLAAM
BLAAM
GAHH!
SO YOU CAN'T HOLD THAT CRAZY WEAPON...
HEY--
...AND CAN'T GUARD A DOORWAY.
YOU NEVER WERE MUCH OF A FIGHTER, KRAGOFF...
DAMMIT TO HELL...

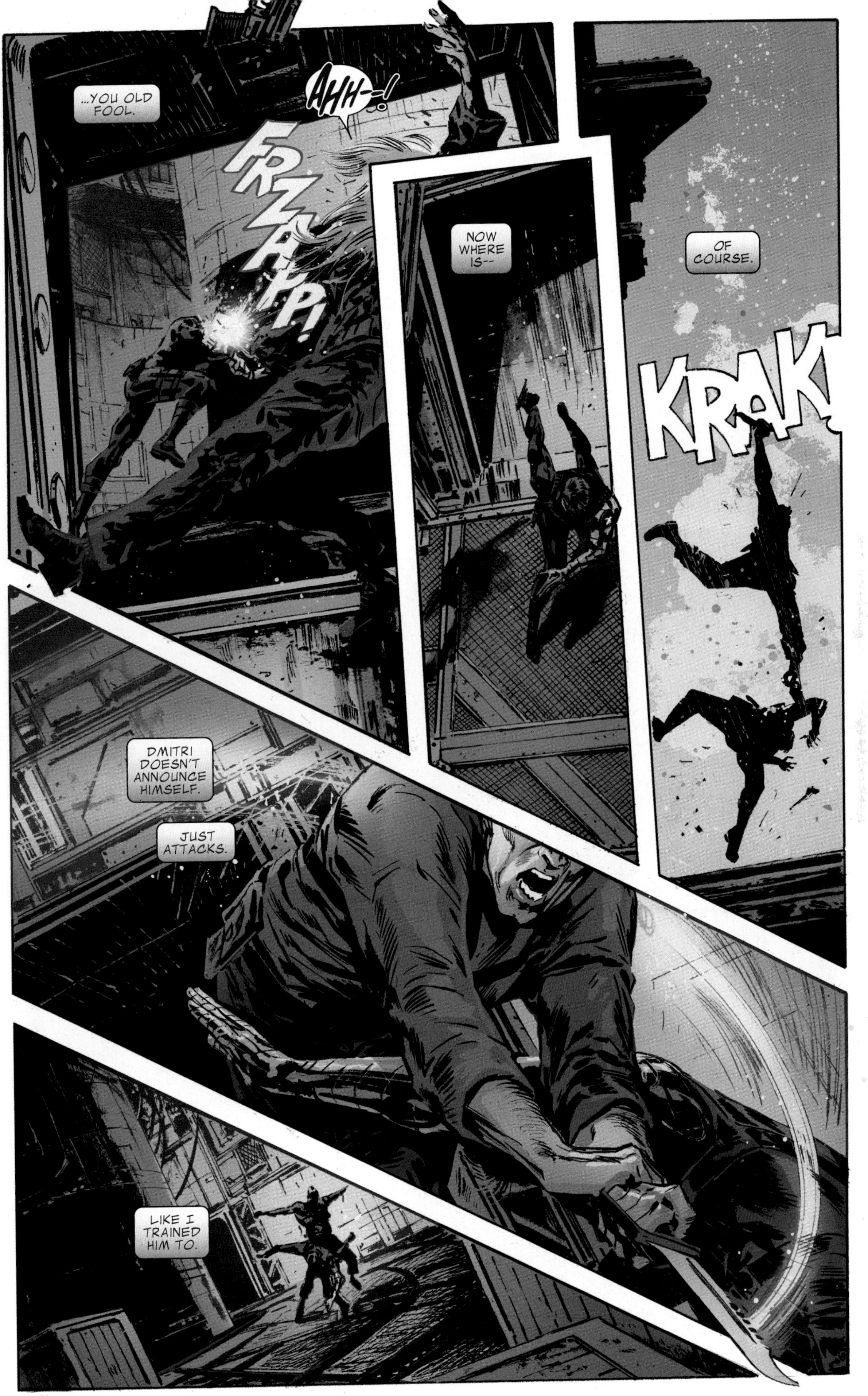

...YOU OLD FOOL.
AHH--!
FRZAPP!
NOW WHERE IS--
OF COURSE.
KRAK
DMITRI DOESN'T ANNOUNCE HIMSELF.
JUST ATTACKS.
LIKE I TRAINED HIM TO.

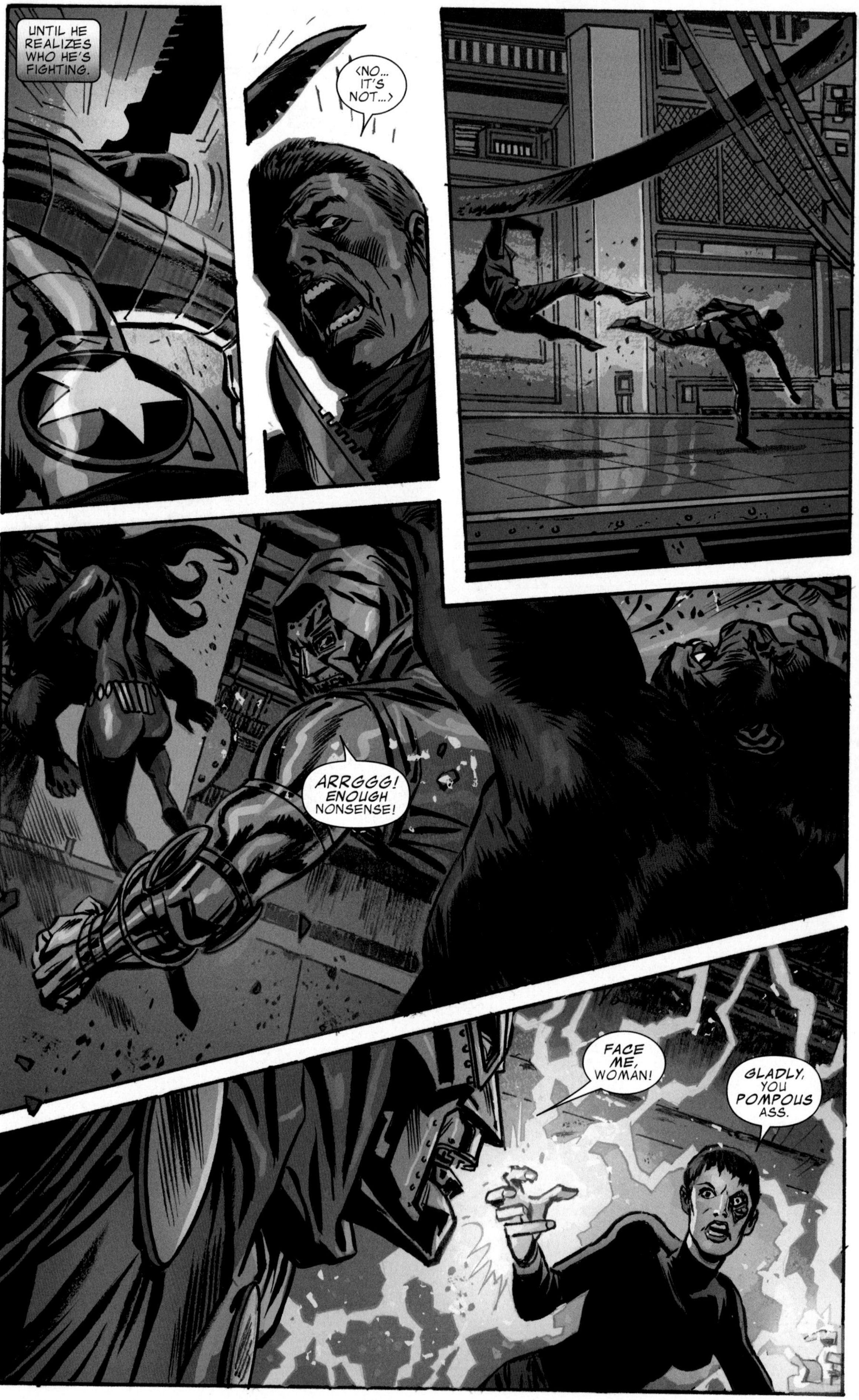
UNTIL HE REALIZES WHO HE'S FIGHTING.
<NO... IT'S NOT...>
ARRGGG! ENOUGH NONSENSE!
FACE ME, WOMAN!
GLADLY, YOU POMPOUS ASS.

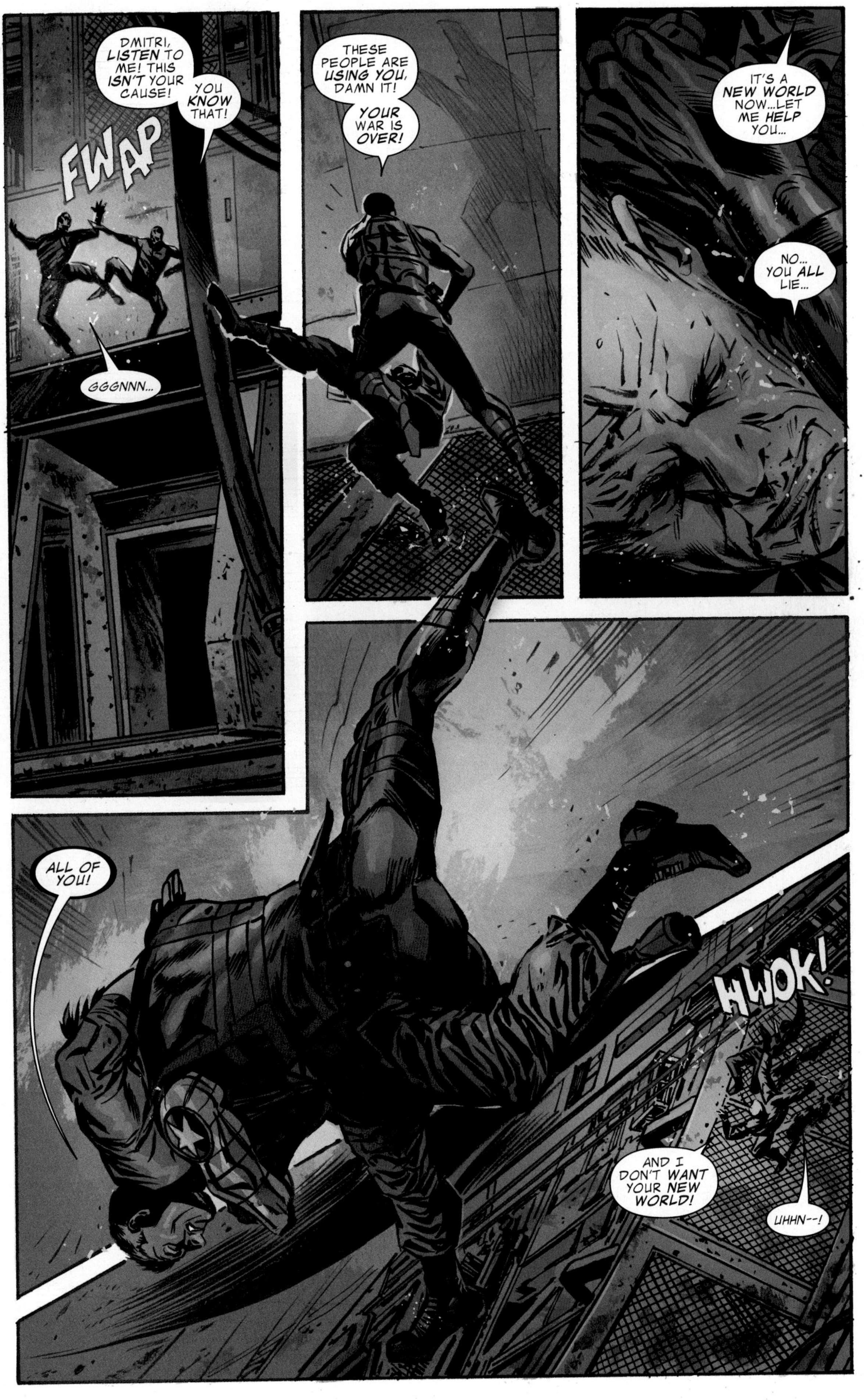
DMITRI, LISTEN TO ME! THIS ISN'T YOUR CAUSE!
YOU KNOW THAT!
FWAP
GGGNNN...
THESE PEOPLE ARE USING YOU, DAMN IT!
YOUR WAR IS OVER!
IT'S A NEW WORLD NOW...LET ME HELP YOU...
NO... YOU ALL LIE...
ALL OF YOU!
HWOK!
AND I DON'T WANT YOUR NEW WORLD!
UHHN--!

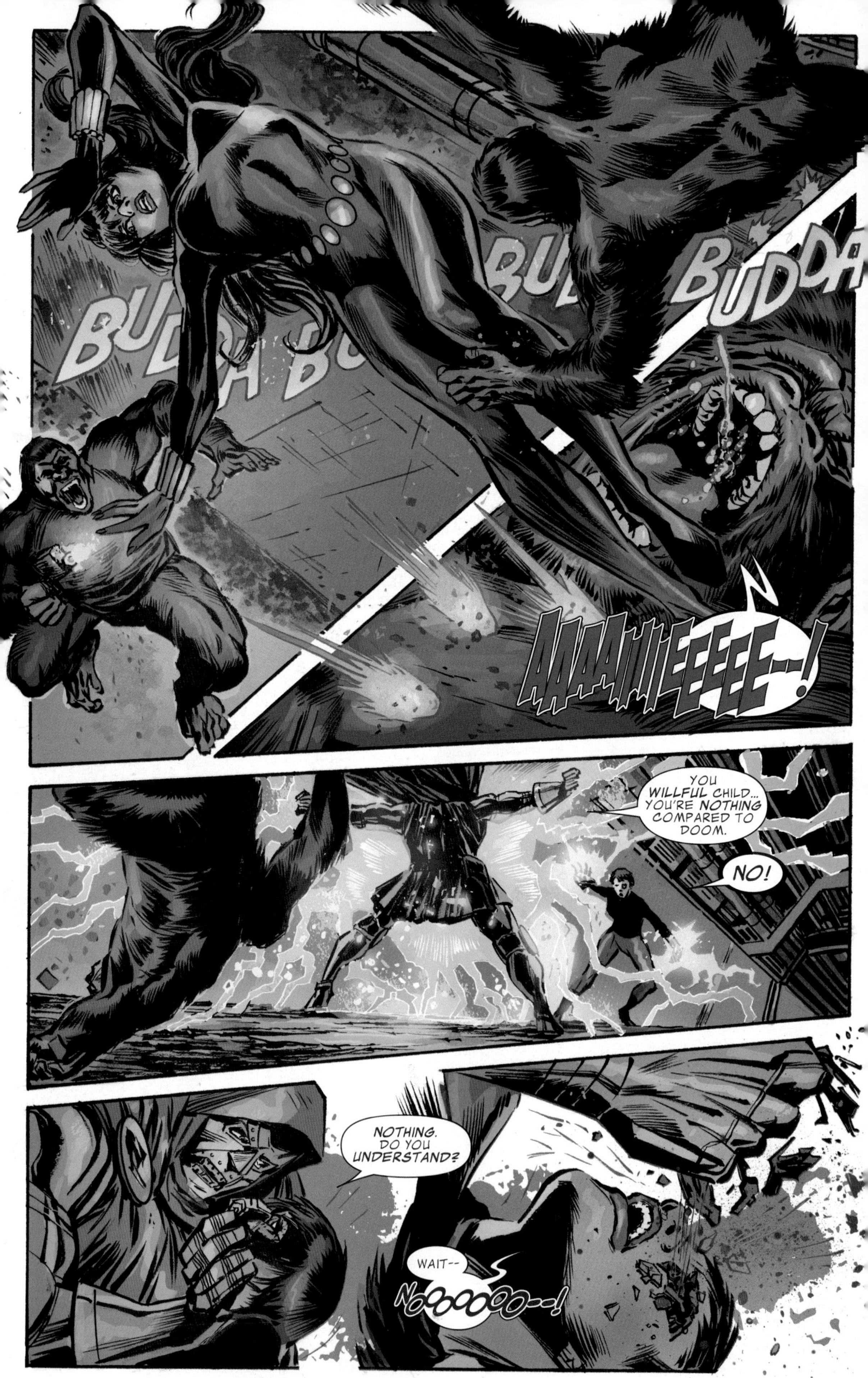
BUDDA BUDDA
BUDDA BUDDA
AAAAIIIIEEEEE--!
YOU WILLFUL CHILD... YOU'RE NOTHING COMPARED TO DOOM.
NO!
NOTHING. DO YOU UNDERSTAND?
WAIT--
NOOOOOOO--!

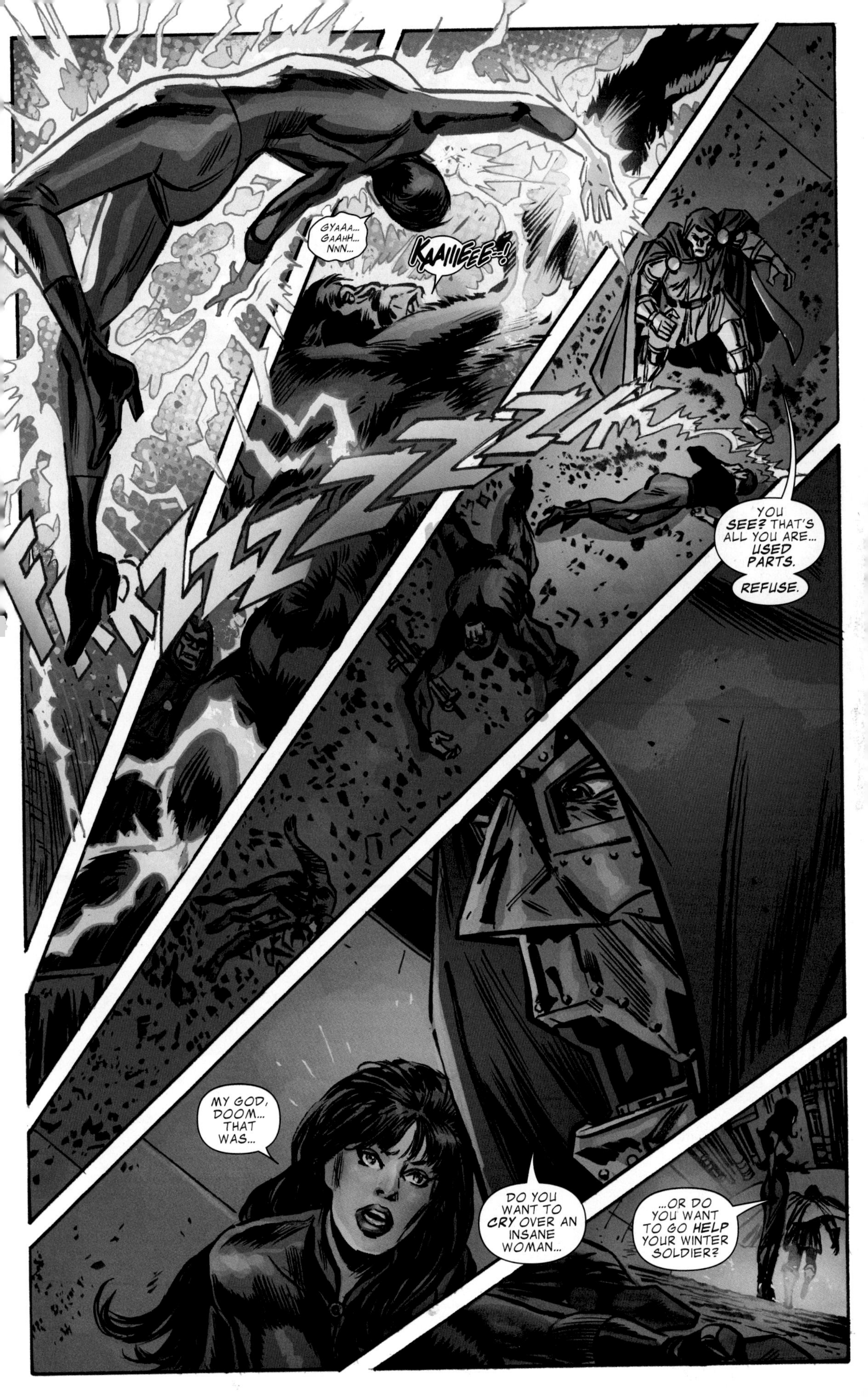
GYAAA... GAAHH... NNN...
KAAIIIEEE--!
FRZZZZZT
YOU SEE? THAT'S ALL YOU ARE... USED PARTS.
REFUSE.
MY GOD, DOOM... THAT WAS...
DO YOU WANT TO CRY OVER AN INSANE WOMAN...
...OR DO YOU WANT TO GO HELP YOUR WINTER SOLDIER?

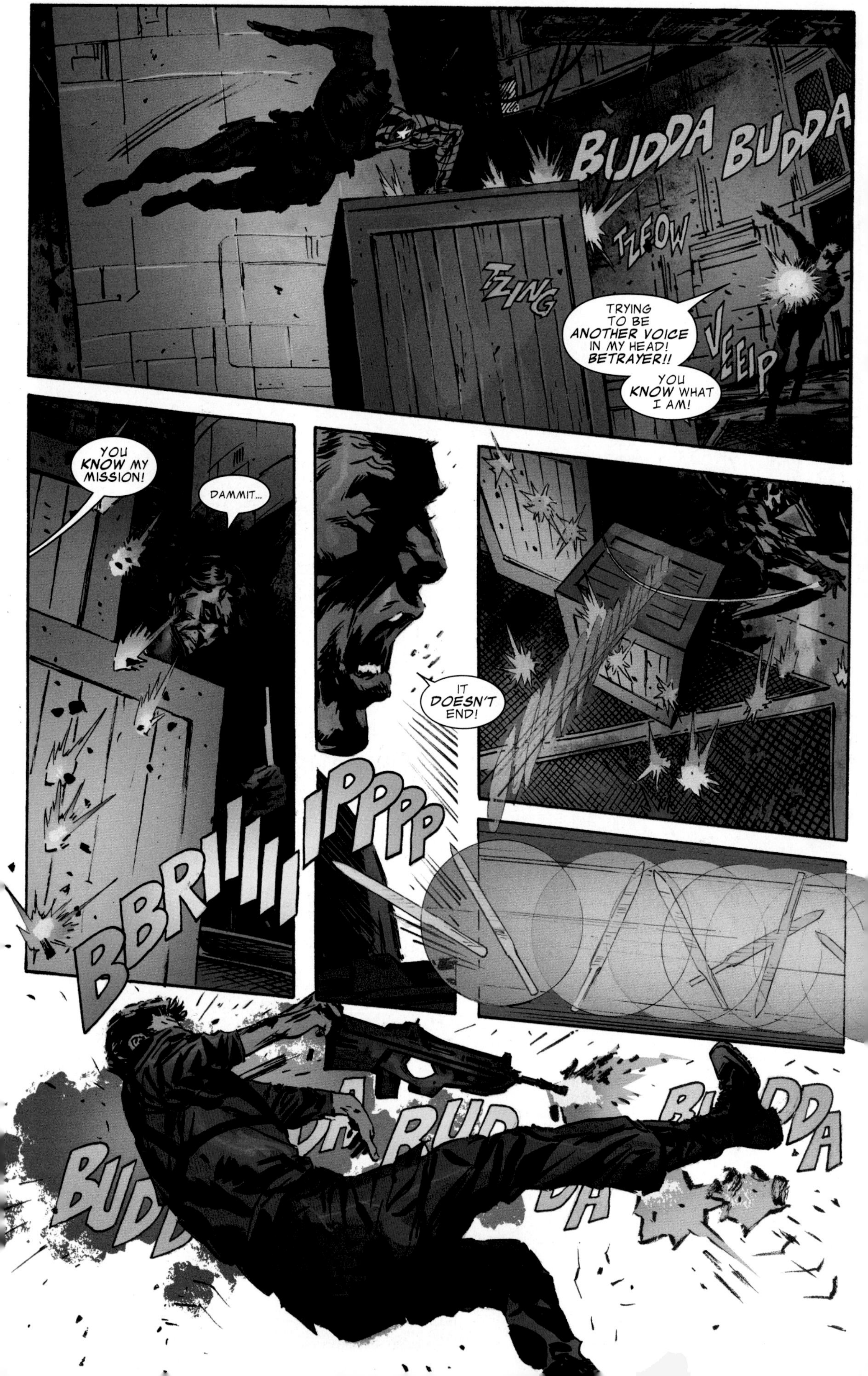
BUDDA BUDDA
TZFOW
TZING
TRYING TO BE ANOTHER VOICE IN MY HEAD! BETRAYER!!
YOU KNOW WHAT I AM!
VEEIP
YOU KNOW MY MISSION!
DAMMIT...
IT DOESN'T END!
BBRIIIIIIPPPP
BUDDA

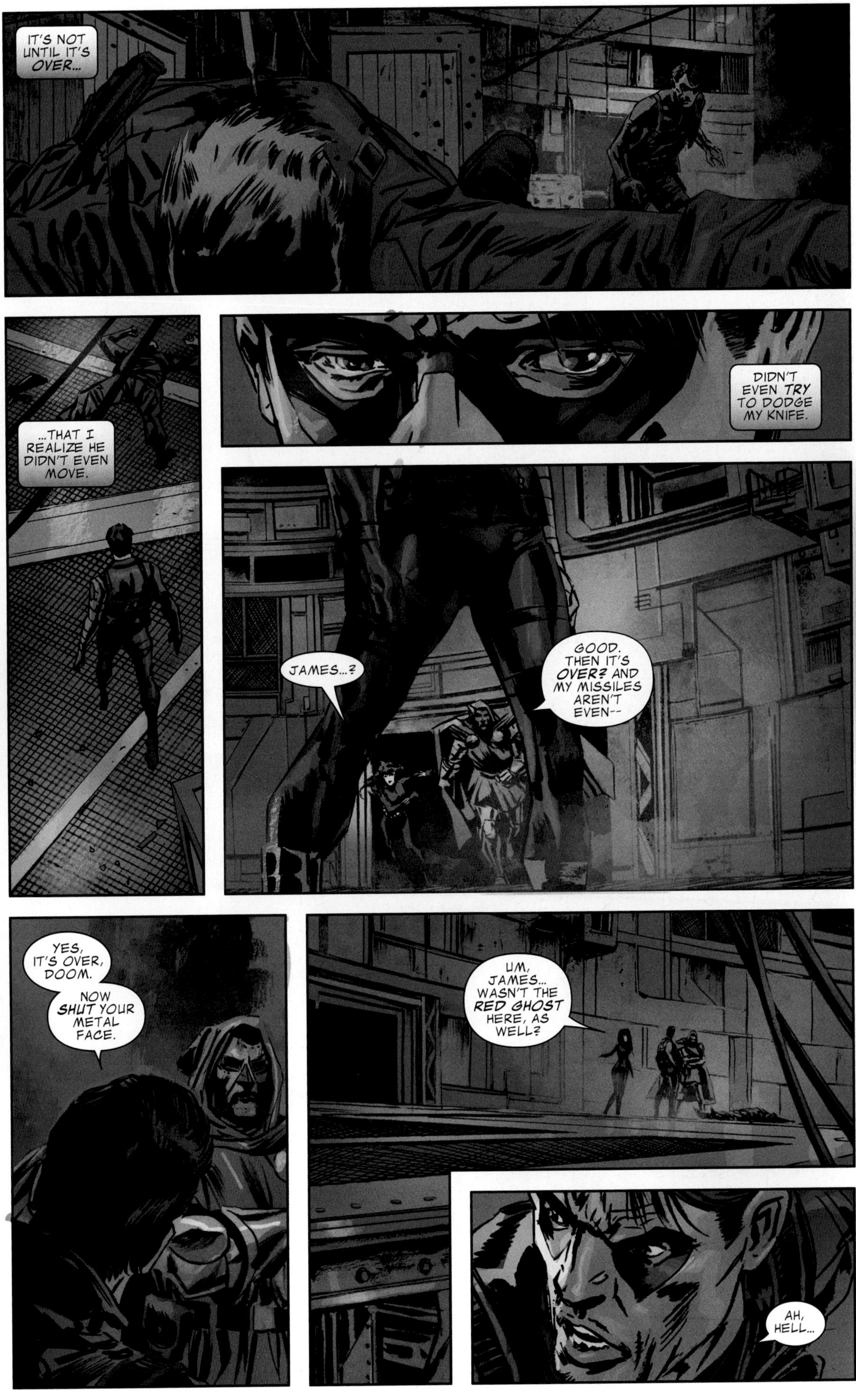
IT'S NOT UNTIL IT'S OVER...
...THAT I REALIZE HE DIDN'T EVEN MOVE.
DIDN'T EVEN TRY TO DODGE MY KNIFE.
JAMES...?
GOOD. THEN IT'S OVER? AND MY MISSILES AREN'T EVEN--
YES, IT'S OVER, DOOM.
NOW SHUT YOUR METAL FACE.
UM, JAMES... WASN'T THE RED GHOST HERE, AS WELL?
AH, HELL...

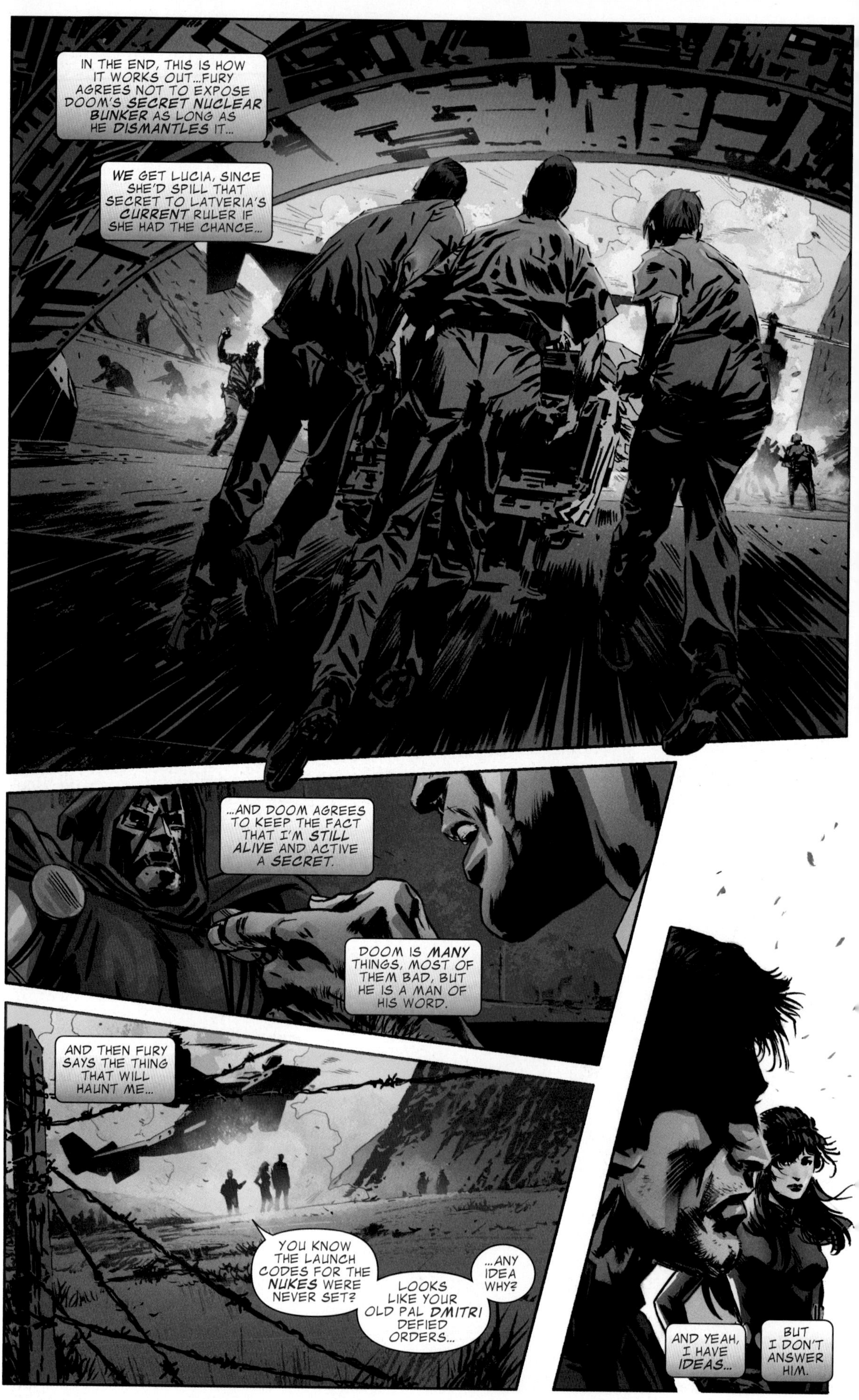
IN THE END, THIS IS HOW IT WORKS OUT...FURY AGREES NOT TO EXPOSE DOOM'S SECRET NUCLEAR BUNKER AS LONG AS HE DISMANTLES IT...
WE GET LUCIA, SINCE SHE'D SPILL THAT SECRET TO LATVERIA'S CURRENT RULER IF SHE HAD THE CHANCE...
...AND DOOM AGREES TO KEEP THE FACT THAT I'M STILL ALIVE AND ACTIVE A SECRET.
DOOM IS MANY THINGS, MOST OF THEM BAD, BUT HE IS A MAN OF HIS WORD.
AND THEN FURY SAYS THE THING THAT WILL HAUNT ME...
YOU KNOW THE LAUNCH CODES FOR THE NUKES WERE NEVER SET?
LOOKS LIKE YOUR OLD PAL DMITRI DEFIED ORDERS...
...ANY IDEA WHY?
AND YEAH, I HAVE IDEAS...
BUT I DON'T ANSWER HIM.

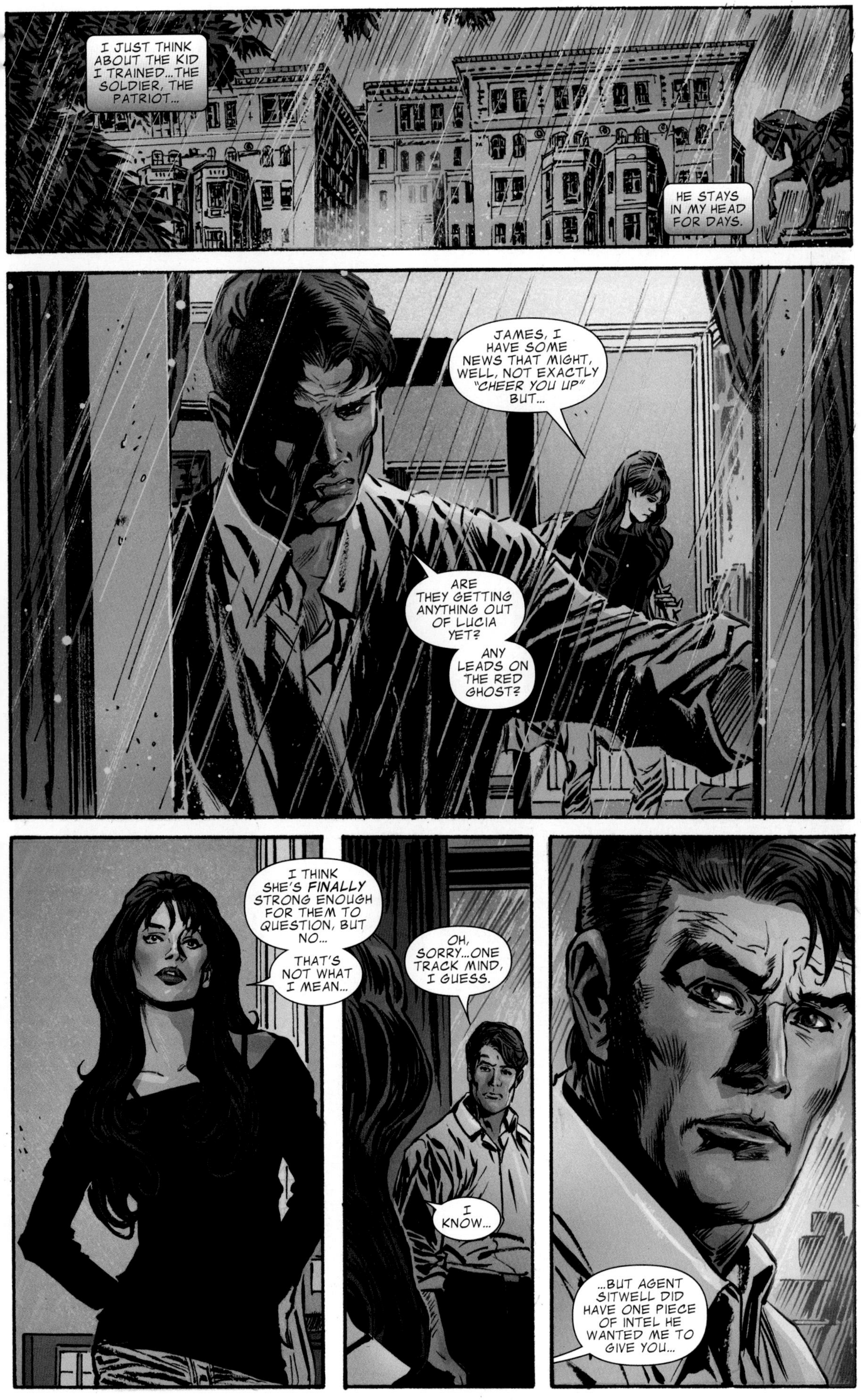
I JUST THINK ABOUT THE KID I TRAINED... THE SOLDIER, THE PATRIOT...
HE STAYS IN MY HEAD FOR DAYS.
JAMES, I HAVE SOME NEWS THAT MIGHT, WELL, NOT EXACTLY "CHEER YOU UP" BUT...
ARE THEY GETTING ANYTHING OUT OF LUCIA YET?
ANY LEADS ON THE RED GHOST?
I THINK SHE'S FINALLY STRONG ENOUGH FOR THEM TO QUESTION, BUT NO...
THAT'S NOT WHAT I MEAN...
OH, SORRY... ONE TRACK MIND, I GUESS.
I KNOW...
...BUT AGENT SITWELL DID HAVE ONE PIECE OF INTEL HE WANTED ME TO GIVE YOU...

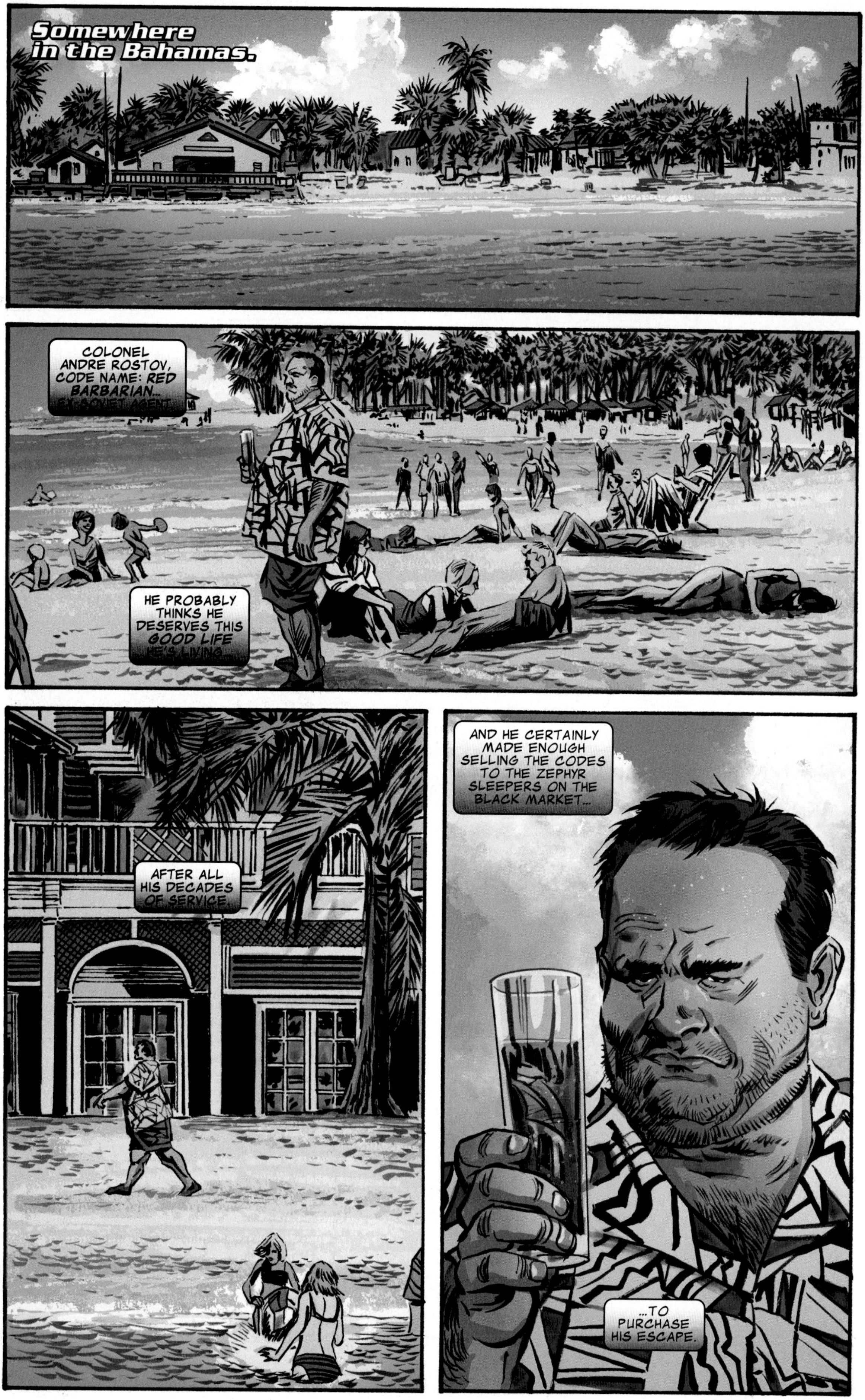
Somewhere in the Bahamas.
COLONEL ANDRE ROSTOV, CODE NAME: *RED BARBARIAN*... EX-SOVIET AGENT...
HE PROBABLY THINKS HE DESERVES THIS *GOOD LIFE* HE'S LIVING...
AFTER ALL HIS DECADES OF SERVICE.
AND HE CERTAINLY MADE ENOUGH SELLING THE CODES TO THE ZEPHYR SLEEPERS ON THE BLACK MARKET...
...TO PURCHASE HIS ESCAPE.

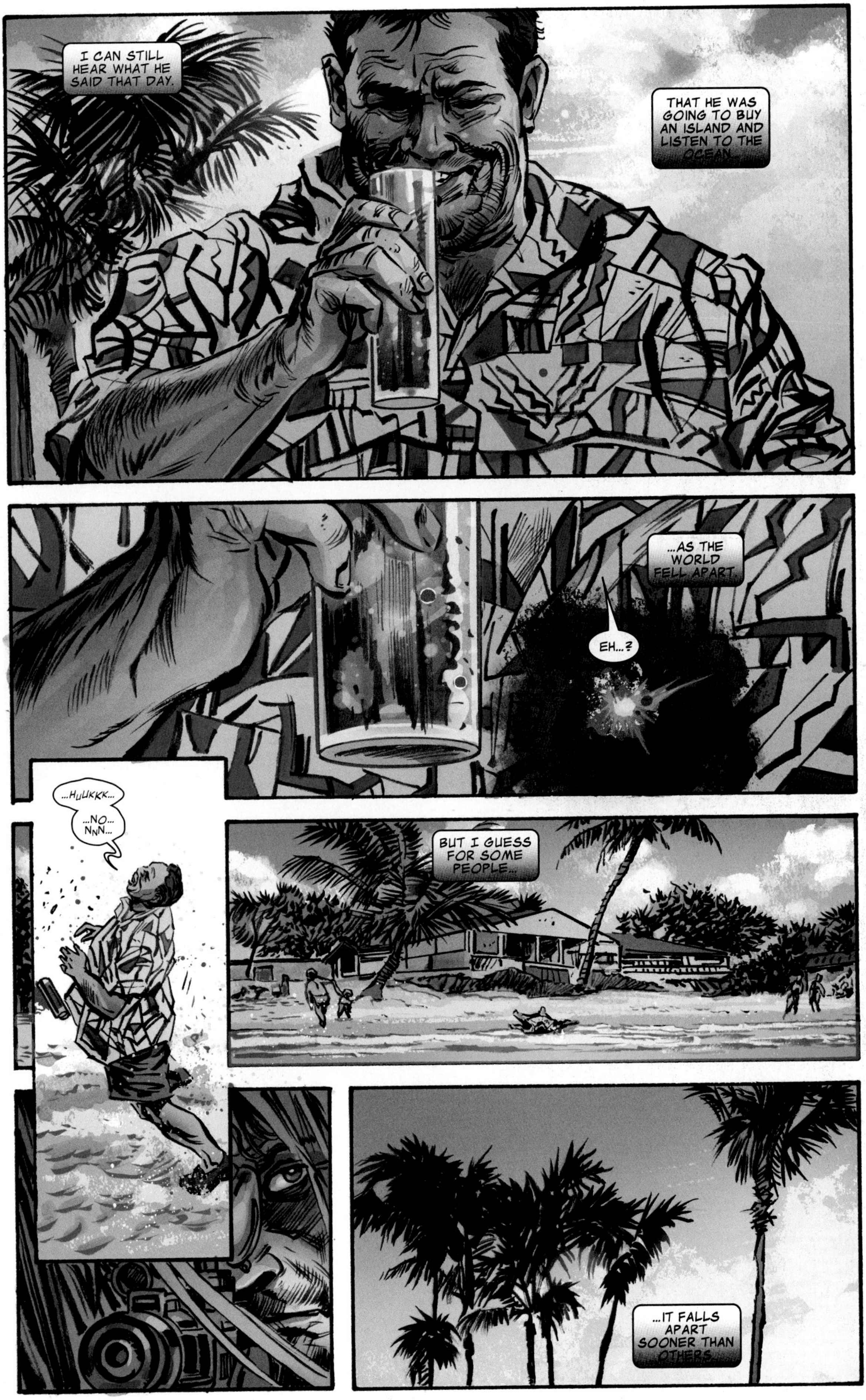
I CAN STILL HEAR WHAT HE SAID THAT DAY.
THAT HE WAS GOING TO BUY AN ISLAND AND LISTEN TO THE OCEAN...
...AS THE WORLD FELL APART.
EH...?
...HUUKKK...
...NO... NNN...
BUT I GUESS FOR SOME PEOPLE...
...IT FALLS APART SOONER THAN OTHERS.

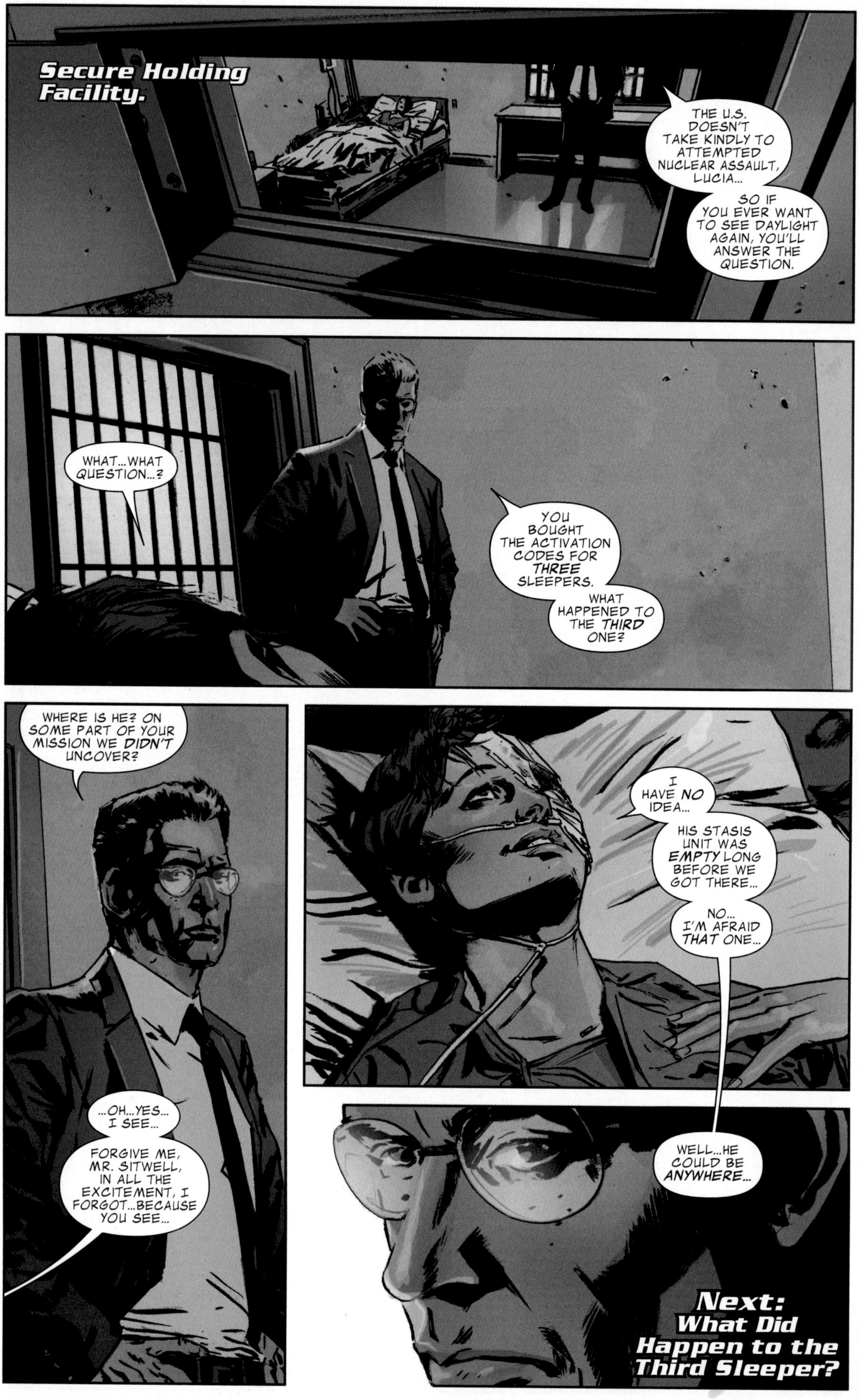
Secure Holding Facility.
THE U.S. DOESN'T TAKE KINDLY TO ATTEMPTED NUCLEAR ASSAULT, LUCIA...
SO IF YOU EVER WANT TO SEE DAYLIGHT AGAIN, YOU'LL ANSWER THE QUESTION.
WHAT...WHAT QUESTION...?
YOU BOUGHT THE ACTIVATION CODES FOR THREE SLEEPERS.
WHAT HAPPENED TO THE THIRD ONE?
WHERE IS HE? ON SOME PART OF YOUR MISSION WE DIDN'T UNCOVER?
I HAVE NO IDEA...
HIS STASIS UNIT WAS EMPTY LONG BEFORE WE GOT THERE...
NO... I'M AFRAID THAT ONE...
WELL...HE COULD BE ANYWHERE...
...OH...YES... I SEE...
FORGIVE ME, MR. SITWELL, IN ALL THE EXCITEMENT, I FORGOT...BECAUSE YOU SEE...
Next: What Did Happen to the Third Sleeper?

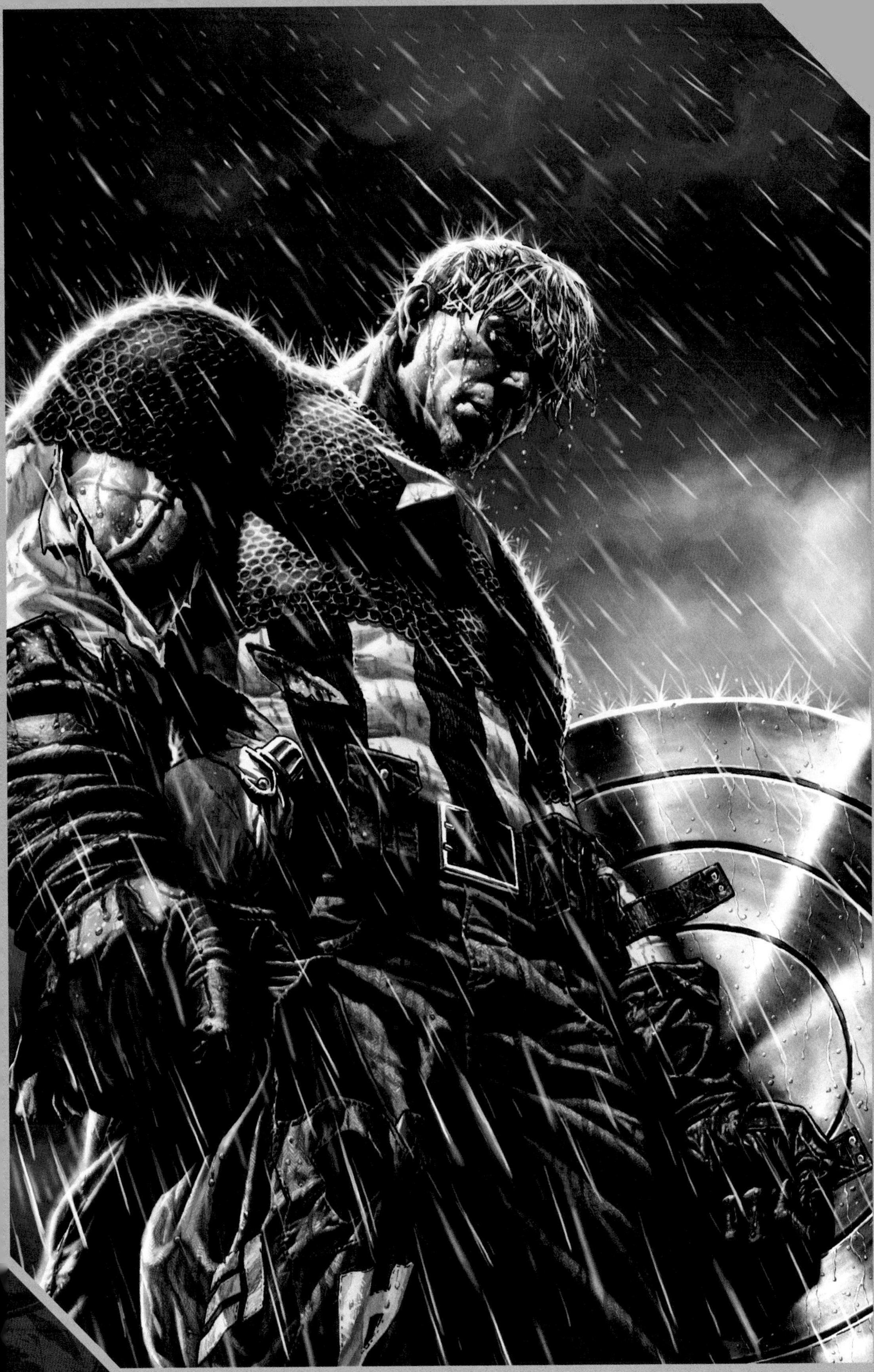

FEAR ITSELF: CAPTAIN AMERICA #7.1 VARIANT BY LEE BERMEJO

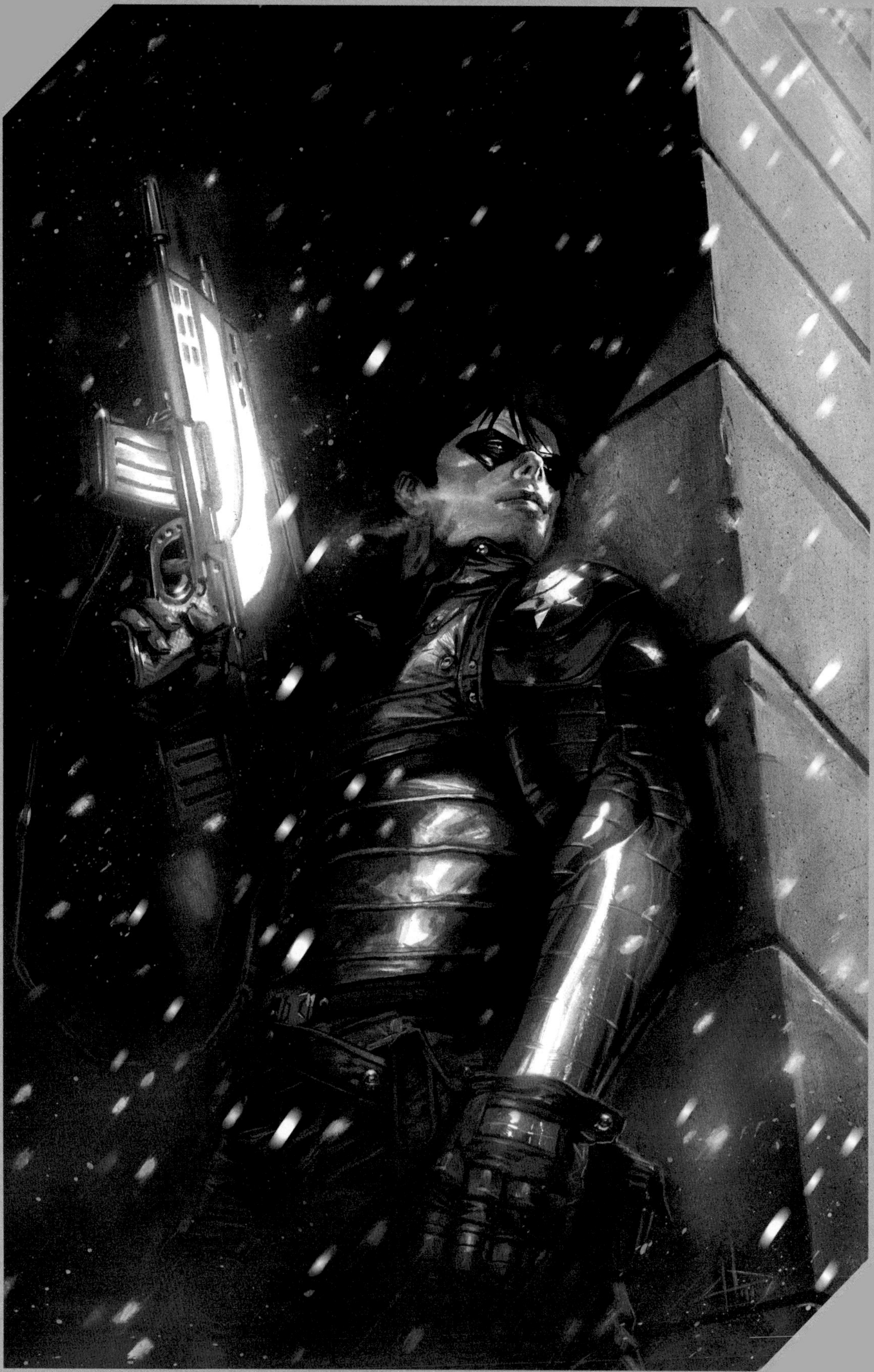

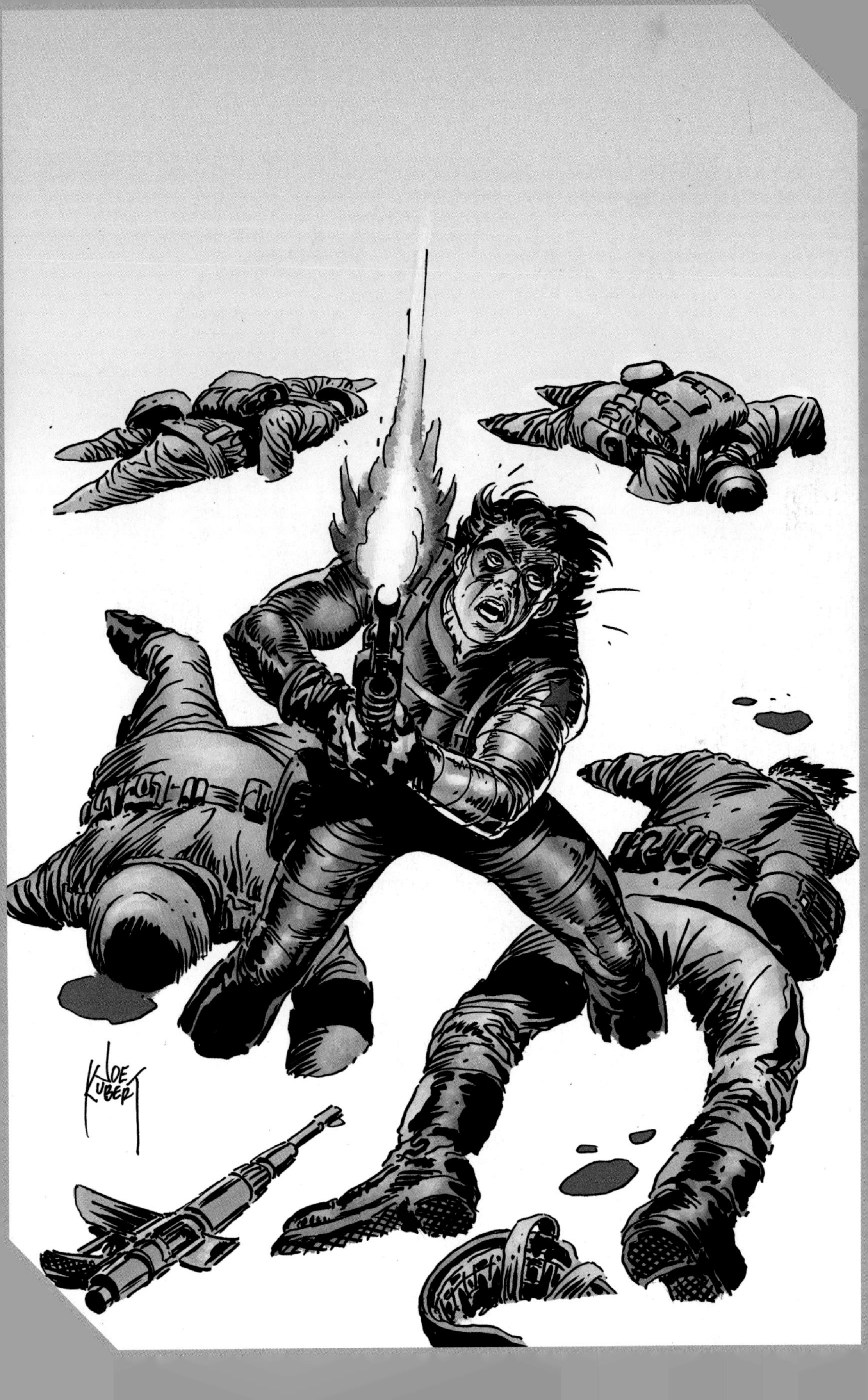
JOE KUBERT

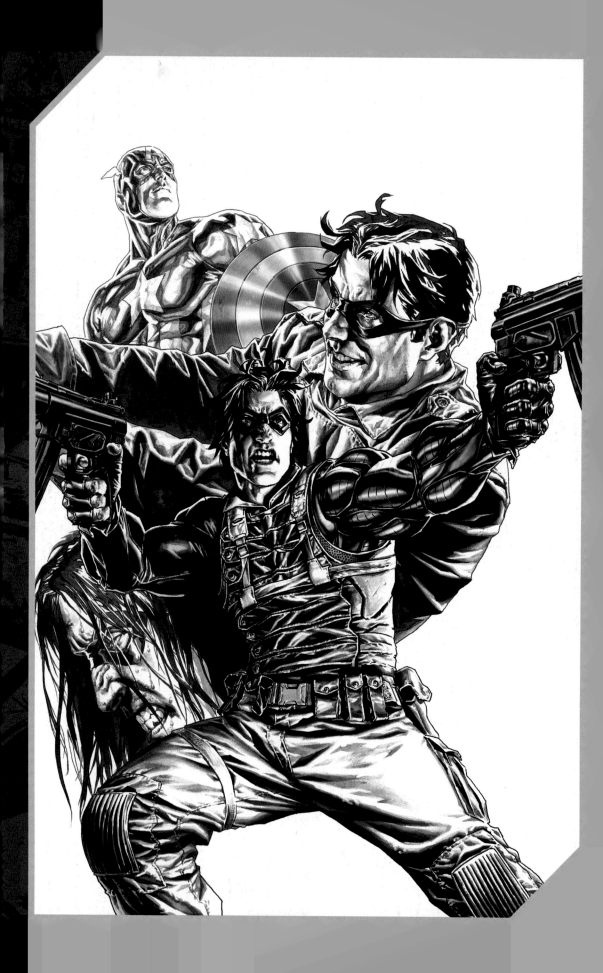